THE BURN ZONE

a memoir

ReNee LiNNeLL

[swp]

SHE WRITES PRESS

Published October 9, 2018
Printed in the United States of America
Print ISBN: 978-1-63152-487-5
E-ISBN: 978-1-63152-488-2
Library of Congress Control Number: 2018940453

For information, address:
She Writes Press
1563 Solano Ave #546
Berkeley, CA 94707

Interior design by Tabitha Lahr

She Writes Press is a division of SparkPoint Studio, LLC.

Names and identifying characteristics have been changed to protect the privacy of certain individuals.

THE BURN ZONE

"Be who God meant you to be, and you will set the world on fire."

—St. Catherine of Siena

I dedicate this book
to the weird girl/boy inside all of us,
the one who never fit in, the child inside of us who knows
we were born to set the world on fire.
When we learn to listen to her/him,
we find our Way.

"What is to give light must endure burning."
—Viktor Frankl

contents

Preface 15

Introduction 21

Part 1: Seeking

Chapter 1: Lakshmi 25

Chapter 2: Childhood. 37

Chapter 3: University of Mysticism 47

Chapter 4: Rage. 59

Chapter 5: Vishnu 66

Chapter 6: Renegade 79

Chapter 7: Chosen. 85

Chapter 8: Hawaii 89

Chapter 9: Arizona. 96

Chapter 10: Tango 108

Chapter 11: Detachment. 114

Chapter 12: Gone. 126

Part 2: Tantra

Chapter 13: Australia 141

Chapter 14: Consort. 149

Chapter 15: Family. 158

Chapter 16: The Decision 166

Chapter 17: Threesome. 171

Chapter 18: Flip Flops 176

Chapter 19: How It Happens. 182

Chapter 20: Outcast. 185

Chapter 21: Karate. 196

Part 3: Crucible

Chapter 22: The Task 201

Chapter 23: Determined. 207

Chapter 24: Hiroto. 211

Chapter 25: Bodhisattva 218

Chapter 26: Spirit Guides 223

Chapter 27: Monster 227

Chapter 28: Shattered. 237

Chapter 29: Oatmeal 241

Chapter 30: Opt Out 242

Part 4: Alone

Chapter 31: Colorado. 251

Chapter 32: Mirrors. 259

Chapter 32: Surprise 267

Part 5: Into the Light

Chapter 34: Tango Lesson. 273

Chapter 35: Awakening 277

Chapter 36: Warrior. 283

Part 6: Whole

Chapter 37: Wild Monk 291

Chapter 38: Graduation 293

Epilogue 295

About the Author 301

Acknowledgments 303

Preface

Every one of us beats ourselves up in the privacy of our own minds. We think that we are supposed to be better in some way: wealthier, stronger, more successful, thinner, smarter, a better parent—you name it. We cannot stand the fact that we are flawed, imperfect, human, so we spend our entire lives hiding our shortcomings, apologizing for them, blaming others for creating them, and hating ourselves for having them. By the time we hit adulthood, most of us have created such a false sense of self in an effort to cover up our inadequacies that we cannot even remember who we naturally are.

The only way to true joy, to true bliss, to true freedom, is to begin the work of uncovering our real selves—to chip away at the parts of us that are false, the façade we created to please our parents, the mask we built so the world would approve of us. Only when we are willing to stand tall in our own uniqueness, with our own idiosyncrasies, will we be able to do the work we came to do, to build the life we always dreamed of, to excel beyond our wildest dreams, and to live in true joy and abundance. When we finally tap into what we naturally are, we discover we already have the exact right skill set to become everything we have always secretly wanted to be.

Every saint—of all the religions—tells us that our differences are beautiful and are given to us for a reason. Every fairy tale and superhero movie shows us how our flaws make us unique and special, that owning our perceived defects makes us powerful, that our difference *is* our destiny. Yet somehow, we still live in a world that yells at us constantly to be like everyone else, to be "perfect," to blend in.

It is our work to not blend in, our work to stay true to ourselves, and our work to unravel and eventually understand the Divine purpose in the parts of ourselves that are not "the norm," to discover the incredible power and wisdom that lies hidden in the owning and forgiving and healing of our wounds. The following Chinese folktale depicts this beautifully. Each one of us is designed differently—and *perfectly*; each one of us is damaged differently—and *perfectly*—in order to fulfill our own unique destiny:

> An elderly woman had two large pots. Each hung on the ends of a pole, which she carried across her neck. One of the pots had a crack in it, while the other pot was perfect. At the end of the long walk from the stream to the house, the whole pot delivered a full portion of water, while the cracked pot arrived only half-full. For a full two years, this went on daily, with the woman bringing home only one and a half pots of water.
>
> The perfect pot was proud of itself and its accomplishments. The cracked pot was ashamed of its own imperfection and miserable that it could only do half of what it had been made to do. Finally, it spoke to the woman one day by the stream. "I am ashamed of myself, because this crack in my side causes water to leak out all the way back to your house."
>
> The old woman smiled. "Did you notice that there are flowers on your side of the path but not on the other pot's side? That's because I have always known about your flaw, so I planted flower seeds on your side of the path, and every day while we walk

back, you water them. For two years, I have been able
to pick these beautiful flowers to decorate the table.
Without you being just the way you are, there would
not be this beauty to grace the house."

If we ever want real peace inside our minds (and subsequently
in the world), we must understand that each one of us is unique,
that there *is* no carbon copy. Only then will we stop expecting
other people to see and do things the way we would. Only then
will we stop expecting ourselves to be further along than we
are, to be somehow "better." Only when we can truly accept and
embrace our own flaws will we be able to accept and embrace
each other's.

Life dealt me some pretty heavy blows early on. I was introduced to death at a young age. Overly sensitive and very small, I
never fit in with other kids and I was constantly teased and beat
up until I became mean. I was raised by an unbalanced mother
and was told continuously that virtually everything about me
was "wrong." I began searching for the meaning of life before I
finished high school and was always desperate to find someone—
anyone—who understood and appreciated me. I spent almost all
of my young adulthood lost and searching. From the outside, my
life looked perfect: I travelled the world as a model and professional dancer, but inside I was soul-sick. I felt incredibly alone.

After a lifetime of trying to be perfect, after subjecting
myself to emotional and psychological abuse in an effort to
become Enlightened, and after paying a small fortune for therapy, I have finally accepted that being flawed is part of the deal of
being human and that getting damaged is an integral part of the
journey—that when we expect ourselves to be somehow "further
along" or "more successful" or in any way different than we are
now, we cause ourselves unbearable suffering. After allowing
myself to be brainwashed in extreme and seemingly unhealable
ways, I have discovered that life wounds us in order to break us
open so that our hearts may finally be exposed to the sun, so

that we soften, so that the Divine seed within gets awakened and begins its true journey towards its full magnificent bloom.

Dr. Maya Angelou once said, "There is no greater agony than bearing an untold story inside you." I believe she is right. I wrote my story as a catharsis—a way to get it out of me so that I could heal and move on. It is my sincere desire that somewhere in the depths of my story you see your own and that my journey into, through, and out of the dark may help shine light on your own rocky path. If you have been struggling to forgive others, maybe my story will help you recognize that everything that has happened to you has happened *for* you. And if you have been struggling to forgive yourself, maybe, just maybe, my story will let you give yourself permission to love all parts of you and all parts of your history.

Embrace your skeletons in the closet. Pull them out and paint them pink. Celebrate them. Your skeletons are probably the most interesting part about you. *Your difference is your destiny.*

"You were wild once. Don't let them tame you."

—Isadora Duncan

INTRODUCTION

All my life I had been searching. For what exactly, I did not know. And then, one evening in June 2006, I walked into a meditation seminar in California. I arrived late, to a crowded room filled with chatter and nervous energy. Fifty banquet chairs faced a low stage, upon which sat a small round table draped in black cloth and a single beautifully upholstered chair. An elegant arrangement of flowers stood in the center of the table. There was one empty chair in the front row on the right. I sat in it just seconds before a woman walked onto the stage.

I had been expecting the speaker to be an older woman with long, gray hair, wearing sandals and a white robe with mala beads around her neck. Instead, she was a young woman, a pretty woman. She was dressed in an expensive black business suit with sexy, sophisticated black stilettos. With grace she walked to the middle of the stage, faced the audience, and then slowly looked from her right to her left, scanning the eyes of every single member of the gathering. She oozed confidence. She radiated power. Her look was piercing. The room went quiet. When she had finished meeting every single pair of eyes, she smiled, placed her palms together in front of her heart, bowed slightly, and said, "Hello, I'm Lakshmi. Let's meditate."

She sat down, connected an iPod to a cable on the table, put on dark sunglasses, and hit play. Her posture was perfectly straight. Her feet rested side by side on the floor. She turned her head to face the audience and folded her hands in her lap, a large gold ring glittering on the third finger of her left hand. Music started. It was loud, and the sound echoing off the walls startled me. I had been expecting spa music, but the song she chose was *Navras*, from one of the final fight scenes in the second *Matrix* movie. Wearing the dark sunglasses in the dark suit, this woman looked like Trinity from the movie. Damn, she was intense. Suddenly, I envied her.

I pushed my thoughts aside, inhaled deeply, closed my eyes, and settled in to meditate. Instantly I felt energy uncoil at the base of my spine and shoot up through the top of my head. Then everything went white and I disappeared; the room disappeared, and I was being held in the hands of God. I had left my body and expanded into Eternity. The peace, the silence, the warmth, the *love*. *This* was what I'd been searching for my entire life. This was *it*. I was *Home*. I had never felt anything so glorious in all my life. I felt ripped apart and filled up with love and energy and white light and pure joy. I felt utter *ecstasy*. I slammed open my eyes, my heart beating wildly, and I clutched the bottom of the chair to keep from fainting. I didn't know who this woman was. I didn't care. I was Home. My search was over.

Part 1
SEEKING

"Religion is for people who are scared to go to hell.
Spirituality is for people who have already been there."
—Bonnie Raitt

chaPteR 1
LaKShMi

"I am not going to sit on cushions on the floor in the dark with a bunch of stinky, patchouli-oil-smelling hippies chanting 'Om'," I said adamantly. It was spring of 2006, and Kate, one of my closest girlfriends, was insisting I go with her to a free meditation class on Tuesday night. She had been suggesting I go for a long time because she loved it and she knew I had been searching and she thought that I would love it, too. But I had no interest in going; it sounded terrible. For a while, I had an excuse: I was teaching a tango class on Tuesday nights. But the series was only six weeks long and the last class ended. So, after weeks of refusing, I went. Begrudgingly. And it was weird. And I didn't love it. But they weren't hippies. And they sat in chairs. And they didn't stink. And there was no patchouli. And it wasn't dark. And I survived. But I was definitely not going back.

The next week rolled around, and there I was again, sitting in the circle of chairs with the non-hippie meditators. Meditating. Or trying to. And it was still all a little weird. And I vowed never to go back.

And the next week rolled around, and there I was, back *again*. I couldn't believe it. This time I had arrived before all of the other students. Only one pair of shoes lay beside the door. *Prada*, they said on the instep—the instructor's shoes.

That's interesting, I thought to myself and entered the room. *Definitely not a hippie.*

After my fourth class, I lingered as the other students packed up their belongings. I had just finished reading a book about a man's evolution to his highest Self, guided by his spiritual teacher. I had never heard of a spiritual teacher and after reading the book decided that maybe I needed one. I had always been so different from everyone else; I had always been searching. Maybe a spiritual teacher could help answer some of my many questions, and maybe this meditation teacher knew where I could find one. Tentatively, I approached the instructor and asked her about finding a spiritual teacher.

She smiled, her eyes kind. She told me that her mentor happened to be in town from Arizona, teaching a three-day public seminar on meditation. In fact, she was teaching the following night.

"Look," she said, pointing to a poster on the wall:

University of Mysticism
More Difficult. More Intense. More Outrageous.
No More Switchbacks, This Path is Straight Up The Mountain

As someone who had spent much of her adolescence dressed in Doc Martin boots, diving off the stage at punk-rock concerts and drag-racing her Mustang, I thought this sounded right up my alley.

Even though I had been to four meditation classes, I had never *really* meditated. I had no idea what to expect. I imagined a relaxing evening spent with an older woman listening to the same type of spa music we listened to in the Tuesday night classes. The seminar was nothing like that.

———

When I opened my eyes, Lakshmi was still on stage, wearing sunglasses, meditating. She had a huge smile on her face. She was utterly motionless. I looked around. The other people in the room still had their eyes closed. My life had just been shaken to the core, and everyone else appeared unfazed. I had no idea what to do, so I sat clutching the chair, trembling, eyes open, heart pounding, staring at the stage . . . waiting for the song to end.

Finally, Lakshmi reached over to stop her iPod, returning her hands to her lap afterward. The tension in the room had dissolved. The peace was tangible. The air felt as if it were filled with white light and tiny little champagne bubbles. We stared at Lakshmi in the silence. She sat as still as a statue, face pointed straight ahead, sunglasses on, hands folded, slight smile on her lips, feet planted on the floor.

Suddenly, as if returning to her body, she inhaled deeply, placed her hands together in front of her heart, and bowed slightly. Most of us bowed with her. She removed her sunglasses, placed them on the table, blinked her eyes a few times, and said quietly, "It's nice to bow in gratitude after a meditation. It's a way of showing thanks for the opportunity to sit in pristine stillness. If bowing makes you uncomfortable, you can simply say 'thank you' inside your mind."

More silence.

More stillness.

She looked around the room and asked, "How was that?" Hands shot up into the air, mine one of them. Lakshmi looked at me and said, "Yes?"

Timidly, I asked, "What just happened to me?"

She smiled at me, with so much love in her eyes, and when she spoke, I felt a tangible current of love flow from her to me. "You are in The Burn Zone," she said. "You may just want to move back a few rows. If it happens again, just open your eyes and look at these flowers." She nodded to the white orchids someone had placed on the stairs leading up to the stage; they happened to be directly between her and me.

I had not described to her what I had just experienced; she seemed to intuitively know. For the next hour I sat pinned to the chair, feeling as though I could not move. It wasn't a heaviness. It was as if my body was made of light. My mind felt so expanded it would not have been possible to think or worry if I had wanted to. Waves of bliss hit me from all angles, pulsing through my skin. I could barely hear what Lakshmi was saying. It didn't matter; I wanted to sit in that chair, in front of her, for the rest of my life.

After an hour, Lakshmi got up and left the stage. Once she was gone, we were ushered to the foyer. One of her volunteers saw me standing against a wall in the corner and approached me with a concerned look on his face. I recognized him from the Tuesday-night meditation classes. He was tall, with dark brown hair. His name was Jake.

"How are you feeling?" he asked.

"I'm not sure," I responded. "A bit shaky."

"You should eat a cookie," he said, walking me over to the table that held cookies and brownies.

"The sugar will help ground you."

He handed me one, and I took a bite. Sugar was the last thing I wanted, but, surprisingly, it did help.

"She's pretty intense, isn't she?" he said.

"Oh my God," I answered. "Yes."

I thanked him and walked back into the seminar, I took Lakshmi's advice and sat toward the back. She was right; the energy was much less intense in the back of the room.

I didn't want it to end. I was hooked. I *had* to know more. I would find a way to stay with her forever. The way I felt in her presence was *magical*. All my doubt was gone. All my questions were gone. I felt as if everything in life was perfect and always had been and always would be. Nothing mattered. Everything was fine. I had never, *ever*, in my life felt this much peace.

On my way back to the car, I stood outside for a minute. I was dazed and utterly transformed. The trees. They were so alive, so green, pulsing with life. I could smell them. I could feel them singing to me. The sky was so dark, the stars so bright. The contrast filled me with ecstasy. The feel of the wind on my skin was so soft and gentle and rich and full of love. I'd only had a hint of this feeling of hypersensitivity once before. I was seventeen tripping on psychedelic mushrooms my brother had pulled from the dirt in a Costa Rican cow field as we walked back from an early morning surf. But this was even more intense, richer. The world was new. I was a child of the universe and everything around me was positively singing with life, with *love.*

Lakshmi had said, jokingly, before she ended the seminar, "Make sure you get in your car before you drive home."

She *knew* we were leaving in altered states of mind.

I simply could not wait to return the following night.

Kate joined me the next night. Our friends Bruno and Emily came along, as well. We sat toward the back of the room. I was so excited for them to experience this with me; Kate, after all, was the reason I was here. When Lakshmi walked onto the stage, my heart began to pound. She wore dark jeans with a thigh-length black jacket cinched at the waist and black high-heeled boots. Her breasts were huge and were much more noticeable in this outfit. She really was beautiful—powerful and feminine.

"Most people think you meditate to relax or unwind," Lakshmi said. "If you want to relax, get a massage; if you want to unwind, go drink a beer and get a blow job. I am going to teach you how to sharpen your mind. It is the hardest thing there is to do."

She went on to explain how meditation focuses the mind to the point that one can actually squeeze a muscle and shut off all thought. She said that once you can work with 100 percent of your focus on the task at hand, your ability becomes close to unlimited.

"This," she said, "is what makes monks so powerful. Imagine being able to walk through this world not affected by anything, not needing *anything* to change. Imagine having a mind so strong that you simply cannot be knocked off balance by the events going on around you."

As Lakshmi spoke, she held command of the room. I could tell she loved teaching. She used her hands expressively, often holding the wire connected to her microphone.

"In the East," she said, "people have strong spiritual practices but have a difficult time making money. They live in poverty. In the West, people excel at their careers but have minimal to no spiritual practice. They become consumed with work and money. They neglect their families, their health, and their own peace of mind."

Gesturing with the right hand, she said, "People in the East are spiritual and poor."

Gesturing with the left, she said, "People in the West are wealthy and soul-sick."

She let that hang there for a moment, allowing it to sink in.

"We can use meditation to sharpen our minds, use our sharpened minds to excel in our work, get promoted, make more money, and use that money to create a life that allows us to meditate better and to give back to the world through philanthropy. This is what I teach."

She sat back down and continued: "There is more . . ."

We waited.

"Mindfulness is as important as meditation. Most of us spend eight or more hours a day at work. It's great if we take the time to meditate in the morning or at night, but what about all those hours in between? What happens then? You meditate in the morning. You feel close to God. Your mind gets calm. You feel centered and at peace. And then you get in your car and someone cuts you off in traffic or you spill coffee all over your suit and suddenly you're an asshole all day long? That's not spiritual. This is where mindfulness comes in. You must learn to monitor your thoughts. It's not easy. You need to stop the bullshit in your mind. And then you need to be focused and awake in your actions. Your entire day becomes your place of worship, your offering to the Divine. This world is dark, and it needs more light. When you meditate, you tap into All That Is, and you shine brighter. When you give the best of yourself in each moment, you tap into All That Is, and you shine brighter. And when you dedicate your work to God or Source or anything higher and larger than yourself and your own measly paycheck, you begin to truly *enjoy* what you are doing, and . . . you shine brighter."

She looked at the crowd. Again, she scanned the eyes of everyone facing her. Her look was fierce. Chills ran up my spine.

Work as spiritual practice—I loved it. I had always felt an innate love for and trust in God, but I resisted the word *God*, and I resisted people who talked about God, mostly because my mother had forced me to go to Sunday school every week, where I witnessed the hypocrisy of the church. It never made sense to me how God could create all of us, yet fill us with desires that were sinful and damn us and judge us and smite us for acting on them. If we believed that God created all of us, then it only made sense to me to believe that God loved us as we were, that we are *all* His/Her children. Even when I was a child it seemed very closed-minded to me to believe there was only one way to find God, only one path to follow, and that anyone that walked a different path was damned. I noticed that when Lakshmi said *God*, I didn't find myself resisting. I found myself intuitively understanding *God* as the intense love and light and peace I experienced in Lakshmi's presence. I loved her irreverence. And I loved that she talked about making money and having a great job and sharpening your mind as a way to walk a spiritual path.

She wasn't saying, *Give up everything and live in an ashram.* She wasn't saying, *Stop having sex and stop eating meat and go get a job as a massage therapist or Reiki practitioner.* She was simply saying, *Use this method to tap into quiet, to sharpen your mind, and use the extra energy and clarity you get from it to rock your career.*

I wanted to be like her. Everything about her was so polished. She was just the mentor I needed. A big sister. A guide. A teacher. I just had to figure out how to become her student.

As I walked through my front door later that evening, my phone rang. It was my Tuesday-night meditation teacher.

"What did you think?" she asked.

"I *loved* it!" I exclaimed. "I love *her*."

"I had a feeling you would," she replied. "She's looking for volunteers to help with next month's event. Would you like to volunteer?"

I immediately agreed.

"Her partner will get in touch with you. His name is Vishnu," she said.

Vishnu called from a private number a few days later. I was driving and quickly rolled up the windows so I could hear him clearly. He was *very* serious. He explained that Lakshmi was an *Enlightened Being* and that she did not need anything from anybody. He said that my volunteering to help her would really be her helping me. And he said it was an immense honor to do anything for an Enlightened Being.

Well, that explains all the light in the room, I thought. In my years of searching I had read books about saints and Enlightened Masters and learned about "selfless service to the guru," so I immediately accepted this as Truth and was utterly thrilled to "serve," ecstatic that I had actually found an "Enlightened Master" the day after I began looking for one. The old adage *When the student is ready, the teacher will appear* popped into my head. I couldn't wait to hear what my service would be.

"Your job will be front-door greeter and ticket gatherer," Vishnu said. "You will need to arrive to the events half an hour early."

He gave me the address of the next event and told me to contact my Tuesday-night meditation teacher if I had any questions. Emily had decided to volunteer as well and got assigned the same role.

At the next event, Emily and I arrived early and got into our positions on either side of a large double door.

I turned to her and said, "I don't know why, but I am *so* nervous." I was wearing a form-fitting turquoise V-neck T-shirt, a really pretty chocolate-brown, turquoise, and tan skirt, and sandals. It was July, and the weather was extremely warm. We were stationed outside a large hotel ballroom and the air-conditioning did not seem strong enough to cool the large space. I lifted my arms and showed her sweat marks that ran from my armpits to my waist. We both broke out in peals of laughter. I kept my arms up, clasping my hands around my elbows on top of my head, hoping that maybe my T-shirt would dry a little.

"I'm nervous, too," Emily said. "She scares me. Her energy is so intense. I feel like she can see right through me."

Just then, Lakshmi walked up, and I slammed my arms back down to my sides. She had materialized out of nowhere. Emily and I held our breath. My heart began to pound.

"Hello," she said to Emily.

Emily replied nervously, through gritted teeth, stiff like a statue.

Lakshmi turned her gaze to me. Her presence was mesmerizing. She smiled.

"Hello," she said to me in a different tone. "It's nice to see you again."

My eyes welled up with tears. She *saw* me. She *recognized* me. She wasn't referring to knowing me from the event the month before. She was referring to knowing me from past lives. I *could sense* this. I could *see it in her eyes*. It was as if her gaze alone was communicating more than words ever could.

I had never *ever* fit in. Anywhere. I had never been like anyone else. I had always been different. As a child I was more sensitive than other children. When someone said something mean to me I felt the energy of the words stab me in the heart. When they made fun of other kids, I could feel the other kids' sadness well up inside my own chest and pour out of my own eyes. If I made eye contact with anyone, I immediately felt inside my body whatever that person was feeling inside theirs. Noises were too loud. Lights were too bright. Adults hugged me too hard. I had a very high moral compass and would not disobey my parents' rules even when they were not around to enforce them. I had hidden these differences because I discovered in childhood that they made me "weird." And being "weird" caused me to be bullied, beaten up, and ostracized. I hated it so I learned to be tough. I learned to bully. I learned quickly how to blend, but I still never fit in. Deep down I had always hoped someone would see my difference and would understand it, that she would tell me I was not "weird" but, in fact, "special."

A few times, in my late teens and twenties, I had gone to see traveling monks or healers and had hoped they would recognize something in me, but it had never happened. Yet here it was, *finally*. Happening before me. With her. Reaffirming that I was, at last, truly Home.

Lakshmi walked through the door and into the event room. Quietly, she walked down the rows and touched the back of every single chair. When she got to the one that held my sweater, she paused and touched it with both hands, lingering much longer than she did on any other chair. She then calmly continued touching the backs of the remaining chairs. At least ten of the other chairs, those reserved by the other volunteers, had sweaters draped over the back. How could she have known which chair was mine? I felt so protected, so loved. I felt like she saw the full, complete me, like she knew how sensitive I was, and like she was somehow energetically protecting my chair, my space, me. Finally, after a very long time, I was not all alone.

Through the three-night seminar, I soaked up every word she said. She talked about religion. She spoke about saints. She explained how important a good career was. But, mostly, we practiced meditation. She insisted that we had to learn to still our minds. We had to create space for the Divine to guide us. Meditation, she promised, was *The Way*.

On the last night, Vishnu invited the volunteers to stay for a quick "surprise" at the end. We stood in a circle in the empty event room, nervously awaiting Lakshmi's arrival. Escorted by Vishnu, she walked in holding a bottle of expensive champagne. Vishnu held a stack of plastic cups beside her. We made space for them in our circle and Vishnu handed each of us a cup. Lakshmi raised the bottle and said, with her charming smile, "Here is

to a job well-done," as she opened the bottle with a loud *POP!*
Next, she walked within the circle and poured a little champagne
into each volunteer's cup, looking each person in the eyes and
thanking each one of us sincerely.

When she got to me, she kept pouring until my cup was
full. She looked into my eyes and whispered, "You need this."

I turned red. She smiled. I smiled back. There was a pal-
pable current of love between us, like big sister and little sister
reunited after lifetimes apart. And then she moved on to the
next volunteer.

All the way home, I was glowing. I couldn't stop wondering
what she could have meant. Finally I decided it didn't matter. All
that mattered was that Lakshmi had singled me out as different.
She had confirmed something I had always known. And she was
clearly telling me what I needed so desperately to hear: that my
"different" was indeed "special."

Emily and I volunteered to help with the August seminar.
In the meantime, I bought Lakshmi's book and read it immediately. I bought and listened to all of her CDs. I began meditating
in the morning. I did everything I could to act as if I already *was*
her student. And when the seminar finally came, I hung, again,
on every word. On the final night my wish came true: Lakshmi
handed out applications to become her personal students.

Perhaps sixty of us remained in our seats to apply as the
rest of the audience filed out. I could not believe my luck. Now
that her summer seminars were complete, she would be leaving
California, and I was dreading having to say good-bye. But if she
accepted me as her student I would not have to. I would have her
by my side, possibly indefinitely, to guide me. I would never have
to be alone and "weird" again. I filled out my application quickly
and dropped it in a pile on the stage, my heart pounding with joy.

On my way out, Vishnu approached me and whispered,
"Are you sure you know what you are doing?"

I looked at him, shocked. "Yes," I replied firmly. I had never
been more sure of anything in my life.

He smiled. "Nicely done," he said.

I got home and called Emily. "I didn't see you in the room," I said.

"I didn't stay," she replied.

"You didn't fill out an application?" I asked.

"No."

I was incredulous. "Why not?"

"Because I was afraid, " she answered.

"Afraid of what?" I asked.

"Afraid she'd kick my ass and break me into a million tiny little pieces."

"Oh," I responded. I paused, then added, "I think that may be *exactly* what I'm hoping for."

Chapter 2
Childhood

The sharks were swimming by, getting closer with each pass. Nurse sharks. They were "only" nurse sharks. But, still, they were bigger than I was. And I was tiny—ten years old and all alone, standing on an inverted bucket, with the tide rising steadily by the minute. My brother, Gary, had dropped me off to collect seashells. He was *supposed* to come back. But that was over two hours ago, and I was beginning to think he forgot.

The year was 1983, and I was on a sandbar in the Bahamas. Well, two hours ago it had been a sandbar. Now it was just water. With nurse sharks all around. Swimming by me in the creepy powerful prehistoric way that they swim: rib cage swinging side to side, tail undulating as a result, dorsal fins rising above the surface of the water and sinking again just as fast, huge heads full of teeth . . . I was scared.

But more than scared, I was pissed off. Where was my brother? This was *just* like Gary to forget about me, to get so wrapped up in fishing he simply forgot. Right now, I had two choices: stand on the bucket and wait for him, hoping he'd arrive before the tide covered it, or swim across the shark-filled water to a bank of mosquito-infested mangroves, then start walking barefoot over hot, spiky lava rock until I found my way to the main island. The swimming would be bad, but the walking would be worse. It would take me a few hours at least, in blazing Bahamian sun, and I had no idea exactly how to get back to the boat we called home.

He'll come back, I thought. *He'll come get me. He will run out of bait.*

I was always waiting for him to run out of bait, only to be terribly disappointed when the "final" fish he caught got turned into bait, and our fishing expeditions were suddenly extended again until he ran out of bait. I hated being stuck on the boat fishing with him, baking in the sun, rolling back and forth in the waves, watching the fish die, smelling the fishy smell, somehow always ending up covered in fish guts and blood, and usually with a fishhook embedded in my skin when one of his casts went awry.

This, in fact, is how I ended up on a sandbar. On this sandbar. Which was definitely now *not a sandbar* . . . but water with sharks.

We were twins, and we were very close. Gary loved me. And I loved him. But at times like this, I wanted to *kill* him. I held tightly onto my bag full of shells, I squeezed my feet closer together on top of the plastic white bucket, I swatted at the horseflies buzzing around my ears, and then I heard it—the faint sound of a boat engine. Slowly, it got louder. A small white Boston Whaler came around the point and slid rapidly into view, and two minutes later, my brother, sunburned and smelling like fish, pulled our dinghy up to my bucket, stuck out a dark brown hand, and helped me into the boat.

For ten years my parents tried to have children. After multiple miscarriages my mother carried a baby to term, a little girl my parents decided to name Renee. She was born dead. My mother told me that while lying in the hospital bed, surrounded by chaos, she had been flooded with an overwhelming sense of peace. She heard God tell her to be patient, that everything would turn out better than she could imagine. She was raised Catholic by very religious parents, and she felt that there was no way God, *her* God, would tease her with something for which she so desperately yearned, only to take it away.

She was soon pregnant with twins. As the pregnancy progressed, my parents discussed names. Gary was quickly decided for my brother, but they struggled to find a name for me. My father was very attached to the name Renee.

"But we already had a Renee," my mother said. "We can't name her Renee."

My father left the room and returned a moment later with a book of names.

"Look at this," he said, showing her the book. "*Renee*," he told my mother, "means *reborn*."

I believe I was that first baby, that I entered this world briefly, felt the extreme psychic pain of it, and left. I went back Home to get a companion, a best friend, someone who would walk next to me through this difficult and, at times, excruciatingly painful world. Gary agreed to join me. He and I have an incredible connection. As far as personalities go, we are as close as two people could get to polar opposites, but on a soul level, we match.

Gary was my closest friend when we were growing up. I was terribly shy and introverted, so I had a difficult time making friends of my own. I hid under the table when guests came to the house. I was socially awkward and afraid. Gary let me play with him and follow him around. He let me play with his friends. He made me feel included.

We shared everything, including a womb for six months. We were born three months early and weighed three pounds each. Our mother was obsessed with the idea that we would get sick and die, so she kept us filled with antibiotics and made us sleep obscene amounts of time. She stressed that we were fragile. She called us *miracle children*.

In many ways, our childhood was not typical. Our father was fifty-four years old when we were born, and our mother was thirty-nine. We spent most of our childhood and much of our adolescence living on a boat in the Bahamas, which made us very different from other children. We very rarely watched television, and we spent ninety percent of every day on or under the water. When we started private school in Fort Lauderdale at age five, our teachers made us work with a speech therapist, because they thought our Bahamian–Bostonian accent was a speech impediment.

We were tiny, different, sickly, extra-sensitive, superskinny, and weird. Gary had glasses, and in fifth grade, we both got braces. When the other kids teased us, we cried. We got made fun of, beat up, and ostracized. We *absolutely* did not fit in. Life in private school was not easy.

Our father had survived five invasions as the Captain of a Landing Craft Infantry vessel in World War II, and his view on life was different from most people's: He felt that every day above ground was a gift, and he lived his life this way. He taught Gary and me to understand that we were incredibly blessed to have three meals a day and a roof over our heads in a country that was not being destroyed by war.

While on that ship, in the war, in the middle of so much death and destruction, my father dreamed of owning his own boat. He imagined calm blue waters with no air strikes and no cannons and no dead bodies. Eventually, he made his dream come true. After the war, he went to night school on the GI Bill. He worked his way up in the world of real estate—from assistant to agent to broker to commercial developer. He made enough money to support himself and his parents, and when he finally bought the boat he dreamed of, he named her the *Chance Two*.

He was old enough to be my grandfather, and everyone at school thought he was, which caused them to tease me more, but it did not matter what the other kids said about how old he looked, my father was my hero, my rock. I suppose being raised by a man that age lends a certain sense of stability that being raised by younger fathers cannot. He instilled in Gary and me a sense of immense appreciation and gratitude for daily life, and he also raised us to be hard workers and incredibly independent. By the time we were ten years old, we had passed all of his sea-survival tests: how to use the radio, how to send a flare, how to anchor, how to tie boat knots, how to know our location and how to read the tides. We could navigate water with coral heads and shallows. We were free to take the dinghy out to explore the island waters on our own, as long as we were back an hour before dark.

I loved the quiet and the serenity of life on a boat. I spent hours on the fly bridge next to my father, sitting side by side in silence, as we travelled from one island to the next, crossing deep and seemingly endless ocean for days at a time. We didn't need to fill the quiet with useless chatter. We listened for hours to the sound of the wind and the waves crashing against the hull and the steady droning of the engine. The salt water caked our skin. The wind whipped and tangled our hair. The sun tanned our faces. Eventually, we would crawl down the ladder, to Gary and my mother in the cabins below, and smile at each other, knowing we had spent the day in a type of church. We never said that to each other. My father was as irreligious as a person could get. He disliked going to church and only went once in a while to appease my mother. His God was nature. His God was silence. And without ever talking about it, he passed that belief, that feeling, that *knowing* on to me.

When I was six years old, my father pulled our little dinghy up near a huge Navy ship anchored off of Nassau. The sailors seemed to be a thousand feet above us, all standing alongside the railing, looking down at us. The ship must have been similar to the type my dad piloted in the war. We waved to the sailors, and they waved back. Then one of them tossed his white hat down into our little boat. It hit the T-top and bounced into the water.

He probably intended it for my brother, but without think-ing, I leapt overboard and dove after it. The water was deep, dark blue and was pierced by magnificent rays of sunlight that illuminated the sinking hat. I kept my eyes open, ignoring the sting of the salt water, and swam as fast as I could—down, down, down—as the hat kept sinking out of my reach. There was *no way* I was going to give up. My eyes stayed locked on my target. And I got it. I clutched it in my tiny hand and swam as fast as I could toward the surface. I came up gasping for breath, with my prize in my hand, which I held out of the water for everyone to see. My father, smiling, lifted me into the boat, and only then did I hear it—the sound of cheering. All those men and women so far above us were cheering—for me!

It wasn't until years later that I realized what I had done. Gary and I were recounting childhood adventures, and he brought up that story, mixed with other stories about my "stupidity."

"Do you realize how deep that water was?" he asked. "It was hundreds, if not thousands of feet deep. We were in the shipping channel. You're lucky you didn't get eaten by a shark or sideswiped by a swordfish."

But thinking of water depth or sharks or swordfish had never even crossed my mind. I was impulsive and not afraid to go after what I wanted, and my father encouraged me. He was proud of me for leaping into the water. He didn't scold me; he smiled.

I was three years old when he taught me to snow-ski, five when he taught me to snorkel, and eight when he taught me to water-ski. I wrestled with him and roughhoused with him and wanted to learn to do everything he did so I could always be by his side.

I was thirteen years old when I found out he had cancer. My mother and I were on a flight from Colorado to Florida when she suddenly exploded in a drunken rage, screaming, "I can't handle this. Your father is dying."

Everyone stared at us. I started to cry. In a high-pitched, breathless voice, I asked her what she meant, and she told me he had leukemia; that he was going to die, and he was going to die soon.

He didn't die soon. He held on for two years. And he hid most of his pain and struggle from Gary and me. We went on about our young lives knowing our father was sick and not as strong as he used to be, but believing he would live forever. His illness was never discussed after my mother's initial outburst. We all pretended it wasn't happening.

When I was fifteen, on the night before Thanksgiving, just as I was drifting off to sleep, I suddenly jumped out of bed, overwhelmed with the urge to go hug him and tell him how much I loved him. We were on our boat in the Florida Keys. He was in his pajamas, in his bathroom, going through his bottles of medicine. He had lost most of his hair from chemo, leaving a fuzzy, bald head that I loved to rub, and he had lost some of his strength, but he still seemed like normal Dad to me.

I stepped up on the toilet in order to sit on the counter so I could be closer to eye level with him. I wrapped my skinny brown arms around him, looked into his sparkling blue eyes and told him how much I loved him and what a great father he was. I told him how grateful I was that he was my dad and that he was the best dad in the whole world. Then I pulled him in close and hugged him with all my might, not wanting to let go.

I returned to my bed and dreamed of chaos and panic. The next morning, he was gone, taken away by an ambulance in the middle of the night. My mother had gone with him. Our boat captain, Dave, and his wife Jeanne (people my father had hired once he got too sick to captain and maintain the boat on his own), told me my father had suffered a mild heart attack and was at the hospital. I had slept through it all, mercifully, but my brother had watched as they pulled my father off the boat on a stretcher. He told me later that our father looked as if he wasn't there anymore, glassy-eyed and panting. I know now that he wasn't; he had left in his sleep, with only a small part of him keeping his body alive in order to appease my panicked mother.

Throughout Thanksgiving Day, Dave and Jeanne (who were like family) pretended that my father was fine, just in the hospital, that we would see him the next day. We had an awkward dinner in a restaurant. Jeanne's eyes were red and puffy; she kept getting up to go to the bathroom. They knew my father had died but were under orders from my mother to keep it from us.

The next day, Dave and Jeanne drove Gary and me to our home in Boca Raton to "see our father." From the backseat I watched the trees and bushes and cars through the window with a nervous heart. I appeased myself with thoughts of hugging my father and kissing his forehead when I got to him. I imagined all of us at home together, making him chicken soup and covering him with blankets, piling in bed and watching movies. Dave and Jeanne barely spoke. Gary and I stayed quiet. It was a long and tense two hours.

When we got to the front door of our house, my father's assistant, Sally, came to greet us, her eyes bright red. "I'm so sorry to have to tell you this," she said. "Your father is dead."

My mother was inside the house, crying. She couldn't bear to tell us herself.

I'm not really sure how I made it through that period of time. Upon hearing the news, I wanted to go straight back to our boat and continue playing with my friends. I had no capacity to hold the information, to grasp the reality that my father was gone, so I just wanted to return to life as usual. I vaguely remember the funeral. I remember kids at school whispering and staring. A few came up to me and offered awkward condolences. Some said things meant to be kind, but that actually made me cry. I really just wanted to pretend it hadn't happened.

Two weeks after he passed, we took the boat to the Gulf Stream to scatter his ashes, per his request. I was standing on the bow of the boat, staring down into the water. Our closest family and friends were grouped along the bow with me. My mother was fiddling with the urn and preparing to read the poem "Sea Fever" by John Masefield, another of my father's requests. A slight breeze was blowing; the boat was rocking gently up and down, side to side, the sun was intense. My mother began reading. My thoughts were elsewhere. I was hot and didn't want to be there. I closed my eyes and remembered hugging my father in his bathroom, realizing some part of me had known I was saying, "goodbye."

Suddenly, I heard my brother exclaim, "Look!"

I opened my eyes.

As far as I could see were dolphins—hundreds of them, maybe a thousand. There were waves and waves of them, surrounding our boat. They stayed there, seemingly motionless, as my mother finished reading the poem, and we threw roses into the water with my father's ashes. Then the dolphins moved. Those closest to the surface grabbed the roses in their mouths, stayed for a moment longer, and then, instantly and all at once, the pod dove deep and disappeared.

The next day at school, my English teacher, Mr. J., called me over to his desk as class was ending, looked into my eyes, and asked me how I was doing. I had always felt close to him. He seemed to care about each and every one of us, as if he was a father to every student. My eyes welled up with tears, and I told him about the dolphins. He paused, smiled, and gently said, "You know, in Greek mythology, it is said that the dolphin carries the soul to the next world."

———

The days and weeks rolled on. At some point, the reality of my father never coming back truly hit me. I cried a lot, alone in the dark at night. My mother started drinking herself to oblivion and spending most of her time in her bedroom. My brother just denied anything had happened.

I struggled with so many unanswered questions. They started with *why*: *Why did God take away my father?* He was such a wonderful man, my hero, my one true love. *How could S/He let that happen? What comes after we die? Where do we go? Is this life, this obsession with wealth, popularity, and buying stuff, all there is?*

I was only fifteen, but so much of my family had already passed away: My father's father died when I was an infant. My mother's father died when I was two years old. My mother's mother, a diabetic, had a leg amputated when I was eight and died of dementia. My father's brother died of lymphoma, and his sister-in-law died of lung cancer. My mother's brother committed suicide by shooting himself in the head. My cousin died of a tooth infection. That is a lot of death to deal with by age fifteen. I felt like there simply *had* to be more to life than what I was being taught in church and school.

And then the book *Many Lives, Many Masters* by Brian Weiss appeared in my life, introducing me to the idea that we incarnate over and over again and that we appear in each life to learn certain lessons. The part I loved the most is that we constantly reunite with souls we love.

All the heaviness surrounding my heart lifted. I had a decision to make: I could believe that we live, we die, and it's over. Or I could believe that we incarnate over and over again, we learn these fabulous and complicated life lessons, and we always and constantly reunite with the people we love. One belief system made me sad and angry and despondent and mean; the other filled me with hope and joy and love and faith. Neither, at this stage in my young life, could be proven, but one offered me despair while the other offered me hope. One offered me death while the other offered me life.

I decided, on that day, at fifteen years old, to believe in reincarnation, to believe in learning life lessons, and to believe in souls reuniting. And with that decision, I planted one foot firmly onto a spiritual path that led me on an adventure I never could have imagined.

chapter 3
UNiVeRSity OF MYSticiSM

After I submitted my application, I heard nothing from Lakshmi or her University of Mysticism. Two agonizing weeks rolled by. I checked my mailbox daily. No response. I checked my e-mail daily. No response. I called my friends who had applied.

"Have you heard from Lakshmi?" I asked.

"No," they all replied.

And so we waited.

I had almost given up when it appeared: a beautiful large crisp envelope, cream colored, with sophisticated font on a perfectly centered white address label with a shining University of Mysticism logo and a gorgeous stamp. I held it in my hands for a moment, studying its beauty. And then I ran inside and opened it. I had been accepted as Lakshmi's student. The first class would be in two weeks. I simply could not wait. The secret door to Lakshmi's University of Mysticism had opened for me.

The program started slowly and magically. Lakshmi assigned wonderful books for us to read, fantastic movies for us to watch, and taught us about different spiritual paths and the Truth underlying all religions. The movies she assigned were mostly mainstream movies, but she showed us how many of the major blockbusters were *dharma films*. (*Dharma* is a term that is difficult to define, but it essentially means "upholding the cosmic order" or "aligned with one's Truth.") Most of the books she assigned were spiritual in nature; many of them on Zen, Buddhism, Hinduism, or mysticism. She taught how the basic thread, the true uncorrupted teachings, of all religions is the same and that one can find mysticism lying beside every major religion: that the difference between mysticism and organized religion is that mystics seek spiritual experiences for themselves, seek to know for themselves what is real and what is not real. She described our path as *tantric Buddhist mysticism*. What made it tantric, she said, was the fact that we used everything as our spiritual path; we did not run or hide from anything in the world.

Close to a hundred of us met with her one weekend every month, in California, in ballrooms in the nicest hotels. She must have accepted *everybody*. I had known all of my friends had been accepted, but I was surprised to see what looked like all of the others, as well. We ranged from teenagers to eighty-year-olds and were a melting pot of ethnicities.

Rather than call our program "University of Mysticism," as she had on the posters and flyers, she called it CDT, standing for "Career Development Training." This put a corporate spin on the events, making them seem more mainstream and less "woo-woo." We were told to dress business casual and to bring a tuition of $150 in crisp, brand-new bills. It was an expression of proper etiquette, she told us, to pay for spiritual teaching with brand-new bills, which, we were told, were energetically cleaner—held a "higher vibration"—than bills that had been touched by count-less people. She called them "tomato cutters."

"Everything is energy," she said. "Everything vibrates. The more you meditate, the more sensitive you will become to energy and vibration." I held a brand-new $20 next to an old, grimy, crumpled $20. She was right; the difference was immense.

During our first class, she rose from her chair, walked to

the front of the small stage, looked at all of us to make sure we were listening, and said emphatically, "*Tantra* does not mean *sex*. How ridiculous. People are confused."

She paused, shifted her weight, played a bit with the wire from her microphone. Then she continued. "Tantra got confused with sex because tantric monks do everything; nothing in life is off-limits for us unless it interferes with our ability to keep our minds stable. Tantric monks have romantic relationships, have sex, eat meat. Tantric monks *live*; they live life. They live in the world. It is the hardest path there is, the most intense, the most difficult, because we do not lock ourselves away from the world in an ashram. Instead, we live in the world and use every-thing—every day, every experience—as our spiritual practice. Our *minds* become the ashram." She paused again and allowed her words to sink in.

"This is a no-bullshit path," she continued. "You have to be a warrior to walk this path. Anyone can act saintly closed away in an ashram on top of a pristine mountain. Try to act saintly jammed in a Manhattan subway car on your way home from a fifteen-hour work day."

She was wearing dark jeans, black high-heeled designer boots, and a perfectly fitted eggplant-colored jacket with a stylish silk scarf tied around her neck. Her long hair was pulled off her face. She was stunning. She looked like a warrior to me. She looked like she could kick my ass in those boots and not even mess up her hair. She sat down. The room was silent. We were all in awe.

She continued, "Our path is the path of the *Bodhisattva*. We are not doing this for ourselves. Everything we do, everything we practice, all the trials we go through will enable us to serve others. If you are walking this path only for yourself, you will fail. It is too difficult. Only with the sincere desire to serve others will you survive. Only with the sincere desire to serve others will you make the changes you need to make."

More silence.

Another dramatic pause.

And then, "Work is going to become your spiritual path. I

will coach you. I will guide you. You will excel in your careers. You will get promoted. You will make more money. You will work your asses off. And you will dedicate every moment at your job to the Divine. Your work will be an all-day—sometimes all-night—offering to the Divine."

She continued, "Almost nobody does this. Nobody spends every second at work utterly focused on the task at hand. Everybody is distracted. Social media, text messaging, online dating. Imagine how quickly you will be promoted if you are the one person bringing the best of yourself to every moment at your job."

She explained more about Bodhisattvas—beings who incarnate over and over in order to help ease the suffering of humanity. She said it was our job to create financial abundance and stability of mind so that we could help others. "How much assistance can you give to others if you are struggling to pay your rent? How much of yourself and your time can you offer if you are obsessed with and bogged down by your own cravings?" Then she told us some of the tasks her spiritual teacher had given her: She had to get a black belt in karate, learn to scuba-dive in freezing polluted water, jump out of an airplane, become a project manager, and get a job on Wall Street—all of which she accomplished before she turned thirty. This path seriously rocked!

I loved that I could be spiritual in a way that increased the size of my life rather than shrank it. I loved that I could be spiritual in nice clothing, driving a nice car, rocking a high-powered career, doing things I loved, rather than stuffing myself in a church or ashram. Everyone I had met in my life thus far that had claimed the title of "religious" or "spiritual" seemed self-righteous and hypocritical and unhappy and mean, as if they were depriving themselves of the fun in life and then angry with everyone else out there having fun. I had tried being Catholic, and it simply had not worked for me. Then I read about other religions, and they all seemed the same: over-structured and damning. Except Buddhism. But I thought all Buddhists lived lives of austerity. Lakshmi was telling me I could still have fun in life, still enjoy the pleasures of it, and *still* be spiritual. And not only could I make money and have nice things and still be spiritual, but that it was my duty to do so. I had never been exposed to anything like this. It was utterly perfect for me.

In the beginning, she suggested we make small changes. "You can tell the state of somebody's mind just by looking at that person's desk or home. The clutter in your home, your car, your computer, and your life is a reflection of your mind. Clean up the clutter in your life, and you will clean up the clutter in your mind," she said. "Think military precision. Those men and women fold their underwear to within an inch of its life. Imagine how sharp their minds are. Imagine how much easier it is for them to meditate."

I went home and tidied up *everything*. Soon, my lingerie was folded to within an inch of its life.

She told us to begin paying much more attention to our thoughts and our words. *Mindfulness*, she called it. "If you want to get rid of the thoughts in your head, and the majority of our thoughts cause us pain, so we do want to get rid of them, start with the negative thoughts. Stop complaining—in your mind and out loud. Stop gossiping. You will have cut down your mind chatter by more than half if you do this." I began to pay attention to my thoughts and was shocked at how much of my mind space was filled up with whining, complaining, and gossiping. I stopped. It felt amazing!

I did everything she suggested. I read all the books. I watched all the movies. And my life started changing. I noticed my mind became sharper. Things I needed to remember would instantly pop into my attention at just the right time. I had much more energy and started to feel happier and lighter. I felt so *alive*. The world suddenly seemed magical. I meditated every morning and every night without fail; I never missed a day.

Lakshmi always opened our sessions with a meditation, followed by a talk, and then she took questions from the students. She ended the first half of the night with another meditation. Next, we had our half-hour break, during which we mingled outside the meeting room and loaded up on cookies, brownies, coffee, and tea. We were told the sugar and caffeine helped "balance out the energy." Lakshmi opened the second half of the night with a meditation, followed by a discussion of the assigned books and movies. She then answered a few more questions and closed with a final meditation.

She taught us to meditate to music, using headphones. Music and headphones, she explained, created a buffer against the psychic noise of seven billion people. "People broadcast thought," she told us, "the way a radio tower broadcasts a signal. Whether we realize it or not, all of us are susceptible to absorbing the thoughts of others. That's why just being around certain people, without even speaking to them, makes us anxious, or angry, or depressed, or optimistic, or calm. We are picking up on the predominant genre, the vibration, of their thoughts. Headphones," she said, "help create a bubble of unimpeded space. The music can be used as a tool to focus in the present. You can focus on each note of the music, or you can focus on your third-eye or heart chakra, or you can chant the word 'Om' inside your mind. You can rotate these tools so that when the thoughts arise (which they always do), you have three different ways to shift your attention away from them."

After the first night with her, we were assigned to meditate twice a day at home: three songs on the third-eye chakra in the morning and two songs on the heart chakra at night. I loved this part of the practice, although I was not very good at meditating. I couldn't stop the thoughts, but I did get rewarded with milliseconds of silence that were so pristine, so peaceful and blissful, that I had to keep trying for more. When these tiny moments occurred, I would get flooded with the knowledge that I was more than just my body, that I was an eternal Being of Light. In this state of mind, no matter how fleeting, I *knew* through the depths of my being that nothing really mattered, that there was never anything to be afraid of, that everything in my life, in everybody's life, was unfolding perfectly. I began to crave these moments the way an addict craves drugs, and I slowly but surely became willing to do whatever it took to access them more regularly.

We typically had no contact with Lakshmi between the weekend classes, and the only way we could speak to her during a class was if she called on us to ask a question. Additionally, we never knew when or where our next meeting would take place; the invitation would arrive by e-mail a week or two in advance, making it very difficult to make weekend plans.

There was, however, a way to have more contact with her. During our first class, Lakshmi said she needed volunteers to help with her events. Those of us who signed up stayed after class and met with Vishnu.

Vishnu was Lakshmi's first line of defense against the outside world; *any* exchange with her had to go through him first. Vishnu was handsome, in his mid-forties, muscular, well dressed, and carried himself like he was Secret Service. He usually wore an expensive dark suit without a tie, mirrored sunglasses, and highly polished black shoes. On the ring finger of his left hand he wore a shining silver ring, like Lakshmi's gold one. He was meticulously groomed and on the rare occasion I got close enough, I noticed he always smelled great.

Vishnu drove Lakshmi everywhere in an *immaculately* clean Audi SUV with heavily tinted windows. When Lakshmi entered a seminar, she did so escorted by Vishnu. They would walk in, we would all stand, and Vishnu would help Lakshmi onto the stage. He would remain standing, legs apart, large masculine hands clasped in front of his pelvis, chest puffed out, until she sat. Then he would sit, facing the audience, in the chair that was always next to the stage. Vishnu looked like a bouncer, but a sophisticated bouncer. And the energy surrounding him said, *I will kick your ass. I actually kind of want to kick your ass.*

When Lakshmi left a seminar, Vishnu would escort her out of the ballroom, and a security team made up of student volunteers, mostly young military men, all dressed in black, with sunglasses and wires coming out of their ears—like mini-Vishnus—would be waiting at the closest exit with the car. They would surround it as he and Lakshmi got in and drove away. We learned that Vishnu was Lakshmi's first student and had been studying with her for close to ten years. None of us knew for sure if they were dating, but the rumor was that they were. They fit perfectly, they matched each other, they both reeked of power, and in our minds they were the ultimate couple. Vishnu treated Lakshmi like royalty, like a goddess, like his sole purpose on earth was to serve and protect her. I have to say, it was *incredibly* sexy.

As volunteers, we reported to Vishnu. We arrived early to events, and we did whatever he asked of us. I was in charge of the linens that covered the tables, including Lakshmi's small stage table. It was my job to place them on the tables, collect them after the event, and get them dry-cleaned and pressed. I was also in charge of picking up the flower arrangements: one for the registration desk and one for the stage. My responsibilities soon increased to handling the audio, as well. I had to test the small clip-on microphone that Lakshmi wore, check the speakers and the volume of the music, and plug in a small device that recorded each evening's talks. Eventually, I was also put in charge of Lakshmi's chair. I would remove it from a cardboard shipping box on Friday nights and would place it back into the box at the end of the seminar on Saturday evening. This, of course, was a *huge* honor. It meant I was "energetically clean" enough to touch her chair; no one else was allowed to.

The events were run with complete precision. Every detail was perfect, from the very simple yet elegant flower arrangements to the meticulous alignment of the chairs to the exact centering on the table of the crease in the linen that covered it. Lakshmi did not mess around; anything out of place was a reflection of her and she took her job "to get us to the highest states of mind possible" *very* seriously.

Volunteers were allowed to ask her one question between events by writing a letter. In my letter, I asked for career advice. I was ready for a change. I had been dancing professionally for close to ten years and wanted something different. Opening a dance studio of my own seemed like the next step, but for some reason, that felt like a dead end to me.

Shortly after submitting my letter, I got a call from Vishnu; he told me to arrive early for the next class and that Lakshmi would meet with me in the back of the event room. I arrived early, incredibly nervous, and saw two chairs set up facing each other in the far corner of the room. A member of the security team approached me and told me to sit in the chair facing the corner. He then disappeared and returned a moment later with Lakshmi, who sat down in the chair across from me, with only two feet of space separating us. She was dressed in all black and looked stunning. She smelled like flowers. Her eyes sparkled. The moment she sat I felt like I was being sandblasted with light and could barely remain in my body. I lost sensation in all of my limbs. I felt as if I was dissolving.

She told me that she read my letter and that she agreed it was time for me to retire from dancing. I held my breath, scared to hear what was coming next, worried she was going to suggest a career I could not do. With her next sentence she suggested that I start a career in computer programming. In ancient times, she explained, monks would stare at mandalas, memorizing the intricate patterns in order to sharpen their minds so that they could meditate better. Computer programming, she told me, was the modern-day version of this. Plus, she noted, a career in computer programing paid very well.

I tried to pay attention. The idea of learning to program computers terrified me. In fact, I couldn't think of anything in life I would be worse at doing. I hardly knew how to check my e-mail.

"Eventually, you will get paid very well to 'meditate' all day long," she said.

I thanked her and bowed, then I left my chair so the next volunteer could meet with her. I signed up for computer-programming classes immediately; they started the following week.

———

The class I chose was Oracle, one of the most difficult languages. I showed up to my first class frightened, filled with self-doubt.

I had to ask how to turn on my computer. I couldn't find the "on" button. I had been used to using a Mac and hadn't used a PC for years. Every other person in the class was a professional computer programmer; I immediately labeled myself the class dunce.

Making it through that class was one of the most difficult things I had ever done. I would get frustrated and start to cry in class and get up and go to the bathroom. Then I would shut myself in a stall and cry harder.

I would quote Lakshmi to myself, "If it is not difficult, you are not changing. Anything worth having in life is difficult. Anything worth having in life takes work. If you want to change, you must be uncomfortable. Get used to being uncomfortable. This path is the path of the warrior."

I would walk to the mirror, look myself in the eyes and say, "If it is not difficult, I'm not changing," and then I would dry my eyes and walk back to class.

On the day of the final exam, I looked at the test and didn't understand any of it. I was going to fail. I closed my computer, I put on my headphones, I meditated for three songs on my navel chakra (my power chakra), and then I opened my computer. I knew almost all the answers. I got ninety-eight percent and an A in the class. The instructor called me to congratulate me and told me he was shocked at my progress.

"You should be incredibly proud of yourself," he said. "What you pulled off is short of a miracle."

I smiled. Lakshmi had explained that when she gave us a task, we were assisted in accomplishing it by our Enlightened Lineage, that Enlightened Beings who were "not in the body" would support us. This was what it felt like to be assisted by an Enlightened Lineage. I felt invincible.

———

It was during our third event, in November, that Lakshmi told us about her "senior students." They were students who had studied with *her* Teacher. She had "adopted" them once he had "left the body," and she taught them monthly seminars, as well.

She told us that when her Teacher died, he left open a portal for them, one through which they had seven years to use his energy to reach Enlightenment. (*Teacher*, we were told, got capitalized when referring to one's Spiritual Teacher.)

The seventh year was almost up, the portal he left open would be closing soon, and as a final attempt to get them through the "door," Lakshmi was taking them on a "Power Trip" to the great pyramids of Egypt. She told us it had suddenly occurred to her that some of us might want to go to Egypt with them. Of course I wanted to go. By this stage, just three months into my classes with Lakshmi, I was obsessed with the idea of Enlightenment.

As far as I could tell, *Enlightenment* meant that one was no longer troubled by human states of mind. One could rise above them. I thought that once I became Enlightened, I would live in peace, *always*, regardless of my outside circumstances; that my mind would remain in a state of grace and peace and love and light, which would radiate from me and touch others, allowing them to feel a tremendous sense of peace and reassurance in my presence. I *yearned* for this. I yearned to soothe souls the way saints did. And it seemed the other students did, too. I had finally found a place where I belonged, a place where I fit in. I had *finally* found my Tribe.

Lakshmi made it sound like we would meditate our way into Enlightenment, that if we meditated long enough and tried hard enough, we would one day blast through a portal into another realm, and life from that point on would be different, we would be utterly changed. If going to Egypt could help blast me into this realm, I was going to go, no matter what.

Those of us who signed up for the Egypt trip had a conference call with Vishnu a few weeks later. I was in Argentina and had to make this call in the middle of the night. He told us the trip would cost $15,000 each. I was stunned, and my stomach sank.

They are using us, I thought.

He continued talking. The first $5,000 would cover the trip costs, and $10,000 would be the "empowerment fee," which went directly into Lakshmi's bank account.

"Money is energy," Vishnu said. I guess $10,000 was equivalent to the amount of energy with which Lakshmi would "empower" us.

A little voice inside my mind told me it was time to stop, that I had gotten myself in above my head.

But I pushed it aside. I had lived life my way for thirty-three years, and it was simply *not* working for me. I was so soul-sick. I was so *lost*. I had to find something new. I needed a radical change. And this was it. I was ready to jump. I wanted to go.

I *had* to go.

By the time I returned to California from Argentina, my investments in the stock market had increased exactly $15,000. I saw it as a sign. I got a cashier's check for the full amount and handed it in with my tuition the following month.

Vishnu came up to me before the event and said, "I want to shake your hand." He looked me in the eyes. "You are the first student to pay in full, and you are a new student. You have some *serious* power," he said.

I loved being singled out, being special. As the nerdy weird kid growing up, the kid who could barely get her mother's attention, I craved this recognition more than anything. Each time they gave it to me, I felt that sad little girl inside of me finally feel worthy, finally feel good enough, finally feel approved of.

What I did not realize is that by paying in full, I had singled myself out as wealthy.

I had always been ashamed of my money, ashamed that I came from an affluent family and did not have to struggle the way so much of the rest of the world did. It always felt unfair to me, as if I didn't deserve it. And so I hid it from people. I worked minimum-wage jobs and drove ratty old junker cars. I lived in tiny studio apartments and dressed modestly. I secretly gave a lot of money to charities and always gave money to homeless people, trying to make up for the fact that I had more than so many others. Suddenly, and for the first time in my adult life, I was blipping on somebody's radar as wealthy. Naïve and trusting, I had no idea what I had just done.

chapter 4
Rage

Gary and I not only lost our father when we were fifteen, we lost our way of life as well. Our mother fell apart; she could hardly function. She sold the boat and fired Dave and Jeanne. She withdrew into alcohol and prescription medication. She had been trained from a young age that a woman's purpose in life is to find a man and become the perfect wife. Without that identity, she had no idea how to face the world. She did not go to therapy, and we did not talk about my father's death.

While married to my father, she had kept her addictions under control. I rarely saw her inebriated. However, she always had wild mood swings. She acted as though she hated me much of the time. She glared at me. She ignored me. When I entered a room, she often turned her back to me, too busy to listen to anything I had to say. If I tried to approach her, she snapped at me, "Not now, Renee." She made it obvious that she was happier when I was not around. When Gary and I fought or argued, she always blamed me. If I got extra attention from my father, she got jealous.

My father, when he was not traveling for work, made up for the neglect I got from my mother. He'd defend me, saying,

"You're always siding with Gary. You never even listen to Renee's side of the story." He would always stop working when I walked into his home office. He would smile and motion me to his lap, hug me and look into my eyes and tell me how much he loved me. He would ask me about my day and was always willing to listen to the long, convoluted stories of a child. If my mother happened to walk in, the color would drain from her face and she would back out of the room quickly.

It felt to me as if my mother never really wanted me. My maternal grandmother told me when I was six years old that my mother didn't feed me when I was an infant and a toddler. My Nana had to sneak food to me, slip slices of wrapped American cheese under my bedroom door. I don't know if that is true. She had dementia so it probably wasn't. But I do know my mother clearly adored my brother and clearly detested me. When Gary walked into a room, her eyes would light up; when I did, she scowled. This is not lost on a young child.

I spent my childhood trying to figure out what it was I did or did not do to upset her so much. Was I really that unlovable? Did me just being me turn her into a monster? An already incredibly sensitive child, I became even more sensitive. *Maybe if I could learn to read her body language and her energy,* I thought, *I could figure out the patterns.* Of course, her mood swings had nothing to do with me, but I didn't realize that as a child. I just learned to believe that I was unlikeable and unlovable and difficult to be around.

Sometimes, especially if my father suddenly appeared, she would catch herself and then overcorrect, telling me I was beautiful and perfect in a sweet, syrupy voice. At other rare times, when she seemed truly happy, she'd hug and love and encourage me.

She taught me proper etiquette and how to be a lady. She encouraged me to eat whatever I wanted whenever I wanted it, saying, "Your body will tell you what to eat and how much." I am grateful for this because I seem to be one of the only women I know who does not have some sort of obsession with calories. She always encouraged me to dance, and she always told me my dancing was beautiful. I cherished these moments with her. Something about my dancing opened her heart. But these moments would never last, causing me to feel even worse when she went back to her regular neglect or nitpicking.

"*Goddammit*, Renee! Close your legs! What the hell is wrong with you—doing that in front of your brother?"

It was a summer day, nineteen months after my father's death, and my mother was screaming at me from the kitchen doorway of a small villa we had rented in the Bahamas. I had danced since I was five, and ballet was my life. I was hoping to get accepted into a major ballet school when I graduated high school the following year. I wasn't as flexible as the other dancers, so I worked on my flexibility daily. The living room floor was the only space large enough to stretch fully. I was off to the side, practically hidden behind the sofa, while my brother and his friend, Teague, watched television. I was not scantily clad, with body parts hanging out; I had on long pants and a baggy boy's T-shirt. Still, my mother had decided I was trying to seduce my brother and his friend. Her anger and the absurdity of her comments hit me like a punch to the stomach. I was stunned, humiliated. I felt sick. I felt as if she had stripped me naked and spanked me in front of my brother and his friend.

"Get in the kitchen and do the dishes!" she screamed.

"Leave her alone," my brother said. "We made the mess; we will clean it up."

"It's a woman's job!" my mother replied. "Renee, get in the kitchen and clean up that mess!"

Another time, she was hosting a Christmas party in her Colorado condo. She'd had way too much to drink, was slurring her words and tripping over furniture, and her wig was sliding off her head (she always wore wigs because she hated to style her own hair). I quietly pulled her aside, into her bedroom, and whispered, "Mom, you have had too much to drink. Please switch to water."

She screamed, "*Goddammit*, Renee! What the hell is wrong with you? How dare you tell me what to do?"

The party screeched to a halt. Everyone stopped talking and stared at us through the open door.

My brother, from across the living room, shouted, "Mom! You are drunk! Stop drinking now!"

All the anger melted out of her body. She looked at him with so much love in her eyes, put down her drink and said, "Gary, you are always looking out for me. Thank you, Honey."

This was life for me with my father gone.

My mother was angry and needed someone to take it out on. That someone was always me. Emotionally abusive tirades like this taught me to doubt myself. They taught me to constantly wonder whether I was being inappropriate. They taught me to tiptoe around the house on eggshells. Her behavior made me want to hide even more, made me more insecure. Everything I did somehow made her angry.

I have blocked out a lot of the pain of my childhood and seem to have mostly happy memories remaining, but very few of these contain my mother. Over the years, I absorbed the message that I was never good enough, never pretty enough, never smart enough, never strong enough, never . . . enough. And I'm not going to lie: it sucked.

The summer after my father's death, I was in the Denver airport with my mother. We were returning from my ballet camp. Suddenly, I couldn't find her. I ran to our departing gate; she wasn't there. I ran back to our arrival gate; she wasn't there. I called for her in the bathrooms; she wasn't there. Then I heard my name over the loudspeaker.

"*Renee Linnell, paging Renee Linnell. Please meet your mother near gate 34. Renee Linnell, paging Renee Linnell . . .*"

I ran to gate 34, but I didn't see her. I turned around, scanning the terminal. My mother was slumped over in a large chair. Her wig was sliding off her head. Her pants were gone. She had squeezed into my white shorts—easily ten sizes too small for her—and passed out. I ran to her.

"Mom!" I yelled.

She raised her head, her eyes dull. She was *wasted*. "I peed my pants," she slurred. "I had your shorts in my purse and had to put them on." She held her head up, crossed her legs, and tried to look refined.

Oh my God, I was horrified. I was a teenager. How was I supposed to get my drunken half-naked mother on a plane? I started to cry.

"Don't cry," she slurred. "It's okay."

"It's not, Mom," I replied. "It's not okay. You have a drinking problem."

"*Goddammit*, Renee, I do not!" Her face contorted with anger. "You are the one with the problem!" She pointed at me as spit flew out of her mouth and rage brewed in her eyes.

With my father dead, and my mother incapacitated by grief and substance abuse, I spiraled into the dark. Sure, I had decided that we all reincarnate and that loved ones constantly find each other in other lives. Sure, I had chosen a belief system that helped me cope with my father's death and filled me with joy. But absolutely no one else in my life believed in anything magical or mystical or spiritual. I had no one to talk to. The only other living relatives I was close to were my godparents, and immediately after my father's death, my mother shoved them out of our lives, telling Gary and me that our godfather had stolen half of our father's estate. I know my mother tried, in her way, to hold it together for my brother and me, but she never suggested we get therapy and she spent most of her time stumbling around the house, barefoot, angry, and irritated, struggling through a hangover.

So, for the last two and a half years of high school, my brother and I were basically on our own. He and I grew apart. He had never been really close to our father because our dad had always been too hard on him, trying to turn him into a man while Gary was still only a little boy. He rebelled from our

Catholic upbringing and chose atheism. He believed that we live, we die, and it's over. We never spoke about our father's death.

Over the course of a few months I went from a shy, quiet, nerdy good girl to a raging, angry insurgent, most of it directed at my mother. I did everything I could to not be the "lady" she was hoping I would be. I dressed in all black: I wore black fishnet stockings, black combat boots, and black bullet-studded bustiers. I cut up my driver's license and made a fake ID. With that, I could get into almost every bar around. My mother was barely parenting me, so I was free to do as I pleased.

One night, in the summer of 1989, just before my senior year in high school, I asked my mother if I could go to Costa Rica. Gary had just returned from a surf trip there with his friends and I wanted to go. She was getting ready for a date; she was a beautiful woman, stunning really, and men were lining up to take her out now that she was widowed.

"Sure, Honey," she slurred, drunkenly.

I hurried to my room to pack as my mother left on her date. I loaded my surfboard and a small bag into my car and ran back into the house to put a Post-It on the refrigerator, *Went to Costa Rica, back in a week or ten days.* We didn't have cell phones then; my mother couldn't contact me. I was *free.*

I landed in Costa Rica at midnight and hitched a ride to Jaco Beach with a bus full of German tourists. I spent a week on the beach learning to surf. I met wonderful people and hitchhiked around the country with some girls I met, surfing and flirting with boys as much as possible. I returned home changed.

That trip ignited a spark within me. It expanded my world. Suddenly, I realized there was so much more out there besides high school and ballet and my sad lonely mother who seemed locked in a life of despair.

I thought, *Travelers, true travelers, are all the same. All unbound, free, liquid, formless, open. Ready to let life carry them where it will. Choosing freedom over security. Willing to be uncomfortable, willing to have no idea what the next moment will bring. They simply surf the flow of life.*

I wondered if maybe they held the answers I was seeking. After that trip, I sat in my history class, staring up at the world map on the wall, planning my trips: Africa, Asia, South America, Australia, New Zealand, the South Pacific, Europe.

My wanderlust had been born.

Chapter 5
Vishnu

In early January, a little more than a month after I submitted my Egypt payment, I received an e-mail from Lakshmi's team asking if I could be available the next day for a call. I was on vacation in Colorado. My heart stopped. Yes! Of course I could be available to take a call from Lakshmi. I e-mailed back a window of time for the following night.

My cell phone rang—a private number. It was Vishnu. He told me to "please hold" while Lakshmi got on the line. I held my breath. This was the first time I had ever spoken to her on the phone. I could *feel* the light flowing through the plastic device in my hand. I felt like I was floating. Again, I was being held in a womb of love and light, by the hands of God. And this was just a *phone call*.

Lakshmi told me I had been doing a great job with the linens and the flowers and the audio and the chair. She said she could tell I was practicing my meditation daily. She said she was very impressed with how quickly I had jumped into computer programming and that I was ready to take on more responsibility. She asked if I would like to accept the task of planning her events.

I was stunned. "Yes!" I exclaimed.

This, she explained, would entail selecting venues for the monthly meetings, negotiating prices, placing banquet event orders, and managing the volunteers. She gave me a list of hotels with which to begin and her contacts at each. From this point on, I would be dealing with Vishnu. She gave me his cell number and e-mail address. She also gave me hers.

When I hung up the phone, I cried tears of joy. I had been given personal access to both of them. I had been *trusted* with this information. I was definitely a *huge* step closer to becoming Enlightened.

Until this point in life, my professional careers had been: massage therapist, bikini and surf model, personal trainer for about a day, and Argentine tango dancer; with brief stints as a booze-cruise ticket salesperson, a barista, and a cliff-diver in Hawaii. I had never had a corporate job, and the idea of it intimidated me. I didn't believe I was capable. Plus, I had the added pressure of wanting to do things perfectly for Lakshmi.

My first call to a hotel was nerve-wracking. I felt like a child playing grown-up. However, I rapidly established relationships with the event mangers at the hotels, and I learned quickly how to find the perfect venue and negotiate huge discounts. I was able to get us into the nicest hotels in town at a third of the price. I loved the challenge of my new job and didn't mind it taking a lot of my time.

There was no pay, of course (it was selfless service to the guru), but I didn't care. I still taught dance on the side and had some inheritance money. The months rolled on. I was so happy. I loved all the changes I was making. I loved my new sangha (*sangha* is a group of people who meditate together). I loved believing I was on my way to becoming an Enlightened Master. And for the first time in my life, I felt as if I had a purpose. For the first time in a very long time, I was truly happy.

In the meantime, Lakshmi began to teach us ways to conserve our energy. One method was *inaccessibility*. According to her, if we were inaccessible, people could not pull on us with their minds, which would leave us free to meditate better and to be less influenced by others. For example, we should make our home phone numbers private and only have people call our cells, because if they call our land lines they have direct energetic access into our homes. We should get post office boxes so nobody knew where we lived. We should not reveal our birthdates (our day of power). We should not have people inside our homes, and if we did, we should rearrange our furniture so visitors could not access our homes in their minds once they had left. We should not give gifts that lasted (people would think of us any time they looked at the gift), and we should accept only ephemeral gifts ourselves. And under no circumstances should we ever be photographed; people would "hit us with their attention" every time they looked at the photo. We should avoid social media and remove every photo and nonprofessional trace of ourselves from the Internet.

She had us read the Carlos Castaneda books and explained that, by changing our living habits, we could increase our personal power. With increased personal power, we could make more money and have more influence in the world. We could get much more accomplished, and we could reach higher states of mind in meditation. It all felt very covert, very James Bond. Suddenly, our new adventure became that much more thrilling. We, like Carlos Castaneda following his Teacher, were on our way to becoming "men and women of power."

We got PO boxes, we listed our phone numbers as private, we stopped inviting people to our homes, we disappeared from the Internet, and we hid from cameras. We didn't even tell people we were going to Egypt (if we did, they would psychically be on the trip with us). We lied to our friends and families. We danced around direct questions about our lives.

In March, we arrived in Egypt. Before I left, I gave a sealed envelope to my boyfriend, a snowboarder I had met just before I became Lakshmi's student. I told him I was going away but that I could not disclose where, and instructed him to open the envelope if I didn't call him ten days later. He looked at me like I had lost my mind. I told him not to worry, that I was going on a retreat and would have a better experience if no one knew my exact whereabouts. He was concerned and began to argue with me but, in the end, agreed to not open the envelope.

In Egypt, we met the senior students for the first time. Many of them were overweight, sluggish, and forlorn. Some of them had been in the program for more than twenty years. They looked worn-out and haggard compared with our group of energetic, fit, bright and shiny eager puppies. I couldn't figure out why they all looked so incredibly dejected. We were walking a path of magic, on our way to Enlightenment. We were learning the secrets of the universe. What the hell was wrong with them?

Very few of them made an effort to interact with us. They seemed miserable, so we, in turn, avoided them as much as possible.

While in Egypt, I had another experience of total dissolution—similar to, but much more intense, than the one I experienced the first time I sat in front of Lakshmi. We were visiting the step pyramid of Djoser, at Saqqara, and Lakshmi told me to touch it with the palm my hand. When I did, I immediately dissolved into white light. I felt myself being drawn toward a gigantic orb of light that was pulsing with love. I knew this orb was my Source. I was absorbed into the orb and was suddenly back Home, where I started, where it all began.

The feeling was so blissful that it is difficult to explain. I wanted to stay there forever. I felt as if I *was* there forever. But, in the far distance, I kept hearing a name: ". . . Renee . . ." Some part of the back of my mind registered that this is what they used to call me. It was one of my many names.

Just then, a hand touched me, and I opened my eyes and returned to my body.

"Please don't touch the pyramid," a guard said.

Emily had been calling my name, trying to get me to take my hand off the pyramid. Even though she was standing right next to me, her voice had sounded a million miles away, and I had barely noticed her touch.

"Where were you?" she asked, slightly scared, slightly annoyed, slightly envious.

"I don't know," I said. There was no way I could possibly explain it.

When I got back on the bus, I asked Lakshmi about it. "What is the deal with the step pyramid? Where did I go? I felt so much more energy there than I did at the Great Pyramid."

She smiled, her eyes twinkling with mischief and love. "I'll tell you this evening," she said.

Later that night, she told us that her Teacher had built the step pyramid and had hidden his power there, away from the Great Pyramid. I glowed in the aftermath of my experience. I felt supercharged with light. The renewed feeling of love and light and God (or Source) and bliss and utter pristine stillness and expansion entrenched me further on this path. I *had* to know more and there was no way I was going to back down before I became completely Enlightened and able to help others do the same.

When we returned from Egypt, my responsibilities grew again. Lakshmi wanted to teach a new series of public seminars over the summer and needed my help booking venues.

She called one day to say, "I have a huge vinyl poster that needs to be picked up from the printer, driven downtown to a movie theater, and then strung up in the lobby. I need you to do this because I know you will get it done properly. So far, you have proved that if I want something done immediately and correctly, you are the person to call."

I felt elated.

"There is a lot of light in this poster," she told me. "You will have to be extremely careful while driving. I want you to get in your naval chakra and stay there until the task is complete. Then I want you to check in with Vishnu and let him know you have safely completed the task."

I felt like a Secret Service agent delivering the President. Over the next few weeks, I helped Lakshmi place radio ads and newspaper ads and helped her print hundreds of posters and postcards. The artwork on her advertisements was beautiful, and each time I looked at the posters and flyers, my mind went completely still from all the energy they emitted and my eyeballs felt like they were floating in light. Lakshmi called this experience "getting baked."

"You are going to feel totally baked after picking up the posters," she would say. I did, and I loved it.

I was now speaking to her or e-mailing with her daily. I quit computer programming classes in order to be more available for her. She approved of this because she knew I could also have a successful career as an event planner or project manager, and she was now leading me in this new direction. I also quit teaching dance, excited about spending the majority of my time in service to my guru.

Lakshmi soon decided to combine the senior student seminars with the new student seminars, so I suddenly had a lot of work to do with Vishnu: changing databases, combining mailing lists, and looking for larger venues.

Lakshmi had told many of us, myself included, that we should learn karate, but we had had difficulty finding a good dojo in town.

"It will make you strong," she said. "It will make you disciplined. It will help you handle the power of this Lineage, and the loud *kiai*—the yell—when you strike will encourage you to be fierce."

Once she found out I had spent most of my life dancing ballet, she said, "Ballet is just as intense as karate, if not more so. It is the same thing, the same training. Ballet is warrior training. You do not need karate, but I still think you should take some classes if you can find a good dojo. Learning to kiai will be good for you."

I was still quite shy. I couldn't imagine yelling like that. She was right; it would be good for me. Apparently, Vishnu was a fourth-degree black belt and, according to Lakshmi, "the greatest martial artist to ever incarnate." I asked her if he could teach us; I mean, if he was "the greatest martial artist to ever incarnate," I wanted to train with him. Lakshmi soon gave Vishnu this new task; he started with just the volunteers.

The small group of us met on the beach to train with him when he was in town. It drew the volunteers even closer together. It also drew us closer to Vishnu; he was now our *sensei*, and we looked up to him with reverence. The training was not easy; he made us run laps in the sand, swim in the freezing water, do tons of pushups, and practice kicks and punches until our limbs gave out. We loved every sweaty, salty, sandy second of it. Most of the volunteers were Lakshmi's and Vishnu's "security team," so I was training with a group almost entirely made up of military men and women. I felt tougher and stronger with every class, and I watched my body change; already very strong from dancing and yoga and surfing, it became even stronger. Stronger mind, stronger body. I was ready for the next step.

Throughout June, July, and August, in addition to our monthly weekend classes and our beach trainings with Vishnu, we also got to attend Lakshmi's public University of Mysticism events. This gave all of us more time with the two of them, which we loved. Lakshmi even organized a Sunday-afternoon beach meditation in June and a Sunday hike in July; we were getting to see her (and Vishnu) seven or eight days a month at this point. By the time September rolled around again, the volunteers were a family, with Lakshmi and Vishnu as our parental figures. We goofed off when they weren't around; we straightened up when they appeared. We looked at both of them starry-eyed. We spent more and more of our time together and less and less time with friends outside the group.

In the fall, Lakshmi decided it was time for Vishnu to teach all of her students karate, and I was asked to help Vishnu locate a training space. He found possible training spaces all over town and requested I show up at these spaces to check them out with him, which I always did.

Each time I showed up to a possible dojo space, he seemed excited to see me and always took the time to ask how I was doing, with a warm smile and sparkling eyes. He told me he trusted my sense of energy and that I would be able to help him decide which space was "energetically clean enough" to become his karate dojo.

One day, as we were walking back to our cars after looking at a space, he casually mentioned that it wasn't appropriate for me to surf in a bikini immediately after the martial arts classes he held on the beach. He said he noticed too many of the male students staring at me, which he explained was "not good for my energetic body." I felt surprised by this. I had spent most of my life in a tiny bikini. But I decided to embrace it. He seemed to really care about me, to be looking out for my well-being. It made me feel protected. I felt . . . *fathered* by him. He said now that I was working so closely with him and Lakshmi that the other students would want to "fuck me or fight me" and that I had to be careful how I presented myself. He began calling me daily.

Over the summer, I had talked three more of my closest longtime friends, Jessica, Matt, and Paul, into joining the group. All three of them came to the public seminars and were awed by what they experienced. Lakshmi seemed to be in rare form. In one seminar, she paced the stage swearing like a sailor.

"Fuck the Dalai Lama. Fuck Mother Theresa," she said. Fuck this, fuck that, fucking this, fucking that.

The auditorium had been close to full when the event began; people started running for the door when she started in with the f-bombs. After more than half the audience cleared out, Lakshmi sat down. She sighed.

"That's better," she said. "Those people didn't want to be here. I helped them out by making them so uncomfortable they had to leave. Now we can get down to business. What do you want to know?"

The remaining people still felt uncomfortable, she could tell, so she said, "It is important not to take life too seriously. I think the Dalai Lama and Mother Theresa are Magnificent Beings that do wonderful work. But it is amazing that we all get so upset by the comments made by strangers. We must learn to control our minds. We must learn to not be yanked around by the events that surround us."

As the public events progressed, she got sillier and sillier, making the audience roar with laughter, shocking them with her profanity. In another event, she explained *The Bhagavad Gita*: She called Govinda/Krishna (the charioteer and incarnation of God) the "taxi driver" and said Arjuna (the greatest warrior that ever lived) was "sniveling like a pussy."

"Stop being a pussy and go do what God made you to do," she paraphrased Krishna. Again, she had us howling with laughter.

Immediately after, she got serious when she read the passage that starts with "*Some say this Atman is slain, and others call it the slayer. They know nothing. How can it slay or who shall slay it?*"

She paused for dramatic effect and said it was her favorite passage in any book. She read it beautifully, and most of us were weeping when she was finished. And, as always, she stressed the importance of sharpening our minds with meditation and rocking our careers.

My friends loved her. All three of them relocated to California in order to become her students. Now, I had five of my closest longtime friends in the sangha. My thrill at having Matt, Jessica, and Paul suddenly in California was quickly squashed, however. Vishnu strongly suggested I not spend time with them.

"They will be changing rapidly and need to integrate on their own," he said. "They hold a lot of energy from your past; they will pull you backward. You have been a student for over a year; you are much more advanced. Now that you are so close to Lakshmi and me, your energy affects us. You don't want to harm us with old energy, do you?"

No, of course I didn't. I allowed my friends' calls to go to my voicemail. Eventually, they became volunteers, and I could spend time with them again, but by then, a distance had formed between us. I was Lakshmi's and Vishnu's "right hand woman." They were simply volunteers. We all knew I was different.

One day, Vishnu told me I was to accompany him to a beach about two hours away to scout out a location for a karate class. He said two others from my sangha would join us and that I should meet him in a certain parking lot at a certain time. This was the first time so few of us had been singled out for an all-day outing with him.

He called as I was on my way to meet him, saying the other two wouldn't be joining us, and asked me to stop in a store and buy two sandwiches.

"I'll take care of drinks," he said.

I was really nervous at the thought of spending so much time alone with Vishnu. With two other sangha mates, it would have been nerve-racking enough, but spending the entire day alone with him made me feel slightly petrified. At the same time, however, I felt extremely honored that Lakshmi would allow me to go on this trip. I imagined her resting after the last event, gathering her energy, and trusting me enough to send me on this outing with her man.

I was waiting in the parking lot when Vishnu showed up in the shiny, sparkling clean SUV with tinted windows. After climbing into the car, I suddenly realized I was sitting *in Lakshmi's seat*. Vishnu was wearing volleyball shorts and a T-shirt; I hadn't expected to see him so dressed down. He looked at my outfit—business casual—and told me I was dressed wrong, that I needed clothing I could get wet and sandy in. My house was three minutes from the parking lot, and he said I should drive home and change, that he would wait for me. So I drove home, changed, and drove back in less than ten minutes.

I barely spoke during the awkward forty-five-minute drive. Vishnu rambled on and on about how you call a gun a *weapon* and about all the different components and how they work, and why different guns are used in different situations. I tried to remember it all, thinking it must be important somehow, but it was too much information to take in at once.

At some point, he said, "We're here," and stopped talking as we passed an empty ranger booth that led to an empty parking lot. In silence, we walked from the parking lot to the sand—a challenging descent on a narrow path through bushes and trees down a rather steep and jagged cliff. When we finally reached the sand, he took a few steps toward the water and sat down, so I sat down next to him. The beach was deserted. As I began pulling the sandwiches out of my backpack, he pulled from his a bottle of French champagne and two glasses.

I was shocked and suddenly afraid. This was Lakshmi's man—wasn't he? At events, she would talk about her journey to Enlightenment and say, "And, as you can see—" she would motion with her head toward Vishnu, "—I think everything turned out okay." All the students assumed they were a couple. They wore matching rings on their wedding ring fingers. Why did he bring a bottle of champagne to drink with me, alone on this beach? He opened it, holding his massive hand over the cork so it didn't go flying, poured it into the flutes, handed me one, and said, "To us."

The color drained from my face, and I held my breath.

"Renee," he said, "you have *tremendous* power. It is an honor to have you work with us, and I look forward to getting to know you better."

I exhaled. I took a few sips. I had not been drinking for months, and I did not want to be drunk in front of my boss, but I did not want to be rude, either. When he wasn't looking, I poured the rest of my glass in the sand. We ate in awkward silence.

Suddenly, he said, "I want to show you something. I want to know if it seems familiar."

He got up, walked about ten feet away toward the ocean, kept his back to me, and started doing tai chi and karate moves.

Familiar? I had no idea what he was talking about, but I wanted to sound evolved, so I said, "I can tell that you had a lot of military past lives."

This made him smile. He loved telling us about his military past lives.

Then he asked me to dance for him. I wanted to disappear into the sand. Dance for him? Alone on this beach? I had on a little white T-shirt and yellow sweatpants with a bikini underneath. Instantly, I realized my outfit was too tight, the material too thin. It was too see-through.

I got up, awkwardly, and walked a few feet away. I did some ballet leaps, a few pirouettes, and then some more modern dance–style lunges and yoga-type balances. I threw in a few Argentine tango moves. I couldn't look at him, afraid to see the expression on his face. The emptiness of the beach scared me. The water was crashing along the shore and I was wondering what on earth I had gotten myself into.

Next, we went for a long walk, and he told me that he was "turning into a force of nature" and that, because of his line of work, he suffered from PTSD. He also told me that being around me helped him, that *I* could help him. I had previously offered, in a thank-you card I wrote him after the first time he taught us karate, to help him in any additional way possible. I did not, of course, mean romantically. In fact, it never even crossed my mind. At the time I wrote the card, I had been dating and was in love with the snowboarder I met in Colorado, and this man, *my Spiritual Teacher's man*, while attractive and sexy in his serving and protecting of Lakshmi, honestly, when he was up close, on this beach, not in his role of bodyguard or sensei, wearing volleyball shorts and a T-shirt, telling me to dance for him, seemed old and overweight to me. He was handsome, yes, but in an older-man, father-figure type of way.

He kept talking. Suddenly I felt sorry for him. As he softened and admitted his vulnerability I wanted to help, felt flattered that I *could* help. I relaxed a little. Although being on the beach alone with him felt strange and uncomfortable and a bit scary, something about it also felt really right. I was so lost, so desperately searching. I had been craving for parental figures since I lost my father at fifteen years old. Walking along the beach with this older man made me feel like maybe I had found the mentor I was looking for. With him and Lakshmi in my life, I was no longer alone. I had older, wiser, *Enlightened* people to guide me.

At the end of the day, we drove home. The ride was less awkward. I felt closer to him. He told me I had spent the day in "a lot of light" and if I felt anything weird to call him at any time of the day or night. He added that he slept alone in a room that was empty except for one bed and that I would not be disturbing him. His eyes lingered on mine as he said this.

I thanked him and quickly got out of the car. Never in a million years would I call that man in the middle of the night.

It would be *disrespectful*, to him and to Lakshmi. I had a quick vision of a bed alone in a cement basement. I brushed it aside and drove back to my house, unsure of how to feel. Part of me felt ecstatic that I was now this much closer to the two of them, that I could help lighten the load and ease the suffering of someone so important to Lakshmi, and part of me felt like I was knowingly covering my eyes as I walked straight into a trap.

chapter 6
Renegade

Not only had my Wanderlust been born in Costa Rica, but my "bad girl" spark had been ignited. I started drag-racing my blue and pink Mustang 5.0 behind the school building. I forged doctor's appointment notes, skipped class, and drove to Alabama Jacks, in the Florida Keys, where I drank Jack Daniels on ice with red-necked fishermen twice my age. I set my cruise control on 135 mph, rolled down the windows, and opened the sunroof, blasting "Magic Carpet Ride" on repeat. Rather than hit the brakes, I would swerve into the shoulder lane to pass cars that were in my way. I dove off the stage at rock concerts, into the mosh pit, where I'd slam my body into people three times my size. I got thrown out of bars for drunk and disorderly conduct. I threw up on my typing exam my senior year in high school because I was still drunk from the night before.

Seriously, I was a mess. I had so much emotion swirling inside of me and so many questions. I felt like a caged animal. All I knew was that I got a lot of attention when I behaved badly. Before my father died, I had been quite possibly the weakest, smallest, weirdest, nerdiest kid in school (besides my brother). Suddenly, I was "cool." People looked up to me. People wanted to be like me. I was an enigma, and the power of it excited me.

My mother had told me things like "a woman only has sex to please a man" and that she had been raised to believe a woman's place was in the home. I could not stand this belief system. By this time, I had watched my mother become so undone by my father's death that she practically lost the will to live. When she did engage in life and social activity, she hid behind her physical beauty and presented the façade of a wealthy, beautiful woman who was kind and gracious, with no problems whatsoever. I vowed I would never let men become that important in my life. I would never become a "prim and proper lady." Whatever she was doing—whatever she had been taught—was clearly not working for her, and I wanted no part of it. I went out of my way to disobey her, to be the opposite of everything she wanted me to be. The rift between us deepened.

Just before my seventeenth birthday, my mother insisted I become a "debutante," something I dreaded. I wasn't sure exactly what it entailed, but when I heard I was to be "presented to society," I wanted to throw up in my mouth.

My father had strongly opposed the entire society thing. He was very humble. He donated large amounts of money to charity, but always did so anonymously. When he built a second story on our house, he had the architect design it so that, from the street, it appeared to still be one story because most of the other homes on the street were only one story. He was very conscious that we were financially better off than most, and he was careful to never act better than anybody else.

My mother, on the other hand, was always trying to show off how much we had, always putting on airs. I realize now it came from a deep insecurity, but back then, when I was a teenager, I just thought she was heartless and superficial.

"It is a privilege to be invited," she said, about being a debutante. "You should be honored." I realize now that she would have killed to have been given this chance when she was young, but back then, I was furious.

The mother–daughter inaugural lunch approached. The other debutantes discussed weeks in advance what they would wear. Each girl got her hair, nails, and make-up done. A photographer would be there, we would be introduced to the other debutantes, and our names would appear in the newspaper.

I didn't want to go, so I did it my way: I showed up straight from the ocean, with sandy feet, wet hair, a crumpled dress I had crammed in the trunk of my car, and a huge hickey on my neck. My mother, who was waiting for me in the lobby, took one look at me and turned beet-red. I thought she was going to start yelling, then she cleared her throat, shook her head, and tipped her nose into the air.

"Well, Honey, I would have preferred you make a little more effort," she said.

She turned her back to me and walked into the luncheon. The photographer, in an effort to hide my hickey, asked me to turn my head as he took my photo, making me the only debutante not to be looking directly into the camera.

Each debutante was supposed to throw a party for the other debutantes, so months later, my mother agreed to host my party in our yard. I cohosted with two other girls, deciding on a reggae theme and a live band. My brother and his friends spent hours lugging coolers, soft drinks, tables, and chairs out to the yard. The morning of the event, one of my co-hostesses called me to go over the details.

She read me the guest list but didn't mention the names of my brother or his friends.

"What about Gary?" I asked.

"He can't come," she replied.

"Why not?" I said.

"Because he is not a debutante or a date of a debutante, and if we invite anyone who is not a debutante or a date of a debutante, it will lower the status of the debutantes," she replied.

I was enraged. "Gary and his friends have spent hours setting up this party. It's at his house. They have to come," I countered.

"No, they are not allowed."

We argued some more and hung up the phone. Her mother called me. Our other co-hostess called me. The consensus was that Gary and his friends were not invited. I screamed inside my mind. This was the kind of high-society frivolous bullshit I could not stand.

I ran to my mother's office and wrote in huge letters on a piece of typing paper:

Come crash my debutante party.
Arrive at 10:00pm sharp and enter as a group.
Live reggae music and free food. BYOB.

I put it in my mother's copy machine and ran off five hundred copies. Then I called a friend and asked him to help me plaster cars at the beach.

That night, hundreds of people showed up. The police arrived to quell the crowd, people ran in all directions, and my mother, to my amazement, appeared in the center of it all, with the bullhorn from our boat, yelling, "Kids, I apologize. This is a private party. You will have to leave. But if you want to come back next Saturday night, I will host a party for all of you." She then found me in the crowd and was—surprisingly—not angry. She was drunk and having fun with so many people at her house and in her yard.

True to her word, she did host a party the next weekend. In fact, once she realized my brother and I were drinking under-age, she allowed us to have everyone drink and hang out at our house on the weekends. She never purchased alcohol for us, but she turned her back on the beer and wine that arrived with our guests. I'd often walk downstairs late at night to get something to eat and find her drinking wine with my friends, all of them sitting around the kitchen table, drunk and laughing.

The truth is, *everyone* loved my mother. She had a great public face for all of our friends. She took everyone in, fed them, listened to them, nurtured them, and sent them home full (in body and in spirit). She let all of them stay as long as they wanted and never asked personal questions. She loaned them money, helped them get jobs, and even made up jobs around our house in order to employ the ones who needed money but were too proud to take a handout.

No one besides my brother and me ever saw her broken side. She was a dichotomy. As we all are. She had such a need to be needed and she was in so much pain. I suppose I was a safe place to let out her hurt and her anger, and in my constant rebellion, I created the perfect target. At that stage in my life, I hated her for disappearing in alcohol and pills. I hated her for being so concerned with her fading beauty. I hated her for acting like she was better than others. I hated her rigid Catholic superiority and her refusal to talk about my father's death. Most of all, I hated that I was there to love and hold and listen to her, but she could not see me or my love, because she was fixated on and only wanting that love from my dead father.

By the end of my senior year, I couldn't wait to get away from her and away from Florida. I was accepted into UC Irvine. My mother spent weeks buying me everything I could possibly need to leave home. This was her pattern: abusive and neglectful, followed by loving, nurturing, and indulging.

Moving to California was the hardest thing I had ever done. I was incredibly homesick. I felt overwhelmed by the enormity of the campus and the sheer number of other students. On Thanksgiving, my mother came to visit, and I fell, trembling and sobbing, into her arms.

"I want to come home," I said.

"Okay, Honey," she agreed.

At times like this, I loved her so much.

I flew home the following week and started school in Jacksonville. I got almost all A's. I qualified to be a member of Phi Beta Kappa and was on the dean's list. I graduated *magna cum laude*, with a BS in psychology and a BS in dance. At night, I worked as a cage dancer at a local nightclub. I was choreographing and rehearsing and going to the gym on my lunch break, surfing in the mornings. I was on fire. In fact, halfway through my junior year, I was diagnosed with chronic fatigue syndrome, and my mother told me to take it down a notch.

"You don't need to get A's in everything," she said.

But I couldn't help myself. It was the way my father raised me: Work hard, do your best, all the time, at everything. And the constant striving, the constant excelling, helped me hide. I didn't have to focus on myself and my mental demons; I didn't have time. I hid in activity, and I pushed the dark, wounded, lost, empty part of myself even deeper. Without realizing it, I put on the *exact* same façade my mother had: happy, sexy, fun, beautiful girl who loves everybody and whom everybody loves.

Chapter 7
Chosen

Vishnu returned to Arizona two days after our beach outing. I had heard very little from him while he was gone and, as always, was not exactly sure when he would return. One morning, my phone rang. Private number. It was Vishnu calling to say he was on his way north from the airport, and was planning to hike a trail near my house. He wanted me to meet him. His voice sounded strained; he seemed distracted and nervous. We met on the top of a hill, took a very short small-talk-filled walk together, and then he told me he had left his car down below; he asked me to drive him back down the hill.

Something about having *him* in *my* car felt really wrong. He seemed too big for it. The closeness we had experienced on the beach had dissipated, replaced by an energetic wall. He didn't speak. I didn't speak. Something major had shifted, and I felt like I couldn't ask him about it. All I could think about was, *I have Lakshmi's boyfriend in my car.* The responsibility of it felt huge to me, and, suddenly, I felt too small and inadequate to handle it. I drove him down to his car in strained silence, each minute lasting an eternity. Quietly, he got out of my car and drove off in his. I was left with no idea why he had wanted me to meet him. Surely, it could not have been just to drive him to his car.

The next day, as the small group of us was arriving for our karate class on the beach, he asked me to join him for a short walk. We walked a few minutes down the beach, along the shoreline, in awkward silence. Suddenly he stopped. He turned to look at me and asked, "Do I seem familiar to you?"

The wind lashed our hair. The waves crashed on the sand. The seagulls' calls echoed quietly against the cliff.

I felt that fatherly connection again. Vishnu was twelve years older than me and so much more mature. It felt like he was filling this void I had held for so long.

"Yes," I responded. "I feel like you were my father in a past life."

He cringed. He looked crushed.

"Father?" he asked.

I felt embarrassed. That obviously wasn't the answer he wanted. "Yes," I said.

He changed the subject. "I want to know about the guy you are dating," he said. "Did you meet him before or after you became Lakshmi's student?"

"Before," I said. "But I'm no longer dating him."

He seemed relieved.

"You have to be so careful," he said. "So many Dark Beings will be drawn to you now. You must be wary of everyone you meet."

By now, the entire group of students had arrived and was lining up for class. He turned back to begin teaching. I followed him, wondering about Dark Beings.

The next week, he called to say we had to go "do recon" on that beach again. The same two students who were supposed to join us before cancelled again at the last minute. Vishnu and I went alone again, and again I felt awkward. We walked along the beach. He talked; I listened. He spoke mostly of what it was like to work so closely with Lakshmi and again brought up his PTSD.

This time, he explained a bit more. He said his PTSD was from "battling the occult," but left that hanging there, like I was supposed to know what that meant.

He looked down at the ground and said again, "You can help me. Just being with you helps me."

This time, it was cold on the beach. The wind whipped the salt water from the waves into our faces and onto our clothes, making us turn around before too long and head back to the parking lot. Before we left, Vishnu sat in the sand to finish what he was saying; I sat down next to him.

After a long pause he looked at me and asked, in an incredibly defeated and humble way, "Renee, would you like to spend more time with me?"

I knew he was asking, *Renee, would you like to see me romantically?* I looked back at him. He was wearing sunglasses, which drew my attention to his short, yellow teeth. I wasn't attracted to him. Or was I? I couldn't be sure. There had been times when I was getting ready for Lakshmi's events that I wondered, as I applied my make-up, *Would Vishnu think I'm attractive?* There were times when I saw him escorting her and protecting her that I thought, *I wish I had a Vishnu in my life.* There were times, when I met him to look at dojo spaces, that I saw him as *strikingly* handsome. When he taught karate, I often saw him as strong and youthful. And there was the fact that he was Lakshmi's consort, her boyfriend—and Lakshmi was God to me.

His question made me feel like The Chosen Child. Out of all the other students, he wanted me. I yearned so desperately to be close to him and Lakshmi, and they were a package deal. Being close to Vishnu meant being close to Lakshmi. I desperately wanted guides, supportive parent figures. I wanted answers to my questions. I wanted to not feel so alone.

And I was afraid that saying no would jeopardize my position with him. I coveted my special position. I was also afraid that if we got closer, he would see my flaws. I did not know if I could live up to his expectations, whatever they might be. I most certainly could not be Lakshmi.

I grabbed a handful of sand and held it up to him. I said, "I feel like I am holding something so precious here. My relationship with you and Lakshmi feels like a precious gem to me, something I have wanted for a very long time." I covered the handful of sand gently with my other hand. "I want to hold it so carefully, with so much respect. Of course, I would like to spend as much time as possible with the two of you. Of course I'd like to see you more."

I had been careful to include Lakshmi in my answer; to show him that I hoped spending more time with him really meant spending more time with her.

"Do you enjoy my company?" he asked.

"Yes," I responded, unsure if it was he I enjoyed being close to or if I just really loved finally being The Chosen Child.

He smiled, stood up, and offered me his hand. It was the first time I had touched him. His hand felt very strong and surprisingly soft. It felt familiar. When I held it, my world turned white. The same feeling I had when I touched the pyramid. He helped me up and, side-by-side, we left the beach.

Chapter 8
Hawaii

Just after my sophomore year of college, I got asked to model for a bikini calendar and was told that one of the models would be selected as model of the year. She'd be given the cover shot and would be taken around the world for a six-month photo shoot, starting the following January. I got picked, and my mother allowed me to take a semester off from school. Her only caveat was that my boyfriend, Matt, go with me.

"We don't know this man," she said, referring to the photographer. "I checked him out as best I could, but I still can't be 100 percent sure he's legit. I want to be sure you have someone you trust with you at all times. I also want you to get your plane tickets for the entire trip from him before you leave. That way, if he's not who he says he is, you can come home quickly."

I loved her for this. She said she was afraid to let me go, afraid of what could happen, but she also realized it was a great opportunity for me to see the world, one she did not want me to miss.

A few months later, Matt and I got our plane tickets and itinerary: New Zealand, Australia, Thailand, Nepal, Malaysia, Indonesia, Fiji, the Cook Islands, Samoa, and French Polynesia. My dream to travel the world was coming true.

The trip had its ups and downs. When we were in Nepal, the photographer and his team of Sherpas abandoned us in the Himalayan Mountains, at an elevation of 22,000 feet. We had to follow donkey poop for ten hours in order to find our way to civilization. The photographer appeared three days later, after we had navigated our way over the top of the mountain pass and down the other side. Apparently, he and the Sherpas had stopped to eat and had started drinking, then could not cross over the pass for three days because it had started snowing.

On the trip, I also bungee-jumped from a bridge three hundred feet high, posed in a bikini inside a New Zealand glacier cave moments before it collapsed, and surfed the biggest waves of my life in Indonesia.

Adventures like this continued through my twenties and into my thirties.

Immediately after I finished college, I moved to Hawaii, to the North Shore of Oahu, the surfing mecca of the world. There, I was trained to surf huge waves by some of the legends of big-wave surfing. I continued work as a bikini model and travelled all over the world, mostly by myself with my surfboards. I met wonderful people, experienced wonderful things.

While attending summer school at the University of Manoa in Hawaii, I met a young guy who was on his way to Tavarua, an island in Fiji. He invited me, saying there would be a world-class tube-riding event, and the owner wanted a bikini model to attend. I fell in love with the place and, a few years later, spent two months managing the island and living in a tiny tree house with white lace curtains. I had everything a young girl could ask for, yet I still felt a void inside. I still felt soul-sick. And it began manifesting in my relationships with men.

In Hawaii, I started sleeping with every hot guy I met, and there were *a lot* of them. Deep down, I wanted love, I wanted true intimacy, but I had been so wounded by life and a part of me craved the power I felt when I got a guy into bed and left before he woke up. I learned to completely separate sex from love. I learned to use my body in the most intimate way with utter strangers and to shut myself, my soul, and my mind out of the process entirely. A part of me really enjoyed the freedom and empowerment of being so promiscuous, especially after being raised by such an uptight, prudish, Catholic mother; however, another part of me knew I was betraying myself.

I picked men who mimicked the love pattern I had learned from my mother: they loved me, then pushed me away. They wanted me, then slept with someone else. If I met a guy who truly loved me and wanted only me, I got bored and broke up with him. I had learned to crave the pull–push, attraction–repulsion, intermittent reinforcement that I had experienced as a child.

Later, I would learn that this insecure, codependent attraction to emotionally unavailable people is common in children of addicts. I, like many children, was taught by my mother that I was not okay the way I was, that I had to change in order to be good enough. The constant refrain of *slow down, be quiet, don't do that, stop crying, not now, be a lady, go play in your room* taught me at a very young age that I had a choice: be exactly the way I was and be shunned and possibly abandoned, or change in order to be loved and taken care of. I picked love and survival; all children do. That's how we end up with screwed-up adults whose insecurities run so deep. Most of us learn in childhood to hide our true selves and become who our parents and teachers need us to be; we learn to turn our feelings off and stuff them deep inside. They reappear, years later, as addiction and self-destructive behavior.

I learned to turn my light down, to blend into the furniture, to not get noticed, to stay out of the way. But I wanted to be noticed. I *needed* to be noticed. So, as a young adult, I used my body to get attention. However, I had grown to believe that if I spent too much time around anyone, s/he would soon get annoyed and shove me away, the way my mother always had, so one-night stands fit my needs. They temporarily filled my void. A man would find me sexy and irresistible, that would feed my ego, and then, if I left before he woke up, he would never get the chance to see my flaws and my wounds and my broken parts.

He couldn't get annoyed or disillusioned with me because I was already long gone.

This pattern of behavior, of course, alienated me from myself even more. I wanted acceptance and friendship, companionship and approval. But by portraying myself as the bad girl who just wanted sex, I attracted the guys who didn't want relationships either and repelled the guys who did. So my wounds multiplied and grew deeper. My belief that I was not lovable, not desirable, not worthy of a close, committed relationship strengthened. So I slept around more. It was a vicious cycle and one I did not realize I was perpetuating. My soul sickness grew more intense with every passing day.

The years flew by. I felt myself going nowhere, so, in an effort to get my life together, I moved from the North Shore to the South Shore, to Diamond Head, and started going to massage therapy school. I got a job as a barista; my shift started at 4:30 a.m. I rented a room in a gorgeous house close to the coffee shop, but I should have paid more attention to the living arrangement. The house belonged to a woman and her daughter living together. The father had just died. The girl, who was a few years older than me, was an alcoholic and struggled with anger and depression. I had landed in the middle of chaos and, subconsciously, I had picked another situation that mimicked my life with my mother. To add to the chaos, a month after I moved in, an exotic dancer took over the last spare bedroom.

We began throwing parties almost every weekend, with loud local bands and people diving off the roof into the pool. The police showed up to shut our parties down. Once, as they were making the rounds, throwing people out of the house, I was in my bedroom screwing a guy I had just met when two police officers entered, flashlights blazing. I was humiliated, but it also woke me up. I was a mess. I had to get off that island or at least out of that house.

I moved back to the North Shore, to a studio apartment. I felt utterly lost. I had no idea what I was doing with my life. One morning I was lying on my bathroom floor, curled in a fetal position, crying my guts out, wondering what to do with my life. I called my godfather for advice. He was very conservative, a staunch Republican, a graduate of MIT, a Harvard MBA, and an engineer. I figured he'd tell me to move to someplace like Boston and get a "real" job in an office.

Instead, he said, "Renee, what do you love?"

I thought about it. "Surfing, dancing, traveling, and speaking Spanish."

He said, "If you can find a job doing something you love, you will never have to 'work' a day in your life. Do what you love for six months, and see where it leads you. Be open to anything."

With that advice, he lifted me up and gave me wings.

But, first, I had to get my ass off that island. I saw before me a life of surfing, surfers, alcoholism, and a dead-end marriage to a Hawaiian lifeguard. I had to do something more with my life than surf and chase surfers. I made a plan—not much of a plan, but a first step: I was going to move to Mexico, learn to speak Spanish fluently, and become a professional massage therapist at one of the fancy hotels. I had just finished massage therapy school. I could do it. I moved to Cabo San Lucas.

I met a cute surfer. I moved into his trailer on the beach and surfed every day. I never got a job. A month rolled by. I *had* to get my ass out of Mexico.

I had travelled to so many countries, most of them on my own. I could work for *Lonely Planet*. I would be the *perfect* guide for them. They had just started a TV show, where they followed a young girl or guy around the world; *I* could be that person. So I sent a letter to their London office telling them so. Then I flew to Europe. I figured I'd walk into the office and simply convince them to hire me.

I started in Italy, visiting a friend and his sister. Then I detoured to Germany, Austria, and Prague. After Prague, I detoured again, to Spain. The *Lonely Planet* idea receded further and further into the recesses of my mind. I spent a week in Madrid and then took the train to San Sebastian, where I had no place to stay. This was how I travelled back then: I'd let the wind blow me and work it out when I arrived.

At the train station, I started calling youth hostels. No availability. Then I tried cheap hotels. No rooms vacant. Then I tried more expensive hotels. Still no luck. Then I tried *expensive* hotels. Totally booked. I was screwed. I sat on the floor and tried to figure out what to do. It was getting dark.

Just then, I noticed a tan, blonde, surfy-looking guy kneeling on the ground, rearranging his backpack. Not sure if he spoke English, I approached him and asked if he had just arrived and where he was staying.

He looked over at me, smiled, and, with a heavy Australian accent, said, "Nah, I'm actually leaving." He looked me up and down and added, "You should come with me. I'm on my way to La Tomatia." I had never heard of it.

"I'll go to La Tomatia with you, if you go to Formentera with me," I heard myself say. What was I doing? I had read about Formentera, the smallest Spanish island, and was dying to go, but it seemed relatively deserted, and I wanted to be sure I had company. He seemed like a nice guy, his eyes were very kind; maybe he'd be a good traveling companion.

He looked at me like he had just won the lottery. "Deal," he responded.

We shook hands and introduced ourselves. His name was Adrian. He was cute—not cute enough to sleep with but definitely kind of cute. We got on the train to Valencia, arriving the next day. After a pitcher of Sangria on a hot Spanish night, I ended up sleeping with him. That's the way I did it then: boys, booze, sex.

We went to La Tomatia, which turned out to be a tomato-throwing festival in a little town near Valencia—30,000 people crammed into a tiny town square pelting each other with overripe tomatoes—then to Ibiza instead of Formentera because it was easier to get to. Finally, ten days later, we arrived in Mundaka to reunite with his friend and a van full of surfboards. Adrian's friend was surfing the World Qualifying Series tour. I decided to move into the van and continue the tour with the boys.

We packed up the van and headed to the next top, Portugal, driving all day long and arriving after dark. It hit me that night, as we were falling asleep in the back of the van, all scrunched together like sardines, that I had spent the last two months in Europe doing the exact same thing I'd done in Mexico, and in Hawaii before that: surfing and sleeping with surfers. If I was ever going to take my life to the next level, I had to make a change.

I woke up the next morning to people screaming outside the van. The surf was pumping, and all the guys in the lineup were yelling their heads off. As I looked out the back window at the surf, I suddenly knew, I simply *knew* I had to move to California to become a professional Latin-ballroom dancer. *That* was my life's next step. It was suddenly crystal-clear. This career choice had briefly crossed my mind the last few months I had lived in Hawaii. I had signed up to take ballroom dance lessons at the Arthur Murray in Honolulu, and while on my way to Mexico, I spent a week in southern California and had looked at a few dance studios in San Diego. As I gazed at the surf, one of those studios flashed into my mind and I saw myself there dancing. This was the answer. I had to fly to California and I had to get a job at a dance studio, and I had to find a Latin-ballroom dance partner, and I had to compete. I got up and opened the back door.

Adrian was surfing. I left him a note:

Thanks for everything. I'm moving to LA. Flying out
of Madrid tonight.
Love and hugs, Renee.

Then I grabbed my backpack, crawled out of the van, and started walking toward the train station.

chapter 9
ARizONa

As Vishnu drove me home from the beach after our "recon," he told me he had really appreciated the card I had given him and was glad we had found some time to be alone. He seemed content. I felt nervous. I had never intended that card to be anything more than a sincere "thank you."

On the ride home Vishnu gave me strict orders not to tell anyone about our outing. According to him, it would set us up—Lakshmi included—for an "occult attack." I most certainly did not want to do that, even though I had no idea what an "occult attack" was. I wished I could talk to someone. I felt truly stuck. This thing with Lakshmi and Vishnu was getting weirder by the minute, but at the same time, it was exciting. I believed in Enlightenment, and I believed I was heading in that direction. I had always been able to talk out my concerns with my friends, but now suddenly I was unable to.

As soon as I got home I called Bruno. I wanted to tell him about my day and contemplated breaking Vishnu's orders, but in the end I simply asked him if we could go see the movie *Alvin and the Chipmunks*. I needed a lighthearted evening to take my mind off all the weirdness.

When I arrived at the theater, Bruno was standing outside with his sister. He had already bought us tickets . . . to see *I am Legend*. I hate scary movies. I had nightmares that night about the creatures in the movie and woke up feeling like something was on top of me, sucking the breath out of my body.

I remembered Vishnu telling me that I could call him if anything strange ever happened, that he slept alone in a room with just a bed. So I struggled through the weight on top of me, reached for the phone, and dialed. It was midnight. He answered and soothed me. He told me to turn on all the lights in my house and make hot mint tea with a lot of honey in it. He said he would wait on the phone until I made it and drank some.

While we waited for the water to boil, he asked what I had been sleeping in. "I will try not to pant," he said.

I cringed and answered, "Sweatpants," even though I had gone to bed naked.

He then explained that all the light running through me from working so closely with the two of them made me attractive in the night to "Dark Beings on the dream plane" and that they came to steal my energy. He told me not to be afraid and explained that they simply used the form of the scary creatures in the movie as a way to frighten me. "They feed on fear," he told me. "Just laugh at them and wake yourself up if it happens again."

I thanked him, hung up the phone, and tried to go back to bed. I could not sleep. Now I was afraid of three things: "Dark Beings," whatever they were; "occult attacks," whatever they were; and a romantic relationship with Vishnu.

The next morning, I ignored his phone calls, letting the messages pile up in my voicemail. I had no idea what to do. I was not ready to be in this position with him. I could see we were headed in this direction, but I also seriously hoped I was wrong. And, part of the truth is that I didn't want to push it away. I was stuck. I wanted to be special, but I didn't want to sleep with him. I was terrified of that step, that radical change in my life, in my path. I was used to being on my own, doing things my way. If I started sleeping with Vishnu, I would be under his command even more. The free spirit in me wanted to run. The soul-sick seeker in me wanted to stay and do whatever it took to become Enlightened. I still had one foot out the door. If I slept with him, I would really be jumping all-in. And what about Lakshmi? Were they dating? Could I just blatantly ask him? Every time I thought about asking him, I chickened out.

At some point, I had to answer the phone. He had called too many times and left increasingly stressed-out messages. When I called him back, we talked only business. We had our last class weekend of the year that night and the next, and we had to discuss the logistics. When class rolled around, I avoided his gaze as much as possible.

The next day, he called again and asked about my change in behavior.

Suddenly, I was pissed off. I did not want to be in this position with him. I told him the beach outings and champagne made me feel uncomfortable, and I said that it seemed like maybe he was implying that we were lovers in a past life. This seemed like the gentlest, most respectable way to say to my boss, my sensei, and possibly my Spiritual Teacher's boyfriend, *Please stop hitting on me.*

By this stage in my life I had been so used to ignoring my inner guidance when it came to men, allowing myself to be in very uncomfortable situations in my effort to be loved, that I was the perfect target for this type of unwanted advance. I had allowed myself to get here, and I had done it with my eyes wide open, wanting to believe he just saw me as evolved, but knowing deep down that he was attracted to me . . . and I had gone along with it because I simply wanted to be as close as possible to Lakshmi, a part of her inner circle. I had always been terrified of confrontation, because I learned as a child that any time I stood up for myself or tried to enforce my boundaries, I got scolded and pushed away by my mother. But I was finally so uncomfortable that I decided I had to say something.

"We have all had so many past lives," he replied, "that we have all been each others' lovers, parents, children, friends, and enemies."

With that, he brushed it aside and went back to talking business. I felt *incredibly* relieved. *I must have been wrong,* I thought to myself.

The event that night went smoothly, and at the end of it, before we all went our separate ways for the winter holidays, Lakshmi—via Vishnu—invited eight of her closest volunteers to meet with her after the event. Once all the other students left, the eight of us went back into the event room and stood in a small circle, nervously awaiting her.

She entered the room escorted by Vishnu. We made room for them in our circle. Seeing Vishnu by her side, protecting her and not focusing his attention on me, I felt reassured. Everything felt normal again.

Lakshmi thanked us for all our hard work that year and told us she wanted us to visit her in Arizona for a special weekend together to celebrate. She explained that we would meet the student who had been mentoring her. This was the first we heard of anyone outranking her; we were thrilled at the idea of meeting *another* Enlightened Master. She told us we would hike in the woods with Vishnu, and we would have a special meditation session with her. Until this point, we'd had only fleeting moments alone with Lakshmi. This opportunity was a rare and precious gift. January could not come fast enough.

A few days later, I flew to Colorado to spend Christmas and New Year's Eve with some close friends. Vishnu was on my mind constantly—dark thoughts of him. He showed up in my dreams: in pain, reaching out. He was grabbing for me. Why did I keep thinking about him? It was such a relief to be away from the intensity of working with him and yet he was still with me. I kept trying to push him from my mind.

He called me on Christmas Day to "check in" on me. I thought I had been plopped back in the "normal student" pile, but it seems as though I was still "special." My heart fluttered at the attention. I excused myself from my friends and retreated into my bedroom. I closed the door, sat on the floor, and listened intently. His voice sounded masculine, mature, protective. And I suddenly recognized that I felt tremendous affection for him.

He asked whether I had received the gift he had sent me. I walked toward the front door to look for it and noticed a small package on the floor under the bench in the entryway. I opened it. It was a DVD of *Conan the Barbarian*. I *loved* Arnold Schwarzenegger. I had learned to love him as a child, while watching his movies with my father.

Delighted by the gift, I thanked him profusely.

"Conan is one of Lakshmi's Teacher's many incarnations," he said. "You can learn a lot by watching the movie."

"Oh," I replied, not sure if Conan had actually ever been a real person, but excited anyway about watching the movie.

I told Vishnu about having him in my thoughts, and he started to explain the occult to me.

He told me that *occult* meant "hidden" and that, because I was meditating and becoming so bright, "Dark Beings" were pushing themselves into my mind. They were "hidden" because they were not "in the physical realm," but, energetically, they could and would hurt me. The brighter I became, the more I had to fear an "occult attack," which would manifest as very dark mind states or extremely vivid nightmares.

I listened, but did not want to believe in "Dark Beings" messing with my mind. I wanted to ask questions, but he kept talking. He went on to explain that when someone thinks about you, there is an energetic line that goes from that person to you and that explains why you end up thinking of each other at the same time. Lakshmi had taught us the proper etiquette is to never focus on another person with our thoughts. Vishnu was adamant that he *was not thinking about me*. If he ended up in my thoughts, it was because Dark Beings were "posing as him" to "gain access to my mind."

If I believed in Beings of Light assisting me on my path, I supposed I had to believe in Dark Beings, as well. *I'm strong enough to handle them*, I thought to myself. We chatted a bit more, and then I hung up and went back to my friends. I had a little glow in my heart. Vishnu had sent me a present. He knew I didn't want to be with him romantically, and he still reached out to me on Christmas. I felt safe putting him back in the "father figure" category, knowing I was still loved, still singled out as worthy of receiving a Christmas gift and call from him, still "different" from the other students.

Two weeks after I returned from Colorado, the eight of us flew to Arizona. Vishnu called me the night before to tell me he was really looking forward to my visit and that my arriving in Arizona would make the state "sparkle with enchantment."

Ugh, I thought to myself, *the romantic overtones are back.* I wanted to believe I had misinterpreted him. I wanted to talk it out with a girlfriend to get clear, but I couldn't tell anyone. Vishnu had specifically told me not to. He said the energy surrounding our times together was so intense it would cause harm to anyone I discussed it with and that the energy would "back up" and harm me, as well. I believed him. I'm not even sure why. I think I had witnessed so much light and magic and intense energy in my interactions with Lakshmi that Vishnu's warnings made sense to me.

I also knew I was one of the only students to ever interact with Vishnu and Lakshmi outside of the weekend classes, and I really believed I would be betraying them if I ever spoke about them to anyone else. I decided I would show up in Arizona and figure it out there.

The morning of our flight, Vishnu sent the eight of us an e-mail with strict instructions: We were told to rent three cars. I was to drive two of the other students, Seth and Lisa. Lisa was to be my copilot, and Seth was to sit behind her in the car.

Seth and Lisa, in fact, were the two students who kept cancelling on our beach outings. I wondered whether they were ever truly invited in the first place, but I never asked them. I was afraid of the answer.

Vishnu had given us a rental-car checklist. It took fifteen minutes to check everything off: tire pressure checked, oil full, mirrors adjusted, no dents, mileage noted, jack in the trunk, all lights working . . . The list went on and we all had to check all three cars. Then we had to drive in a caravan from the airport. Our first stop was at Whole Foods where each of us had to buy Lakshmi and the senior student an arrangement of flowers. This took forever, because eight of us showed up and asked one flower arranger to arrange sixteen complicated bouquets of flowers. By the time we were finished, we had only twenty minutes left to find our hotel, check in to our rooms, shower, and change for dinner.

When we arrived to the restaurant the hostess led us upstairs to a large and sad room that held nothing but our table for thirteen on a thin, stained, green carpet. There were a few sizeable windows, but otherwise the walls were bare. Awkwardly, we stood in a semi circle facing the door, unsure of what else to do.

We heard Vishnu in the hall moments before he and Lakshmi entered the room with Shiva, a shriveled older man with wild hair, oxygen hoses in his nose, and two younger, *much* younger, consorts by his side. Vishnu and Shiva approached our semicircle with Vishnu wheeling Shiva's oxygen tank along side him as he introduced Shiva to each of us. When he got to me, he said, "Shiva, this is Renee" and then dropped Shiva's oxygen tank, which hit the ground with a loud crash and strained the tubes in Shiva's nose.

Lakshmi, Shiva, the consorts, and the other volunteers looked stunned. Vishnu flushed red, bent over to pick up the tank, and introduced Shiva to the next volunteer. As soon as all the introductions were done, we sat down around the table, Lakshmi on one end and Shiva on the other. I was told to sit next to Shiva and across from Vishnu. Shiva's consorts sat on either side of Lakshmi. I noticed Shiva and his consorts all wore rings that looked like Lakshmi's. All the other volunteers sat nervously in the center.

Dinner was weird. The restaurant was run-down, the food mediocre. Shiva and Lakshmi did most of the talking. At one point, Shiva looked at the necklace I was wearing, a string of hand-painted porcelain beads. With a strange expression, he said to me, "That's an interesting necklace. Where did you get it?" He added, "It has some very . . . interesting energy."

I told him it was my mother's, and he made a face. "Should I take it off and put it in the far corner of the room?" I asked, horrified that I was wearing something harmful.

He said, "It may be better if you don't wear it, but putting it in your purse is fine."

Once I removed it, he quickly switched the subject to something more lighthearted. Sitting so close to him, I felt the same way I did next to Lakshmi: like I was being sandblasted with light, dissolving into bliss and peace and love and silence and God. He was an old man, with long, stringy hair, trembling and weak, but I was overwhelmed by the light I felt in his presence.

As we left the restaurant that night, Vishnu pulled me aside and said quickly, "You may want to get rid of all of your mother's jewelry. We need to discuss this when we're back home."

The next night, the eight of us went back to Whole Foods to buy everything Lakshmi told us we needed for our special meditation event with her: Burrito Night. We met Lakshmi and Vishnu at a beautiful house—not Lakshmi's house. They had rented this one for a few hours because none of the students could be allowed to know where Lakshmi lived. According to Vishnu, it would be "far too dangerous for her energetically" because we would hold the image of the house in our minds, and our impure energy would harm Lakshmi.

Burrito Night was a blast. The ten of us filled the small kitchen and divided cooking tasks among ourselves. Then we stood around a huge table in the dining room, chatting and laughing as we built our burritos. Everyone was in great spirits; we were all "totally baked." Many of the volunteers, myself included, got caught staring at Lakshmi in awe. She just smiled her charming, light-filled smile, and we would look away, embarrassed. We sprawled out in the chairs and on the floor to eat.

While the others were finishing their burritos, Vishnu and Lakshmi asked me to go outside with them for a moment. Suddenly, Lakshmi seemed upset. She told me that teaching the group took a huge toll on her and that Vishnu had suggested they bring in somebody to take over her tasks in running her company. With all the senior students and the new students, as well as the Power Trips and public seminars, Lakshmi had built a sizeable personal/professional development company.

"Vishnu suggested that this person be you," she said. "I'm not thrilled with the idea. I love running my company, but my energy is diminishing, and I need help."

She turned to look me in the eyes, grabbed both of my hands, and said, "We will have to trust each other."

It was the first time I had ever touched her. Her hands felt like light: soft, as if they were not really hands but balls of energy. She seemed so vulnerable. I wanted to protect her. I would do anything for her. Of course I would help run her company.

When we returned to California, Vishnu and I made an appointment to go over the details of my new responsibilities—at his house. Vishnu and Lakshmi had led us to believe they always stayed at hotels. I myself booked the rooms for them—always two separate rooms—so I was surprised when he gave me an address that sounded like it belonged to a house. I wondered if Lakshmi would be there, and if I would see her today, too. Had they moved from Arizona to California? I drove up to the house and Vishnu was standing outside. I suspected I would not be invited in and I was not.

The morning of our meeting, he called to say, "I'm about to go for a hike. Would you like to join me? If so, bring beach clothing." The hike was long and hot and very fast. I quickly regretted saying "yes," although I'm not sure I had really been given an option; I had assumed we were going to discuss my new job while hiking. Instead he took off ahead of me in silence. As I walked behind him, struggling to keep up, he took his shirt off, and I cringed at his sweaty, pale skin and the rolls of fat above his volleyball shorts. He walked ahead of me with his left hand raised, making funny motions with his index finger. He wore a fanny pack. I began to think how odd Vishnu was, how repulsed I was by him. And then suddenly my thoughts switched to compassion. He seemed to be in great emotional pain, struggling with something, and trying so hard to become Enlightened like

Lakshmi. I still could not figure out if he and Lakshmi were dating. The more I interacted with him, the more it seemed he was always alone.

Suddenly, as if he felt me thinking about him, he turned around and told me to do a karate *kata* that he had taught before the holidays. I felt completely caught off guard. I hadn't thought about that kata for over a month. I wanted every position to be in perfect form, to show I was a good student, but I simply could not remember it all, especially with him staring at me. I did it poorly and I felt embarrassed: I suddenly felt small again, weak, vulnerable, flawed. I felt like a failure. He said nothing when I finished, just turned on his heel and continued hiking. I hurried along after him.

When we returned to his house, Vishnu told me we needed to get into the hot tub because we "cleared out a lot of energetic lines on the hike" and the hot tub would "make sure they left our bodies." I wasn't sure why, if we cleared out lines, we still needed them to leave our bodies, but I decided not to ask.

Vishnu opened the hot tub cover, removed his shoes, dropped his shirt and fanny pack in a pile on the ground, and crawled in, sweaty and sandy. I realized I was supposed to do the same. I had a blue bikini on under my hiking clothes and awkwardly peeled off my socks and shoes and then my t-shirt and shorts. I looked at the ground, pretending to focus on my balance as I removed my clothing. I couldn't bear the idea of him watching me undress.

The hot tub was large enough for four to five people and I stayed curled in a ball in the corner, as far away as I could possibly get from him. This felt *way* too intimate. He leaned back and kept his eyes closed most of the time. The jets made a lot of noise. We were on the side of his house, halfway between the front sidewalk and the back yard; he had chosen a corner by the back yard so I was closer to the sidewalk and turned away from him, looking out onto the street, pretending to be fascinated by the cars and people that passed by. Eventually, he got out. I got out with him and stood awkwardly by the hot tub. He went inside and came out with two towels. Then he told me to follow him as he showed me to the guest shower. He told me to shower and change and meet him on the upper deck to discuss my new job.

I showered as quickly as I could, worried about keeping him waiting. Then I nervously climbed the stairs. I had to walk through a bedroom to get to the deck. I tried not to look around, but I could not help noticing that I was walking through *Lakshmi's bedroom*. I could tell it was hers by the few items I saw. So they *did* live together, at least when she was in California. There was no sign that Vishnu shared the bedroom. I had noticed that he walked downstairs in the three-level house after he showed me to the guest shower. I tried not to look at any more of Lakshmi's room as I walked through it to the deck. I did not want to "harm her with my attention." I couldn't believe I was being permitted to walk through her bedroom.

When I got outside, Vishnu was waiting on the deck dressed nicely, in dark jeans and a dress shirt. I was wearing the same sweaty clothing I had hiked in. He looked annoyed and asked if I had something nicer to change into.

"No," I said. He had told me to come dressed in beach clothing, not in anything nicer. I had assumed we were going to hash out the details of my new job while hiking. Plus, the last time I showed up in business casual attire for a beach outing, he had told me to change. Again, I instantly felt criticized—small, flawed, and vulnerable.

We discussed the job; well, he talked and I listened. He said my life would change drastically, that I would no longer be able to come and go as I pleased. Most of my time would be spent with him and Lakshmi. He told me I would have a lot of responsibility, but he knew I could handle it. He was very clear that it would no longer be appropriate for me to spend as much time with the other students. He told me I would be his personal assistant and do "anything and everything that needs to be done," that I would basically be on call for him 24/7. He said I would help with shopping and errands and cleaning and cooking when Lakshmi was in town, and that I would help him run her company. He was vague about time off and he never mentioned pay. His soliloquy lasted fifteen minutes, because he repeated himself often; he never asked if I had questions, and then he dismissed me.

"Go home and change," he said. "We are going out to dinner to celebrate."

I arrived at the restaurant in dark jeans, heels, and a maroon sweater. I did not see him near the front door so I looked past the hostess and noticed he was already seated. I approached his table slowly, nervously. He smiled at me and stood up and pulled out my chair, waiting for me to sit before gently pushing it back towards the table. He then immediately ordered two glasses of champagne and told me I was going to eat filet mignon because I needed to start eating meat if I was going to be working so closely with him and Lakshmi. Meat, he said, would ground me, would help me meditate better. I had been a vegetarian for over ten years, but I couldn't imagine saying no.

Then he said, "Lakshmi and I have never done this."

I didn't understand. Never done what? Eat dinner together? Drink champagne together? Go out to restaurants? I could not figure out what he meant by the comment, but I was too nervous and intimidated to ask. He had set himself up as so far above me—not on Lakshmi's level, but definitely very close. And I was terrified that, if I asked him about his relationship with Lakshmi, he would come right out and say he wanted to sleep with me. Shiva had two consorts. Maybe Vishnu could have two women, as well. I wanted so desperately to believe he had my best interests at heart, that he was looking out for me as a mentor and guide. I wanted to believe he loved Lakshmi, was devoted to her, and that I was brought into the picture to assist the two of them. I simply would not allow myself to believe differently. I choked down the meat and drank the champagne and decided tomorrow would take care of itself.

Chapter 10
Tango

I went from Portugal to Madrid by train and flew from Madrid directly to Los Angeles. As soon as I landed in California, it became clear I had made the right choice. My path unfolded quickly and easily. The girlfriend who picked me up at the airport agreed to let me stay with her until I got settled. The next day, I bought a used car and drove to every Arthur Murray dance studio along the coast between Los Angeles and Mexico. I was surprised to see that, while the instructors in each studio appeared to be decent ballroom dancers, none of them had been trained in classical dance. I reasoned that, with all my ballet, jazz, and modern dance training, I would be the best dancer in those studios within a month. I wanted to be with *real* dancers, trained in classical dance. If I was going to learn to compete in Latin-ballroom dance, I wanted to be trained by the best.

A few days later, I walked into a small studio near the beach; the studio from my vision in Portugal. In the center of the dance floor a man was teaching a woman the cha-cha. The studio was otherwise empty, but the energy in the room felt great. Floor-to-ceiling windows flooded the large wooden floor with natural light.

"Excuse me," I said, interrupting them. "I am interested in applying for a job here. May I leave my resume? I want to become a professional Latin-ballroom dancer."

He stopped dancing and walked toward me. "This is an independent studio," he said. "Independent contractors teach here. We don't 'hire' anyone. And I'm not the owner, anyway."

However, while he was saying this, he extended his arm and took my resume. He scanned it and looked at me.

"You have an extensive background," he said, "and you would be shorter than me in heels. Do you already have a partner?" he asked.

"No," I responded.

"Well," he said, "Let's see if we can dance together." We set a two-hour window for us to practice the following day. It went really well, we were the right size for each other, and I learned very quickly. He was impressed and we were both thrilled to have found each other; plus, I *loved* the way I felt in that studio.

We practiced together daily, with him teaching me the fundamentals of Latin-ballroom dance. Shortly after our first practice, he told me who owned the studio. I had no idea who she was.

"Who is she?" I asked.

He stopped dancing and looked at me, incredulously.

"The world champion in Latin-ballroom dance," he replied.

It was my turn to be incredulous. I had been in California for less than a week, and not only did I find a studio and a partner, but the studio I found was owned by the world champion at exactly what I wanted to learn. The best dancers in the world came there to practice and teach when they were in California. That's why the energy in there felt so good.

Before long, I was taking lessons with the owner of the studio. I had a small part in her holiday show. I wore a French Maid costume and strutted across the stage holding a tray with empty plastic martini glasses, but—still—I was onstage with some of the best ballroom dancers in the world. Ultimately, I began helping her business partner, Sara, teach evening group classes in return for ballroom dance training. I was also offered free coaching once a week by two other US Champions who used the studio. I had found my people. I had found my next step in life. I couldn't believe how quickly it had fallen into place.

I helped Sara teach salsa on Monday nights, West Coast swing on Tuesday nights, and Argentine tango on Wednesday nights. Tango was my favorite. I knew the leader's part better than the follower's for most of the dances, because the majority of students in the evening group classes were women. One day, Sara told me a professional Argentine tango dancer from the Middle East was coming to the studio for a week to teach a workshop and give private lessons; she suggested I sign up for a private lesson, which I did immediately.

Halfway through the lesson, the instructor stopped dancing and said, "We are going to do a tango show tonight."

"Oh good," I said. "I have never seen a tango show! With whom will you be dancing?"

"You."

"What?" I asked.

"You are good enough. You follow well. You are a nice dancer. I will be dancing with you." He started to lead me through the basics again.

That night, at the *milonga* (tango dance party), he and I performed. I realized later that this was his thing: to perform with a brand-new dancer, to show off how well he could lead "anybody." But, at the time, I felt extremely flattered that he had picked me. At the end of the weekend workshop, I had fallen in love with Argentine tango.

There is a saying: "You don't find tango; tango finds you." Tango had found me and wound me around its little finger. I had to learn more.

As all the students were saying good-byes and gathering their things, the instructor and I were sitting side by side on a step outside the back door of the dance studio. He inhaled the smoke from his cigarette deeply, held it in his lungs, exhaled, and said, "Renee, you must go to Argentina. There is no one in the States who can teach you."

I turned to look at him.

"I am serious," he said. "If you really want to learn Argentine tango, you must go to Argentina."

Shortly after the workshop, I flew out to Colorado to visit my mother. I told her about tango. I told her about Argentina. She smiled. She had always encouraged my dancing. That afternoon, she drove me into Aspen to meet a man she knew named Jimmy, who had started a tango night at his restaurant. Jimmy was a tall man, probably twelve years older than I was. He had a deep baritone voice and a very kind smile. I liked him instantly. I went back to his restaurant for tango night and danced with him. We danced well together. Even though I was still so new to tango, I could follow him. He told me he had been asked to cater a tango workshop the following week in Steamboat Springs and suggested I go, which I did. Daniel Trenner, the man credited with bringing Argentine tango to the United States, was running the workshop. I loved every second of it. I fell deeper in love with tango. I *had* to go to Argentina.

At the end of the workshop, Daniel and Jimmy told me they were going to be in Argentina at the same time, and they suggested I meet them there.

I booked my flight for the following month.

———

After eighteen hours of travel, I landed in Buenos Aires, *exhausted*. The man sitting next to me on the plane discovered I was travelling alone, that my Spanish was not great, and that it was my first time in Argentina. He said the hotel I had booked was crap and that his wife was going to pick him up at the airport. He insisted that they give me a ride to a hotel that was better, one owned by a friend of theirs.

I agreed and secretly decided that if his wife was not his wife or did not show up, I would take a taxi to the "crap" hotel I booked. His wife did show up, and they helped me check in, got me a great deal and a great room, and insisted I call them to go to dinner while I was there, or if I had any problems. I thanked them profusely, and they drove away. When I got to the room, I immediately fell asleep.

I met Daniel, Jimmy, and Jimmy's new girlfriend, Heather, at a *milonga* the following night. We arrived after 1:00 a.m. at an obscure building on the outskirts of town. A few taxicabs sat in front, the drivers standing nearby, smoking cigarettes and talking with each other. There were no streetlights. We entered through a small unmarked door, and a heavily made-up woman seated in front of a fold-up card table took our money and gave us paper tickets. We continued down some stairs to a large rectangular basement that was half-empty. Tables sat around the edges of the concrete floor, and a few couples were dancing in the middle. Daniel led us toward the bar in the back, stopping to greet people along the way. Apparently, he was a big deal in the Buenos Aires tango scene and always had a prime table reserved close to the dance floor. He walked us to his table and sat down just as a server arrived with a bottle of champagne.

As the night progressed, more and more dancers arrived. By 2:30 a.m., the place was packed with people of all ages, locals and tourists alike. I learned that night that the "good" dancers arrive around 1:30 or 2:00 a.m., rarely before—unless they were legends like Daniel, in which case they arrived to a reserved table whenever they pleased. As the crowd filed in, Daniel introduced me to some of the masters of tango, and they all invited me to dance. I wasn't great, but I was young and pretty and had potential, so I was in. I did not realize it at the time, but it was an amazingly rare opportunity for me: it set me up to be trained by the best tango dancers in the world.

I stayed in Argentina for two weeks, going out with Jimmy, Daniel, and Heather every night. The milongas were scattered all over the city, but were usually in the poorest neighborhoods. They were loud, sweaty, hot, smoky affairs, and I loved every second of them. The music was fantastic, the outfits outrageous, the rooms and dance floors packed. I continued to dance with the masters of tango, often taking lessons with them during the day in Daniel's apartment. Tango music played everywhere.

Often Daniel or Jimmy, and sometimes even Heather, would invite me to dance while walking down a cobblestone street or while waiting for a meal in a café. Bystanders would watch and applaud, but our random dancing was not out of the ordinary. This was the Land of Tango. I left Argentina in love— with tango, with Buenos Aires, and with Argentine men.

I flew back to California and began focusing on Argentine tango. I still helped teach the group classes, but I had switched my career aspirations from professional competitive Latin-ballroom dancer to professional Argentine tango dancer. There were still not many people teaching Argentine tango in the US, and I saw it as my niche. I learned as much as I could from tango dancers in California and started acquiring students.

I had done it: I had found my next step in life. I was dancing with some of the best dancers in the world and was still surfing great waves. I was speaking Spanish and traveling to Argentina. I had found a way to combine traveling, speaking Spanish, dance, and surfing. For the first time in my adult life, I felt content and happy. I felt at peace. I felt like I had found my way. And then I got a horrible phone call from my mother.

Chapter 11
Detachment

"**O**h shit!" I said, as my brand-new leather Armani jacket sailed through the air in a perfect arc, landing exactly in the middle of the fire. That was *not* supposed to be in the pile.

Detachment, I reminded myself. *I'm learning detachment. Out with the old, in with the new. But, shit, that jacket rocked.*

Lakshmi had told us to get rid of everything old, everything from our past.

"Anything you wear that you do not feel beautiful in," she had said, "get rid of. Anything you would not wear on a first date, get rid of. Anything that reminds you of your past, get rid of.

"We do not donate our used clothing and furniture, because it is covered in our energetic lines. Instead, we burn it or cut it up. If you want to donate, you can donate money.

"We do not display photos of people in our homes. When you display a photo of somebody, you allow that person's energy and state of mind to enter your home and your attention through the photograph. We display photos of beautiful places in nature instead. Get rid of old photos. You do not need them; they weigh you down. They trap you in the past."

I went home that night and hit "select all" and then "delete";

I deleted every single photo I had in my computer. I piled up all the photo albums I owned and dumped them into cardboard boxes. I went through my closet and pulled out almost everything in it. I went through all my files. I went through my entire house. And then I loaded all of it into my SUV.

By this stage in the University of Mysticism, Lakshmi had raised our tuition to $500 per month and changed our dress code to "business professional." *Tonal*, she explained, is our energetic presentation of our Self to the universe. We were told it is proper etiquette to always have a "tight tonal," which meant dressing well, with neat hair and nails and great personal hygiene, at all times. Lakshmi had insisted we upgrade our wardrobes to more expensive labels. She even gave us a task to try on a suit at JC Penney and feel the vibration of the suit and the dressing room and the store, then go try on a suit at Armani and feel the difference.

"Everything is energy," she said. "Everything vibrates. There is a huge difference between the vibration of a suit made by someone who is not paid enough to feed his or her family and one made by someone who, with immense pride, gives total attention to every detail."

She told us it was our duty to wear highly vibrating clothing, that it would help our light shine out into the world. It was amazing to watch the change come over the students. Many of them were misfits and hippies and had shown up to the public events in old jeans and old T-shirts, with long straggly hair. As the months rolled by, these same people started to slowly and magically change into suit-wearing, well-groomed versions of themselves. They carried themselves straighter; they walked and talked with more confidence. You could see that they began believing anything was possible for them, that they had pride in their appearance and in themselves. Paying the higher tuition created more dedication and commitment in the students. So, when Lakshmi told us to get rid of everything old, we were more than happy to oblige. In a sense, we were burning and tearing up and purging these older, outdated versions of ourselves.

Lakshmi also told us to stop smoking pot. "Pot," she said, "breaks down the structures in the mind, making it very hard to have a tight attention. In meditation, we are building structures in the mind, structures that make our minds sharp and focused and strong. Pot makes the mind loose and wobbly. Your mind *cannot* soar in meditation if your attention is loose, just like a kite cannot soar with a loose string. If you want to sharpen your mind, if you want to build your personal power, if you want to have magical meditations, you *must* stop smoking pot."

Matt, my hippie surfer ex-boyfriend who had relocated from Hawaii to join the sangha, when asked by a friend if his life was improving, said, "Hell yeah, my life is improving. I used to sit around on my sofa all day smoking pot if the surf was flat. I was barely making my rent waiting tables. I watched a ton of TV. Now I'm in grad school getting my Masters in architecture. I stopped smoking weed, and I never watch TV. I'm on fire, man."

This shit was working; we were changing. And we were changing in *magnificent* ways.

I asked Jessica to help me take everything to a fire pit at the beach. We filled up her SUV with the rest of my old stuff and she followed me. We brought logs and fire-starters and loads of paper from my file boxes to use as tinder. We even brought lighter fluid to keep the flames revved to maximum force.

The clothing went first. Sweaters and jackets melted into toxic puddles and made the flames turn blue. Next came the boxes of childhood memories. I grabbed the largest one, walked to the side of the fire, and lifted it.

"Don't you want to see if Gary . . . " Jessica started as I tipped the box over and let the contents dump all at once into the flames. "That's a negative, Houston," she finished. We stood there and watched it burn. Baby bracelets, baby photos, baby blankets, my parents' wedding album. Box after box, bag after bag, photos, clothes, furniture went up in a massive blaze. The smoke reached over forty feet into the sky.

A man walked over, an old surfer. "What are you two doing?" he asked, incredulously. I had just thrown into the fire a beautiful framed wall hanging of two photos of me surfing a huge wave in Santa Catalina, Panama—photos taken by a professional photographer.

"That's a huge wave," the guy said as the three of us stood there and watched it burn, first the corners, then the loud "pop" of the glass as it cracked from the heat, and finally the beautiful glossy photos of me in the middle.

"Shame," he mumbled as he walked away.

Next was my bed. Jessica had helped me take it apart and load it into the car. We piled the headboard onto the fire, followed by the frame and the wooden slats. The sheets and pillows and duvet got dumped on top. The pillows melted. The fumes were toxic.

"Is this even legal?" we asked each other at the same time.

It burned so fast, all of it gone so quickly—my entire past, my entire life. We did this multiple times as the months rolled by. I burned carloads of my belongings. Each time I thought I had gotten rid of everything old, I discovered even more stuff that was possibly "trapping me in the past." I was so desperate to get rid of old versions of myself, so sure they were wrong and holding me back from Enlightenment.

I gathered all of my mother's jewelry, gifts my father had given her, beautiful antique rings, bracelets, and necklaces that she had inherited from her mother and aunt—items I loved—and stuffed them into my wetsuit. I paddled out on my surfboard as far as I could into a stormy winter ocean and let all of it fall into the water.

I was so proud of myself. It was so liberating: detachment, total detachment. I had burned and chopped and hacked and dumped my entire history, almost everything I loved—gone.

I had a dream one night that I drove up my street, and my house was on fire. "My cat!" I screamed. "Where is my cat?" As I got to my driveway, I saw her safely curled up on a tree branch. She was all I cared about. "Let it all burn," I said in my dream, as I grabbed my cat and walked away. I was on my way to total liberation. I was hacking through the chains that bound me to this world. I was doing *everything* that Lakshmi suggested. And I was sure it would lead me to freedom and nirvana.

I began my new job, working closely with Vishnu, learning to manage his Excel spreadsheets, answering hundreds of e-mails from students, planning Lakshmi's events, managing her company, and doing her errands when she was in town. My life was now consumed with meditation practice and working for her. Over the fifteen months I had been Lakshmi's student, I had slowly disengaged from most of my friends outside the group.

"They will hold you back," Lakshmi said. "You are changing, evolving, growing into the true you, and they will peg you into the mold of the old you and not allow you to change. In fact, they will get angry at you for changing."

So I gradually abandoned them. I stopped returning phone calls. I stopped going out to dinners. I took meditation, finding God, this path to Enlightenment so seriously that I was not going to jeopardize it in any way. I saw the light coming out of my Teacher, and I wanted to be like that. She seemed so free—free from doubt, free from fear, so connected to God and her own Divinity, so knowledgeable. I wanted all of that and was willing to do anything. In fact, I fantasized about radiating peace and love and light and God the way saints did. That was my goal in life. I figured if I could do that, I would finally be happy.

So I clipped my friends. And then I changed my phone number and my e-mail address. I wiped myself off the Internet. To most of them, I offered no explanation, simply disappeared. To the closest ones I explained a bit: "I'm trying to find God, studying meditation seriously, and am going to drop off the map for a while in order to do this." Reluctantly, they agreed; they had no choice. A few of them cried. God bless them for loving me enough to cry.

For a while, I had my new friends, my sangha mates, to hang out with. I couldn't tell them anything about the work I did for Vishnu and Lakshmi, but when we were together, we spoke about meditation and walking a spiritual path and about the books and movies Lakshmi assigned. Vishnu repeatedly suggested that I spend less time with the other members of the sangha now that I was working so closely with him. So, gradually, I disengaged from them as well.

It all happened so subtly. Slowly, I left my life to be consumed by Lakshmi's and Vishnu's. Slowly and without knowing it, over sixteen months, I erased my entire foundation, my whole support system, everything that I loved, everything that made me *me*. And just around that time, Vishnu asked me again if I was interested in seeing more of him. I was alone, lonely, lost, with no life besides the one I had built around him and her, but she was never there. I was always dealing with him. She still lived in Arizona; he had moved to California. She still only flew to California one weekend a month, so I barely saw her. I worked with him every day, saw him every day. And I was becoming attracted to him.

I started imagining sleeping with him. I started imagining loving him. One day, I boldly asked him—I had to know, and I was finally willing to jeopardize my position and our "relationship" by asking—"Aren't you with Lakshmi? I thought you were her consort."

His reply was, "There is a field beyond right and wrong. Meet me there."

What the fuck was this man talking about? I was sinking fast into something—into what? Was it love? Was it grace? Or was it something dark and sticky? I couldn't tell. I loved him, didn't I? I was attracted to him, wasn't I? I truly and honestly had no idea. My friends were gone. My dance career was gone. My sense of the world was rapidly disappearing. They taught that tantric monks lived in the world, yet slowly and surely, they were teaching me to leave the world, to hide, to stay inside, to stop going out. Everything and everyone was going to drain my energy and interfere with my meditation.

I began spending almost every day with Vishnu. When I wasn't with him, I was usually on the phone with him. We started having lunches and dinners together.

And then it happened. After a particularly trying day, I complimented him on a job well done and he grabbed me and kissed me—a wet, slobbery, brutal kiss. We were standing by the sink in his kitchen. He took a breath, opened his mouth wide, and jammed his tongue as far down my throat as it would go.

I was shocked. I stood there, my head cocked back, my neck arched until it nearly broke, with this man's rough tongue jammed down my throat, and I thought, *How on earth can a man his age kiss this badly?* Later, he would tell me it was the best kiss of his life.

The next stage entailed *a lot* of kissing—no sleeping over, no sex, no clothing off, just kissing. Wiping-your-entire-face-with-the-back-of-your-hand kissing, for weeks. And I just assumed this was part of the tantric practice. I didn't know if tantric monks slept over each other's houses or went down on each other or even had sex. I assumed they must, but still was just so unsure of it all. I didn't know if I even liked him in that way. I honestly could not tell.

Meanwhile, I thought Lakshmi knew all about this, and I felt so honored to be so close to her in this way, taking care of her best friend and closest student so she wouldn't worry about him and could keep meditating. He presented himself as there only to serve her. I figured someone had to help him. Someone had to take care of him. I assumed she was thrilled about it, and I felt honored to be the woman she trusted with her best friend.

Vishnu drank an entire bottle of Veuve Clicquot every night, and he wanted to see me every day. They taught "moderation." They taught us to "touch the world lightly." Lakshmi had explained to us, numerous times, that the human tendency is to find something we love and indulge until we hate it—especially with people.

"You suck the magic out of your relationships," she would say. "You insist on seeing each other every day until you are utterly bored with each other. You turn the magical into the mundane with everything: food, music, booze, people. You must learn to touch everything lightly."

She assigned for us to read more Carlos Castaneda books, making sure to point out how his teacher, Don Juan, repeatedly teaches Carlos to "touch the world lightly." Vishnu had been at all of the events. He had done the reading. He knew about "touching it lightly," but still he insisted on seeing me all the time.

So now my "job" included doing his errands, buying his groceries, tidying up around his house, cooking for him, and making out with him for hours. After over a month of making out, we still had not slept together. Kissing was as far as we were "allowed" to go. I'm not sure who was doing the "allowing." I assumed it was Shiva, but maybe it was Lakshmi. I did not know. Vishnu just seemed like a tortured man who had to take his orders from higher up.

One night, he came over to my house to watch a movie. We made out on the sofa for a bit, and then he walked outside. He was gone a long time, so I went to look for him. I found him leaning against the wall on the side of my house, crying. When I asked him if he was okay, he quickly stopped and said, "My job is hard, Lady."

I hated being called "Lady."

"One day, I will tell you all about it," he said and walked back into my house.

I started to ask a few more questions, and he shifted back into Teacher mode and told me he was under occult attack. He gave me a list of groceries to buy for him and left.

As I look back on this, I wonder how all of this was okay with me. I wonder how I let it even get this far. But the answer comes quickly and easily: I was in love with God. I was in love with the idea of nirvana and Enlightenment and I was sure this was the path and these were the guides. Raised Catholic, I had been repelled by the fear and rigidness of that practice, but this tantric Buddhist mysticism, on the other hand, seemed real, like something I could do. It seemed like it was filled with life and love and hope and gratitude, rather than fear and hate and judgment and restrictions. I never doubted for a second that Lakshmi would lead me to my own Enlightenment, my own understanding of the Truth, by helping me finally merge my mind with God in an experience of nirvana that all the saints talked about.

Meanwhile, Lakshmi seemed to be getting brighter and

more powerful with each passing month. She would have us do open-eye meditations during her events, and many of us could see gold light and colors shooting out of her hands as she performed mudras. I saw her shape-shift into Jesus and Padmasambhava and Saint Clare of Assisi and Mary Magdalene. I began to believe she had either been these people in past lives or studied with them. My ability to meditate was improving, so I would be blasted into seemingly higher realms of light when I was around her, which filled my mind with the most exquisite silence and peace, as if I had been carrying two thousand pounds my entire life and was relieved of the load each time I was with her. I became even more willing to do whatever she suggested.

One day, on the phone, she told me I still had "too much time on my hands" and assigned *The Gospel of Sri Ramakrishna*—over a thousand pages of tiny font. It taught me that one should view one's guru as God. That step for me, at this stage, was not too large to take. I became convinced that Lakshmi was an incarnation of God. I became even more willing to serve her in any way she needed.

"When you travel, you should fly in first class and stay in only very expensive hotels," she told us. "Everything is energy, everything is vibration. Even the scientists will tell you so. If you fly in first class and stay in nice hotels you will be less energetically drained, leaving you in higher mind states, with more energy to meditate and to apply to your job."

She also told us that as we meditate more and more, we become more open and will be able to feel much more, including all the people who have slept in a hotel bed. I believed her. I put my head on a hotel pillow and saw thousands of faces flash through my mind. I felt unbearable psychic pain in the mattresses. It wasn't very long before I couldn't sleep in a hotel bed. I had to pull the bedding off and sleep on the floor. Meditation was making me so sensitive that the only people I wanted to be around were Lakshmi and Vishnu.

And I have to admit: I liked the nice hotels. I liked flying first class. I liked wearing designer business suits and running a company. I really liked this new version of me, and even though she was so drastically different from the old version of me—maybe *because* she was so drastically different—I believed I was headed exactly where I wanted to go: freedom, nirvana, Enlightenment.

———

Valentine's Day approached, and Vishnu told me I would be spending it with him. I wondered if it meant we would finally have sex. I spent the day getting ready—manicure, pedicure, and a bikini wax. I shopped for a new outfit and sexy lingerie. I got my hair cut, colored, and blow-dried. I arrived at his door, nervous and insecure, a bit frazzled from running around town all day. In my mind, I had prepared for him the most sacred gift I could: my body.

He looked incredibly handsome when he answered the door. He was barefoot, wearing dark jeans and a black Italian dress shirt open to the middle of his chest, framing a beautiful turquoise and silver ankh that Lakshmi had bought him in Egypt. In the time we had been "dating," he had whitened his teeth and switched from glasses to contacts. He had gotten a much more flattering haircut. Since he had started teaching karate to the sangha, he had gotten back into fitness, and his body had gone from lumpy, pasty, and white to muscular, lean, and tan. His open shirt showed off his strong chest, and the necklace glistened against his brown skin. His thick, dark hair was styled and combed back. The sight of him took my breath away.

He had made me dinner. It was very romantic. The dinner was quite good, and so was the wine; I allowed myself to become tipsy for the first time around him. After dinner, he took me up to the deck. He poured us each a glass of champagne and raised his glass to the sky, saying, "Here's to Robert Linnell, a wonderful man and a wonderful father. Happy birthday."

I started to cry. He had remembered that my father's birthday was Valentine's Day. I felt loved. I felt supported. I felt *safe*. Truly, for the first time with this man, I felt safe. And I felt *incredibly* attracted to him. He was not treating me like a student, like an employee, like a peon. He was finally and for the first time treating me like an equal, like a *woman*.

We went back downstairs and started making out. He sat on the sofa, and I climbed on top of him, facing him, with my legs wrapped around his waist, my arms wrapped around his neck.

He said, "One day I would like to show you what tantric sex is."

Well, there I had it. We definitely weren't going to have sex that night. After what felt like an hour of kissing, I went home.

He called the next morning and said, "You made a mistake last night."

My heart dropped. "What did I do?" I asked.

"I can't tell you," he said. "It's your task to figure that out."

I hung up the phone and cried. I thought about it all day long. What could I have possibly done wrong? What mistake could I have made? I had purchased all the groceries and the wine and dropped them off earlier in the day. It's not like I had not contributed to the meal. Plus, I had been willing and even planning to sleep with him. At the end of the day, I called him.

"I can't figure it out," I said. "I truly have no idea what I could have done wrong."

"Keep thinking about it," he replied and hung up.

I cried again. Oh my God I was so confused. The night before had been so lovely. I finally felt attracted to him—*truly* attracted to him. For the first time with him, I finally felt safe— *truly* safe. And then this. I had no one to talk to about it, of course. I couldn't tell anyone in the sangha, and I had no other friends left. I wished I could ask Lakshmi. I wished I could talk to my parents.

That night he called me. "So," he said. "Did you figure it out?"

"No," I replied.

"Drive over here, and I'll tell you."

I did. When he opened the door, I felt sick. I couldn't bear the sight of him.

"Come in," he said. We sat down. He was very serious.

"You brought no offering," he said. "I am your Teacher, and you brought no offering. You should have brought flowers."

Instantly, he reminded me of my mother. As soon as she allowed herself to open up and love me, as soon as I let my guard down and loved her back, she would close herself off and shoo me away. I hated this feeling. I hated him for making me feel this way.

First of all, he *was not* my Teacher! Lakshmi was my Teacher. Second, I had spent the entire day preparing the most precious and sacred offering I could for him: my body! I had no response.

I started to cry.

He hugged me and said, "You're a new student, so you don't know. It's my job to teach you."

I stayed as long as I felt I had to and then went home, where I continued sobbing. Why was I doing this? How could I let someone treat me like this? I cried all night long and woke up the next day ready to forgive. My self-doubt had kicked in, my clarity gone. I had been wrong. I should have brought an offering. I went back to work for him, back to running his errands, back to tidying up his house, back to making out with him as if nothing had happened. And I shoved my intuition and my power and my true sense of self just a little bit deeper into a very dark hole.

Chapter 12
Gone

In a child psychology class I took in college, I learned about *intermittent reinforcement*. In an experiment, chickens were taught to push a button with their beaks. In one group, each time the chicken pushed the button, a food pellet appeared. The chickens would peck at the button until they were full, then they would stop. In the second group, the chickens got rewarded with food at first but then consistently got nothing when they pushed the button. These chickens pushed the button a few times after the food stopped but soon grew bored and quit. In the third group, the chickens sometimes got a food pellet and sometimes did not. It was random. These chickens pecked the button until their beaks bled . . . and kept on pecking, never knowing if just one more push of the button would reward them with food. The result of the experiment: To strengthen behavior of any kind, use intermittent reinforcement.

Seeking love from an addict or a narcissist is an example of this. Sometimes you get the reward: love, warmth, acceptance, encouragement. Most of the time, you do not. The fleeting moments in which the person is loving and kind are random and unpredictable, and the desire for reward becomes unquenchable because you constantly believe it could come again with the very next attempt. You peck until your beak bleeds, and then you peck some more.

My mother was an alcoholic and a pill addict. In her dealings with me, she alternated between emotional abuse and absolute neglect, with a little bit of love and fun doled out in between. Our relationship scarred me deeply; it set me up to mold my romantic relationships on a toxic model, to seek emotionally unavailable men who loved me intermittently. But scattered among the bad times, she and I had a lot of good times together—laughing until we both peed in our pants. In those times, I felt she truly did love me, and I loved her. I was as codependent as a child could get; I always forgave her. I had to; she was my mother. And as a teenager, I went out of my way to antagonize her, to get the attention I knew it brought.

One of my favorite memories is when she came to visit me in California and we laughed ourselves to exhaustion trying to wrestle a very old queen-sized futon out of my apartment and down multiple flights of stairs to the dumpster because she wanted to buy me a "real" bed. That thing was so heavy. She kept talking to it, as if it were alive, "Come on, Futon. You can do this. Work with us, Futon. Just a little bit further, Futon." We had to keep stopping not because we were exhausted but because we were laughing so hard we couldn't breathe.

Another happy memory is of when I dragged her to the Amazon River for an adventure. She hated every second of it but tried so hard to pretend she was having fun, showering in cold water and schlepping through the jungle, getting attacked by mosquitos. At times like that, she was adorable. And so kind to so many people. And so giving to so many people. She was every-thing, really. Everything that we all are—all the dark and all the light. She had so much fear and pain inside her, and bless her little heart for overcoming it as well as she did in order to raise Gary and me. She was terribly abused by her own mother. She and her brother both were. Her brother couldn't take it, killing himself when I was a kid. To get away from her, my mother married young to a man who also abused her. He pushed her down a flight of stairs when she was pregnant with his child. She miscarried, and then he abandoned her at a train station in Europe. Her mother would not let her return to the family home, saying she had disgraced the family, so she moved in with her aunt and put herself through school. Eventually, she got a job working for my father. She came a long way, from utter poverty and total abuse. In so many ways, she was *incredibly* strong.

A few weeks after planes flew into the Twin Towers and the Pentagon, I got a very strange call from my mother. She was in Colorado. I could hardly understand her. It sounded like she had a mouth full of marbles.

"I've had a stroke, Honey," she managed to say. "But don't worry. I'm fine."

Fine? She sure as shit did not sound fine. "I'm flying out there today."

"No," she responded slowly, the word straining out of her mouth. "Don't. Bill arrives tomorrow, and I want to be alone with him."

Bill was some Australian man my mother had met online. He was scheduled to arrive the next day to meet her for the first time. There was no way my mother was meeting anyone for the first time sounding the way she sounded. I demanded to speak to a doctor. She refused and hung up the phone. I called the hospital. I explained the situation and asked for someone to please tell me what was going on.

"Your mother had a massive stroke," the nurse said. "In fact, it's a miracle she survived. You need to get here immediately."

I hung up the phone, quickly packed a bag, and drove to the airport.

It turned out my mother's brain had started hemorrhaging the night before, but she didn't know it. She got out of bed and fell, twisting her ankle and badly hurting her foot. She then waited until the morning, her brain hemorrhaging the entire time, and drove herself to the hospital, where she walked into the emergency room and said there was a problem with her foot. The triage nurse instantly noticed the stroke and got her to the proper doctor.

I arrived at the hospital to see my mother next to the registration desk, slumped over in a wheelchair. Apparently, she was on her way to the shower but had been left near reception by a nurse. Her hair was crazy, long and stringy and wild. She was wearing a faded, worn hospital gown. Her chin was resting on her chest. Her left arm hung limply in her lap, with her hand dangling between her knees.

"Mom," I said.

She couldn't raise her head. I kneeled next to her wheelchair and started to cry.

"Don't cry, Honey," she managed to slur. "I will be home tomorrow. Bill is coming to visit."

I called for a doctor. A woman in a white coat approached.

"Please tell me what is going on with my mother," I said.

"She had a massive stroke. She will never walk or talk again. She will need to live in a nursing home." She checked her clipboard and walked away.

A nurse appeared. "I'm going to bathe your mother. Do you want to come?"

I followed, too stunned to speak. She wheeled my mother into a shower stall, removed the gown, and then turned the showerhead on full force while aiming it at my mother's slumped-over head. I felt my mother grimace as the cold water hit her.

I grabbed the showerhead from the nurse and said, "May I please do this." It was not a question.

I turned the water to warm. I made sure the temperature was right and then gently placed it over the top of her shoulders and covered her body with the warm water, the way I would start my own shower, the way I would shower a child. Then I moved it to the top of my mother's head while tilting her head back; I held her head and was careful not to get the water on her face.

My mother looked at me with so much love in her eyes. I gently washed and conditioned her hair and did the best I could with the rest of her. Then I softly toweled her dry. I got her dressed in a new hospital gown and back to her bed, where she fell asleep instantly. I called my brother, who was in Florida, and broke down. I was sobbing so much that at first he couldn't understand me. He said he'd be on the first flight out in the morning. I drove back to my mother's condo but couldn't sleep. I was panicked. My mother would be incapacitated from now on. Life as I knew it was over. I spent the night staring at the ceiling and weeping.

Gary met me at the hospital the next day. I happened to be outside just as he walked up, and I collapsed into his arms, sobbing. I couldn't pull myself together. I had never been happier to see him in my life; I had never needed to see him more.

We went inside to see a different doctor. He was kind and lovely and answered all of our questions. He showed us the images of our mother's brain and explained everything that happened. He told us that no one can ever say for sure what will happen after a brain injury, because a proper diagnosis can't be made until the swelling goes down. Then he said that getting my mother to a great stroke rehabilitation facility would radically improve her chances of recovery.

Gary immediately started making phone calls. He found a rehab facility in South Florida, near her home in Boca Raton, and made plans to leave the hospital as soon as we were allowed. We were told she was too disabled to leave unless she was in a medical jet, accompanied by a nurse. The kind doctor helped us secure one and told us we could possibly leave the following day.

The next afternoon, we left on the jet, with my mom on a stretcher and a nurse by her side. We arrived to the rehab facility after dark. It was a terrible place, a giant hospital filled with the dying and nearly dead. The nurses seemed more interested in what they were going to eat for dinner than in our crazy-looking mother. We knew we had made a mistake as soon as we arrived, but we had to leave her there overnight. They put her in a room with another patient, who looked like a snoring corpse. It broke my heart to leave her there. I had never seen my mother so weak, so incapacitated, so *vulnerable*.

"We'll be back first thing tomorrow," we told her.

I had flown from California to Colorado two days before, had not slept for three nights, and was now in Florida. I was exhausted. Gary and I took a taxi to our mother's house and tried to sleep, but sleep wouldn't come. I spent another night staring at the ceiling and weeping.

When we arrived at the rehab facility early the next morning, we found our mother lying in bed, with her breakfast on her chest and her head sticking up at a ninety-degree angle. Someone had raised the head of the bed so it resembled a lounge chair, but my mother had slid so far down that her body was flat, with only her head propped up.

I ran to her, surprised she could breathe in that position.

"I have to pee," was the first thing she slurred. "No one will take me to pee."

Gary and I hoisted her out of bed and into a wheelchair. I wheeled her to the bathroom and managed, with her help, to lift her onto the toilet.

"We're getting you out of here today," I said.

Gary made some calls. He had a friend who had access to the best private stroke rehab facility in South Florida. It would cost us a fortune, but we didn't care. The nurses told us we couldn't leave, that we couldn't take her, that she would have to wait to be seen by a doctor and properly discharged. Gary wheeled her past the nurses and out the front door, saying, "Try to stop us."

The new place was amazing. She got a private room with a huge window. She got a private nurse. I could tell immediately that she would be taken care of. Her therapy started that day. All I could do was wait and hope that it worked. I spent a week in Florida, most of the time in my mother's room, washing her and moisturizing her and stretching her limbs, combing her hair, feeding her, watching TV with her. I flew back and forth between California and Florida each month, praying that what the first doctor said was not true.

My mother's progress was slow at first but rapidly improved. By December, she moved back into her home, attended by visiting nurses and daily trips to therapy. My brother moved in with her.

After close to a year of great therapy and incredible will power, she recovered enough to talk, walk, drive, live on her own, and even ski again. The woman was incredibly strong. Her brain was altered but in amazing ways: Her façades were gone. When she hugged me, instead of keeping her body stiff and hard like she used to do, she melted into my arms and allowed me to hold her. She lost her desire to go to church twice a week; instead, she turned to introspection. She was kinder. She was happier. She was frustrated with her new limitations, yes, but her spirit seemed lighter, like a child's. She left the house dressed however she pleased, no longer concerned with looking "perfect." She told me she loved me all the time. And she laughed a lot—full-throated, hearty belly laughs. It was adorable to watch. It was as if the stroke had stripped her down to her true essence, her magnificent, original, lovable Self.

Even though she healed so well, she still had trouble with daily tasks. One day, I noticed she was making beef stew and had put the package of meat, still wrapped in plastic, in the slow cooker. The plastic was melting and slowly poisoning the food. Another day, she was leaving the house and my brother noticed large lumps on her back. He got closer and realized she had put her bra on backward, the padded cups protruding through the back of her shirt. She would run a bath and forget, allowing the bathtub to overflow and flood the bathroom. A few times, she ate old expired food and ended up so sick she had to dial 911. My brother was exhausted from living with her and dealing with all of it on his own.

I decided to move to Florida to be with her so he could move out. As life would have it, I woke up one day and my hip no longer worked. The joint felt like a sliding glass door that was off its hinges. I could barely walk. I saw doctor after doctor, and they all said the same thing: "No more dancing." As if my mother having a stroke wasn't bad enough, suddenly my dance career was over. The next step was obvious: My mother needed me. I moved out of my apartment in California, packed up my car, and drove to Florida.

Two weeks after I arrived, she told me she was moving to Colorado. I wanted to kill her. It was *so* like her to do this.

She moved to Colorado the following week—jumped on a plane with her cat and left. I was beyond pissed off, but I was also relieved. Clearly she was willing and able to live on her own. I called a few more doctors. Maybe I could get my hip working and dance again. I drove to Miami to see the joint specialist for the Miami Dolphins. He put me in an MRI machine and decided to inject the sheath of my iliopsoas with cortisone. It hurt like hell, but it worked. I could walk again, and surf.

I went to Panama for two weeks to surf and clear my mind. My hip responded well to the ocean. When I returned to Florida, I had forgiven my mother and talked my brother into flying to Colorado to visit her with me. We spent a week together. She was a little slow, a little off, but she could live on her own, and she was happy, so I flew back to Florida to figure out the next step in my life.

Two weeks later, as I was having lunch with my brother and some friends, my cell phone rang; it was a Colorado number— Audrey, one of my mother's closest friends. I picked up.

"When was the last time you spoke to your mother?" she asked.

"Three days ago," I responded. "Why?"

"She drove to Denver for a doctor's appointment and was supposed to return yesterday. We were going to meet for dinner. I haven't heard from her, and I'm a bit worried. She asked me to watch her cat. It doesn't seem like her to not call me if she planned on staying longer in Denver. She would be too concerned about the cat."

Where the hell was my mother?

I called my father's personal assistant, Sally, who still worked for my mother two days a week out of our home in Boca; she happened to be in her office at our house.

"When was the last time you talked to my mom?" I asked her.

"I'm not sure . . . " she responded. "A few days ago. Why?"

I told her about my call with Audrey.

"Gary and I are on our way to the house right now," I finished and disconnected the call. On the drive home, my mind
went into overdrive. Where the hell was my mother? Dead in a
ditch on the side of the road? No, traffic patrol would have called
us. Still in Denver at a hotel? No, she would have called Audrey.
Drunk in a bar? Possibly, but she'd be too concerned about her
cat to not go home. She had to be okay. She had to be okay. She
had to be okay, right? She simply had to.

Sally opened the front door just as I was reaching for the
door handle. She had the same look on her face as she had fifteen
years earlier. "Your mother is dead," she said. "I'm so sorry."

———

After calling multiple police stations in Colorado, Sally found my
mother's body in a morgue. She had been discovered dead in the
bathtub in her hotel room in Denver, drowned. I crumpled to the
floor. She was only sixty-eight years old. She had healed from her
stroke. She was happy and living on her own. How did this happen?

I had an autopsy done. I had to know. Was it suicide? I got
the results a few days later: Apparently, it wasn't. There was no
"foul play," and the toxicology report showed therapeutic levels
of her usual medications (blood thinners, Ambien, Zoloft) and
one glass of wine. There was no contusion; there was nothing
abnormal. The report deemed her death an accident. How does
a grown woman drown in a hotel bathtub? It made no sense.

That night, I cried my guts out. It could have been suicide
or just a lethal combo of drugs and alcohol; I wasn't sure. I felt
so sad for her. She had called me just a week before to tell me she
felt lonely and was thinking of returning to Florida. I was still
pissed about her move to Colorado right after I arrived to help
her, and I reacted poorly.

"Well, I won't be here," I said. "I'll be in Australia. Gary is
never around; he just bought a new house with his girlfriend.
You'll be alone here, too."

She said, "Well, at least Sally is there a few days a week. I
think I'm going to come home."

It was the last conversation I had with her.

I continued to sob. I was a horrible daughter. I felt like a horrible daughter. I cried and cried . . . and then I tried to talk to her. I couldn't sleep, so I went downstairs in her house, in the house I had grown up in; I sat on the floral sofa, and I spoke to her, out loud, alone at midnight.

"Mom, what happened? I miss you. I'm so sad."

I got an instant response; it appeared as her voice in my mind.

"Honey, please don't be sad. I was done. I didn't want to be here anymore. You know that. I got into a warm bath and simply left my body. I'm Home. It's where I want to be—here, with your father; here, with God."

I sniffed. I wiped the tears from my eyes, the running snot from my nose. And then the most surprising words came out of my mouth in the stillness of the night.

"It's not that I loved Gary more than you; it's simply that you needed me less."

Oh my God. It was true. I didn't need her the way my brother had. Gary had always been so clingy, so needy, so *adoring* of her and her love. I had always been independent, always wanting to be off on my own, too sensitive to be around other people for extended periods of time. She hadn't been neglecting me. She just needed to be needed. She yearned for it. She could hardly live without it. Suddenly, I understood. So, right then, in that moment, I let her go. I forgave her. And I loved her for being the best mother she could have possibly been.

———

With my brother's girlfriend, I flew out to Colorado and took a taxi to the morgue. We collected my mother's personal effects, but I refused to identify the body. Some things you just can never unsee. Then we took a cab to her hotel, where her car was still in the parking lot. We drove it back to her condo, packed up all of her belongings, donated them to a women's shelter, collected her cat, and flew back to Florida.

Having no idea what to do next, I flew to Argentina. I

figured I'd start my dance career again. But when I got there, all I did was sleep and cry. I could barely leave the apartment. I was an orphan. My parents were gone. I felt so alone.

Eventually, I realized I had to get myself back to the United States and get on with my life. My brother and I sold the family home; I used my half of the money to buy and remodel a little house in Cardiff. I started teaching dance again, built a new life for myself. I returned to Argentina, and, because the peso had been devalued 400 percent when the economy crashed, I was able to buy a brand-new apartment that I rented out to traveling tango dancers when I wasn't there. I also began importing tango shoes to the United States.

I got invited to join a burlesque dance company, owned and run by two of the top ranking Latin-ballroom dance champions in California. My part in the company was small: I danced a ménage-a-trois tango with the two owners of the company, and my dress came off at the very end, as the lights dimmed, to reveal my nearly naked body clothed in only a jeweled G-string, flesh-colored fishnet stockings, rhinestone-covered nipples, and flesh-colored high heels.

Slowly, I began recovering from my mother's death. I loved my life as a dancer and I loved living in Cardiff. I was traveling back and forth to Argentina. I had great friends. I was surfing a lot. I was being coached by, and dancing with, some of the best tango and Latin-ballroom dancers in the world. But I was *still* soul-sick. I had a void inside of me that simply *could not* be filled by anything in this world. I felt like an alien living in a human body, pretending I fit in, but all the while knowing I did not. I could find no one else like me, no one else who saw the world the way I did. I missed my mother terribly. Even though our relationship had been tumultuous, I missed having her to talk to. There had been times, especially after her stroke, when she had given me great advice. I missed knowing that if my life exploded, I had her as a safety net. My brother had gotten married, and we hardly ever spoke to or saw each other. He was on his way to building his own family. I felt very alone.

And then my godmother got diagnosed with a brain tumor—incurable. She tried radiation and chemotherapy to prolong her life, but neither worked. I flew to Boston every other week to be with her. She died slowly and in agony in August of 2006.

Her death was another loss that cut me deeply, another loss that left me undone, another deep wound in my psyche. And a month later, when Lakshmi handed out applications to be her student, I grabbed the opportunity like a drowning person grabbing a life ring.

PART 2
TANTRA

"Love nothing but that which comes to you woven in the pattern of your destiny. For what could more aptly fit your needs?"

—Marcus Aurelius

Chapter 13
Australia

Shortly after Valentine's Day, Vishnu returned to Arizona, as he did every month, to be with Lakshmi. Usually, when he was there, he became cold and distant with me. When he called or e-mailed, it was strictly business. He seemed to have no time to talk to me about anything else. He never mentioned Lakshmi or what she was doing, he was always very secretive about that. At the end of a phone call, he abruptly told me I needed to get blood work done.

"I want you to get a full CBC, and I want you to get a gynecological exam. Get tested for every STD, as well. When you have the results, please fax them to me. I want to see them."

He then asked, "Are you on birth control pills?"

"No," I responded.

"Ask your doctor to write you a prescription for birth control pills." He hung up. I guessed Vishnu and I were finally going to have sex.

I had the blood work done, got the exams, and started taking The Pill. I faxed him my results: I was healthy—nothing to report. He told me he would be back in town the following week and wanted to take me out to dinner. He suggested I walk around a sacred site three times. "It will purify your energy field," he said. Apparently, this man needed me clean in every way possible if he was going to screw me.

When he landed, he called to tell me when he'd pick me up and suggested I pack a sleepover bag. I couldn't bear to; it just seemed too premeditated and unromantic. Again, my emotions were mixed. I wasn't ready for this step, and yet I knew I was going to take it . . . even if I didn't really want to. I had turned the volume down so low on my true feelings, my true emotional guidance system, that I wasn't sure *what* I actually felt.

I wore a sexy brown backless dress with beautiful bronze strappy high heels. He wore dark jeans with a pale blue long-sleeve dress shirt and a sport coat. He looked handsome. He appeared nervous. He ordered a bottle of Dom Perignon. Half-way through dinner, he asked me if I noticed anything different about him.

I did not.

He wiggled his left hand a bit.

I still didn't know what he was asking about. He wiggled his hand again. Then I noticed his ring. It was the dragon ring, designed by Shiva. It was *beautiful.* It used to be silver; now it was gold. Lakshmi wore a gold one. Shiva wore a gold one. Shiva's consorts each wore a gold one. And now Vishnu had a gold one. He explained the fact that his ring was now gold meant he was close to Enlightenment.

I wanted one. Silver or gold, I did not care.

Then he looked at me and said, "Renee, you are magnificent. I love you. I'm in love with you."

Before I could respond, he raised his glass of champagne and said, "To us."

I sat across from him and decided he truly was very handsome, incredibly sexy. I decided he was a good man, an honest, hard-working man and that he would take good care of me. Everyone in the sangha looked up to him. The military guys practically worshipped him. The female students swooned over him. And Lakshmi clearly saw him as incredibly powerful and evolved. Any issues I was having with Vishnu must be problems with my own ego, I decided. If I ever wanted to change, if I ever wanted to take my life to the next level, this was my chance.

I'm going for it, I thought to myself, *no turning back.* I suddenly began enjoying the evening and looked forward to the rest of our night.

We went back to his house after dinner. He poured more champagne, and then we went down to his bedroom. It was the first time I had ever been down there. He was right: He had a bed, queen-size, no headboard, in the middle of what would be an otherwise empty room except for a dresser, in the basement level of the house. The bedspread was dark blue and some type of cotton/polyester mix. Not very inviting, but not the concrete bunker I had imagined. He put on classical music.

I asked if we could change it. If I was really going to do this, I needed something unromantic. I was going to have to jump over my own walls, and the only way I knew how was to resort to the behavior I had learned in Hawaii: remove my mind and heart from the situation at hand. I asked him to play some techno. It was loud and took my mind off what was happening.

Sex with Vishnu was the same as the kissing: detached, rough, and sloppy. It was the kind of sex that is meant to be hot and heavy but is obviously just forced acting, purely physical, with no true emotional connection at all—none of the feeling of loving the other person so much you simply want to get as close as your two physical bodies will allow. There was just a strange, distant, insecure separateness, along with animal-like or porno-like grunting from him, and it was over. He didn't use a condom and ejaculated inside of me. I had not expected that. This was the first time a man had ever ejaculated inside of me without a condom; it would be dripping out of me all night long.

He fell asleep immediately. While he snored, I looked up at the ceiling feeling used, alone, afraid, violated, and disgusted.

I wanted to love him. I wanted to be insanely attracted to him, but I simply wasn't. When he was dressed up, on stage, protecting Lakshmi, I did love him; I was insanely attracted to him.

But when he was with me, in moments like this, I was repulsed. I tossed and turned all night and thought about sneaking out while he was asleep.

I woke up the next morning exhausted and drained. He was filled with life and energy. We had sex again before we got out of bed. It wasn't any better. I went home and cried. And then I took a nap. And then I reminded myself that I was "The Chosen Child," that I had yearned for a Vishnu of my own, and that I had gotten what I prayed for. I decided to embrace it. I decided to focus on the positive. I decided I would find a way to love and be attracted to Vishnu even if it killed me—exactly what I had done at dinner the previous night, exactly what I had done after Valentine's Day, exactly what I needed to do in order to keep walking this crazy path to Enlightenment.

As time passed, I became more comfortable around Vishnu, more confrontational. I told him that if he truly loved me, he had to treat me better. He tried. He would have dozens of long-stem white roses delivered to my home, usually after we had an argument of some sort. He told me he loved me, but he also insisted I do all of his errands, buy all of his groceries, cook his meals, clean his house, and lug his briefcase like a Sherpa. Maybe this was all very sexy to him, but it sure as shit was not sexy to me. I hated it.

Well, I loved the attention. I loved being part of the Lakshmi and Vishnu team. I loved my elite status. But I hated being treated like a servant and a concubine. And I *hated* the way he kissed and touched me. I simply could not get used to it; I could not understand how a man his age could be so lacking in this particular skill set. And I could not understand how a man would think it was okay to have his girlfriend be his servant. It just made no sense.

My intuition told me to run, but I heard Lakshmi's voice saying, "This path is incredibly hard. You will want to quit. Only if you are doing this for others will you stick it out. Only if you are doing this for others will you do what it takes to change."

I *was* doing this for others. So I convinced myself my task was to take care of Vishnu. I convinced myself that *this* was my selfless service, an extreme way for me to "sand down my ego."

I had been reading about Sri Ramakrishna cleaning the latrines with his long hair in order to sand down his ego. If he could do that in India, I could certainly do this.

And so I stayed.

———

And then Vishnu became our Spiritual Teacher.

By this time I was practically living with him. He told me the week of the event that Lakshmi would not be flying in to teach, that he would do it instead. I helped him prepare. Suddenly, he was taking Lakshmi's place, and I was taking his. I cooked him dinner before the event, then I rode with him to it. I was escorted by the security team the way he and Lakshmi would have been. I sat with him in the green room, and when he entered the ballroom, I walked behind him, dressed in a gorgeous suit with my hair slicked back in a low ponytail, carrying his briefcase, struggling in high heels to keep up with him.

When everyone stood up as we entered, they stood up for *us*. I sat in a designated chair in the front row. When he ended the first half for break, I followed him out of the room. We repeated the same entrance and exit the second half of the night. My status had been immediately elevated in the eyes of the other students. Suddenly, it was very clear to the rest of the sangha that I was a part of the inner circle. The volunteers had probably suspected it, but up until now it had been mostly hidden.

Vishnu was a disaster on stage. He was nervous and awkward. He shook his leg and clicked a pen for the entire three-hour seminar. He constantly moved and fidgeted, in ways that created weird shadows on his face, making him look distorted and grotesque. The event was a shit show. And, to top it off, at the end of the second night, he demanded that everyone stand up and bow to him—low, Japanese style, the way you would bow to a Japanese emperor. I was *appalled*. Lakshmi had never asked us to stand and bow. We did so because we adored her, and when we bowed to her, it was a slight tip of the head over hands pressed together in *namaste*. It was *never* a full-torso bow. It was never *subservient*.

When Vishnu and I got back to his house that night, I couldn't look at him. I made myself busy cleaning up his kitchen, until I simply couldn't hold it in.

"Lakshmi would never make people bow to her." I blurted out. "Lakshmi would never end an event the way you did."

He replied, "Well, it felt right to me. We're both tired; maybe you should go home."

Lakshmi called me the next day to ask about the event. I told her we all missed her terribly. I also told her about Vishnu demanding we bow to him. She went quiet. Then she sighed and said with sadness in her voice, "I was a bit worried about that." And then she quickly changed the subject.

The next month, Vishnu taught again. This time, he insisted that everyone bring a notebook and write down every word he said. The man never stopped talking. Ever. He told me that when he talked, he was getting a "download" from God. He called his ramblings "Master Teachings." The students pulled out notebooks. We wrote down what he said.

Many of the students were upset. They asked when Lakshmi would return. He got annoyed and said he couldn't answer that. Many of the senior students quit; those who had looked the most forlorn on the Egypt trip left first.

"We didn't sign up for this," they said. "We signed up to be taught by Lakshmi."

But, where *was* Lakshmi? Nobody knew. It looked like Vishnu was now going to be our regular Spiritual Teacher. *And* our sensei. This meant we were his captive audience at least four days a month.

It also meant he was harder on me. Now he was "more exhausted" and had "more pressure" on him. He needed me to cook for him and wait on him more often. He suffered more "occult attacks," so he was nasty more often. I felt as if I was dating a five-year-old. His moods were mercurial, his temper tantrums rampant.

We had another Power Trip coming up, to Australia, and everyone hoped Lakshmi would be there. I had no idea where she was, but I was so busy planning and organizing the trip and struggling through my feelings about Vishnu that I had little time to focus on her. I assumed she was meditating her way toward becoming a *Mahasiddha* (an even higher level of Enlightenment) and that we would see her again once she had reached the next level.

A few days before the trip, Vishnu called to tell me he wanted me to fly with him instead of with the rest of the sangha, to help him set up. He booked us both first class tickets and spent much of the flight sitting cross-legged with his hands placed on his knees and his eyes closed, meditating with a ludicrous grin on his face. He kept the dome light on overhead, illuminating himself. The flight attendants must have thought he was crazy. I was embarrassed and shrugged each time they gave me a WTF? look.

We had been in Sydney less than 24 hours when I discovered that Lakshmi did not know I was there with him. When she'd call, he would motion for me to leave the room. As I walked away, I overheard him speaking to her coldly. He was mean and authoritative. He spoke to her as if *he* was the Spiritual Teacher and she was his student.

The afternoon of our second day we were sitting outside at a café by the water, halfway through our meal, when he went quiet and then started to cry. He told me Lakshmi was possessed, that she was not really Enlightened. He told me he was probably going to have to "go on without her."

I had no idea what any of this meant, but I did know that she had taught me to meditate. She had taught me that God was within all of us, and if we just got still enough, we could feel Him/Her. She had taught me that Enlightenment was real, and she had dedicated her life to finding students like me and showing us The Way. There was no way I was going to leave her behind to be possessed by herself, whatever the hell that meant.

"Can't I stay behind with her?" I asked. I didn't even know what "stay behind" meant, but if it meant me living with her and helping her by cooking and buying groceries, and running errands, well, I was basically doing that already for him, so why not move in with her to do it?

He began to cry again. "I'll stay with her, too. We won't abandon her." He grabbed my hand. "I'm so relieved to hear your reaction. Shiva had told me I might have to leave her and become the Big Dog, but now I realize that Shiva was wrong."

What the *fuck* was this man talking about?

He shifted his mood to manic and ordered champagne to celebrate. I drank until I was drunk. I hated this man. I could not wait to see Lakshmi. I prayed she would appear when our event began.

The next day, Vishnu flew to the Outback just before the rest of the sangha arrived in Sydney. We would meet him there the following day. Lisa, by now one of my closest sangha mates, and I were roommates and once she arrived and Vishnu left, it felt so good to be a "normal" student again. I could let my guard down. I did not have to be perfect. I spent the day and evening with all of them, walking around the harbor, going out to dinner.

But as I watched all the other students and heard them speak of Vishnu and Lakshmi with such reverence, my thoughts and feelings shifted. I was excited that I had a special little secret. *I* was Vishnu's consort. It made me see him through their eyes and it flooded me with love for him. As I spent the whole day with my sangha, I noticed how much I had grown apart from them, how much more comfortable I felt with Vishnu. When he called me that night I told him I missed him so much it hurt. I told him I was falling in love with him. And I meant it.

chapter 14
consort

The flight to the Outback was early; Lisa and I both fell asleep on the plane. When we landed, Vishnu was in the airport waiting to welcome all of us. He flushed red when he saw me. I wanted to run up to him and throw myself into his arms, but instead, I smiled and approached him the way a regular student would, with distance and respect. When we got to the hotel, Vishnu called a meeting in the event room with the volunteers. We sat in chairs facing him, listening as he went over the details of our week there.

I sat next to Seth, who had become one of my favorite people in the sangha; I adored his girlfriend, Tiffany, as well. At one point, Seth said something funny, and I turned to him and smiled. I even reached out and touched his arm. He was always cracking us up and I greatly appreciated his humor.

Soon, we were dismissed and went to our rooms. Vishnu was talking to the security team, so I smiled at him and walked out with the others. I figured I would get alone time with him later.

As I entered my room, the phone rang. It was Vishnu. He started screaming at me. He said Seth was in love with me and that I was encouraging it. "You need to stop blowing your pussy all over the place," he yelled through the phone. "Shut it down right now!" He hung up.

I slid to the floor and began sobbing. "Blowing my pussy all over the place?" What did that mean? I couldn't understand what had just happened. Seth was not in love with me; he was in love with his girlfriend, who was on the trip with him.

Lisa walked in just as I hit the floor. "Honey!" she exclaimed. "What's wrong?" She ran to me and sat by my side. In between sobs, I told her everything—that I was Vishnu's consort and it was a huge secret and no one could know and that he had just accused me of making Seth fall in love with me. I told her about the vulgar language. I told her I didn't understand what I was doing that was so wrong.

Her face turned red. She hugged me and held me and said, "There is a lot of energy here. He is probably very stressed. Don't take it personally." Then she smiled and said, "You're Vishnu's consort. That's *really, really* cool. Renee, that's a huge honor. You should be proud of yourself; not many people could handle that much energy."

She gave me chocolate and made me instant coffee from our mini bar and made me laugh. She reminded me that this path was supposed to push us to our breaking points, so that we could be Free. "This is all part of The Path," she said with a sparkle in her eyes. I felt a lot better.

The phone rang again.

We both stared at it and then looked at each other.

"I guess I should get it," I said. It was Vishnu. He told me to go up to his hotel room. I didn't want to see him, but I went. That's what consorts do.

Vishnu opened the door and let me in. The sight of him made me sick. We sat on the back of his sofa, and he asked if I had fallen asleep on the plane.

I told him I had.

"You got slimed by the occult," he said. "You will have to be very careful. You are making mistakes. You cannot afford to make mistakes. I forgive you." Then he grabbed me and kissed me—another rough kiss, gagging me with his tongue.

He looked at me longingly and said, "I wish you could stay."

Fortunately I could not. We had an event to get ready for. I wiped my face off and went back to my room.

The phone rang again. It was him.

"That kiss was so hot, so romantic," he said. "You drive me crazy. You are magnificent. I love you. Go buy flowers and vases for the event room. I told all of the students to bring some from Sydney, but there aren't enough."

We were in the middle of the Outback of Australia. I didn't have a car. Where the hell was I supposed to buy flowers and vases? I ran around the resort in 120-degree heat looking. I actually found some and bought everything I could find. I filled the room with flowers and just barely had enough time to shower, get dressed, and arrive on time to the event.

Lakshmi walked onto the stage, and we all gasped. We had not seen her for so long. She shined with gold light. The energy coming off her seemed even more intense. As we began the first meditation, I closed my eyes and felt myself transported to the top of Uluru. I had a vision of myself in between Vishnu and Lakshmi, holding hands on top of that massive rock, spreading gold light in waves across the Outback. I was filled with peace and love and the feeling that everything would be okay. Lakshmi was back, and it was magical. She seemed much more powerful; she must have been away meditating, just as I had imagined. All of my worries disappeared.

Vishnu sat on stage with her, but instead of guarding her as he usually did, he sat in half-lotus on his chair, with his eyes closed and a smile on his face, his shoes placed side by side on the floor beneath him. When the event ended he walked Lakshmi out of the auditorium, but quickly returned and asked me to join him for dinner; he apologized again for his outburst, telling me he had been under occult attack. He was so sparkly, so full of light, and looked so masculine and so handsome. I was so filled up with love from the event. I agreed.

At dinner, he held my hand under the table and even leaned over and kissed me, not worrying whether any of the other students saw us. As he walked me back to my room, he looked at me yearningly and said he wished he could spend the night with me.

"Let's have breakfast together in the morning," he whispered as he kissed me goodnight. He pointed to a bench in the garden and said, "Meet me here at 7:00 a.m."

In the morning, I got up and showered, meditated, and walked down to the bench. Vishnu was not there. I waited fifteen minutes. He did not show up. I walked into the restaurant. He was not there. My time to eat before we departed the hotel was quickly diminishing.

I figured Vishnu must have gotten held up helping Lakshmi or a student, so I sat down with Bruno at a table that gave me a view of the bench in the garden. Just as I was finishing breakfast, Vishnu walked in. He saw me and motioned for me to join him. I walked over, and he walked outside. I followed him.

He grabbed my arm roughly and said, "What is wrong with you? Where were you? Why were you eating with Bruno instead of me?" There was so much anger in his voice. I felt like a child being scolded and started to cry.

"I waited for you," I said.

"You didn't wait long enough."

"I thought you got held up. I could see the bench from my table, and I never saw you there. I was planning to walk out the second I did," I said.

"*I* was watching the bench, and I never saw *you* there," he said. "The next time I tell you to meet me somewhere, you need to meet me. Don't have breakfast with another man instead."

He walked away. I was dumbfounded. No matter what I did, I simply could not please this man.

That day, we followed Lakshmi around Uluru. There was so much light coming off of it that I could barely feel my body. It was hot and dry; the sun scorched our skin. Lakshmi walked slowly, waddling side to side, like an old fat lady. I wondered why she walked so slowly. I worried about her health. On stage she had been radiating light, but up close she did not look well. She wore black cotton pants and a black tank top that hung low and covered her bottom. Her arms were turning pink, so I asked her if she needed sunblock.

"No, thank you," she replied. She was wearing sunglasses, so I couldn't see her eyes, but there was ice in her voice.

Her arms continued to burn. When we had completed a full circle of Uluru, we were allowed to climb it. I decided not to. I could feel the spirits of the Aboriginal elders pleading with us, *Please do not climb our sacred site*. Instead, I lay on my back on a bench in the shade, peering up at the sky. Waves of white light pulsed through my body, expanding me as far and wide as eternity Herself. I was incredibly confused about Vishnu, but too "baked" by Uluru to care.

When we returned to the hotel, Vishnu announced that he would be teaching karate in one hour. Almost all of us, close to one hundred students, showed up to the room forty-five minutes later and waited outside patiently. The doors were closed. Vishnu must have been running late. The minutes ticked by. We sat quietly. Finally, Vishnu opened the door from inside the room and spoke to James, one of the security guards. James turned to us and said fifteen of us could enter.

Vishnu was visibly upset and kept making mistakes: counting out of order, forgetting to do kicks on the left side after kicks on the right, telling us to do one combo of moves and then doing something different. After the warm-up, he walked to the door and admitted everyone else but told them they had to sit in *seiza*, a formal Japanese kneeling position, around the edge of the room. When their legs started falling asleep and they began fidgeting, Vishnu yelled at them to stop moving. This was mean—incredibly mean. Some of the students were sixty or older.

Finally, he stopped teaching the first group and told us to kneel, as well. He started screaming at us: "Every one of you was late! And not a single one of you brought me flowers! It is a sign of disrespect to not bring an offering for a Spiritual Teacher, much less to show up late for class. This is unacceptable! In a traditional dojo, your sensei could kill you on the spot for this kind of insolence. How dare you?"

The whole time, his fly was open.

I raised my hand timidly and said, "Sensei, all of these people were here early. They were waiting quietly outside the room."

The other students looked incredibly relieved.

Vishnu grew quiet and turned slightly red. He said, "Well . . . you all are forgiven. You are invited to join class. But every single one of you should have brought me flowers."

We responded in unison, "Osu, Sensei."

As we left the room after class, many of the senior students thanked me. Vishnu called the volunteers aside and asked us why no one had told him earlier that everyone had shown up on time.

"Sensei, you are a bit intimidating," Seth said.

"Well, someone needs to tell me in the future," Vishnu replied, as if it were our fault. He dismissed us.

As I walked to my room, I hoped I would not have to be near Vishnu again for the rest of the trip.

At dinner, I was assigned a seat at Lakshmi's table, to the right of Vishnu. My heart raced. I was so mad at Vishnu that I couldn't look at him, and I was really nervous about being so close to Lakshmi. I barely spoke to either of them. I simply ate my food quietly and let the other students ask questions. At one point, feeling the need to say something, I looked at Lakshmi and said, "It is so good to have you back."

"I never left," she said. "I have always been here, always teaching you." She had an edge to her voice, something dark below the surface. Up close, she looked like the magic had been sucked out of her. In her time away from us, she had gained weight and gotten soft. Her clothing was baggy, boarding on frumpy. I had a fleeting glimpse of her as a pudgy, white, privileged Jewish woman, not a god. It disappeared as fast as it arrived.

When dinner was over, I walked back to my room, desperate to have some time to myself. Vishnu called before I went to bed, to tell me Lakshmi had told him I had incredible etiquette around him, that she was very impressed. I guess my being pissed at him and ignoring him mimicked proper etiquette. I got off the phone as fast as he would allow.

The next day, as we were all learning to make Aboriginal art, Vishnu pulled me aside and had me walk with him to the back of the building.

He looked at me with tears in his eyes and said, "I'm becoming Enlightened. Renee, will you be there for me? Will you stand by my side? I need to know I can count on you."

I was a bit baffled. To me, he seemed further from Enlightenment than anyone else in our group, but what did I know? Of course I would be there for him. Enlightenment was the most important thing in my life. I wanted it to happen to all of us so we could make the world a better place.

"Of course I'll help you," I said.

He hugged me and cried into my hair and told me he loved me. Then he pulled himself together and we walked back to join the rest of the group.

Lakshmi watched us as we entered the room. Her gaze lingered a bit too long. I quickly picked up my art and continued making little dots.

That night, Vishnu called me again, this time to tell me Lakshmi was having a meltdown. "She called me to her room and asked if Shiva told me to have a tantric relationship with you," he said. "I told her no."

My stomach sank. This entire time I thought she knew about us. This entire time, I thought she was relieved to know Vishnu had someone to take care of him and to love him. This entire time, I thought I was *helping* her. How could he lie to an Enlightened Being?

His lying about us confirmed something else for me: Vishnu and Lakshmi were in a relationship. Otherwise, why would he lie about us? I was angry, and I was so sad inside.

"I'm shocked," I said. "I can't sleep with you anymore until I'm sure Lakshmi not only knows but also approves of it. Once a woman trusts another woman, there is a sacred bond of trust that cannot be broken."

I hung up the phone and curled into a ball and sobbed.

Then I went out to my patio to meditate. Instantly, I saw myself sitting in front of Uluru. I was on dry, cracked red mud, and there was no one else around. In my vision I surrendered totally, offering my spirit to Uluru and my body to the parched earth below me. I imagined leaving my body and allowing it to decompose, to feed and nourish the Outback. And then my heart chakra exploded into white light, and I saw that the love and grace I kept hoping for had to come from within my own heart and radiate out, not the other way around. I suddenly understood why all the senior students looked so dejected. They had been waiting twenty years to be blessed and Enlightened, never realizing it wouldn't come from a Teacher; it had to come from within themselves.

I opened my eyes. The phone was ringing.

"Hello, Renee. It's Lakshmi. Do you have a moment?"

Of course I had a moment. I loved her so much. My heart began thumping.

"Can you please come up to my room?" she asked.

Suddenly, I was terrified. What was she going to ask me?

When she answered the door, she hugged me. It felt like being hugged by light.

Her eyes looked red and swollen, like she'd been crying. She told me she had a gift for me and handed me a stuffed koala holding its baby in its arms.

I started crying. She asked why, and I said, "Because I want to be able to hold and protect you the way the larger koala is protecting the little one."

"Well, we can take turns protecting each other."

I stood there awkwardly, holding the child's toy, until she said, "That's all. I saw them in the gift shop and they told me I had to buy them for you. I hope you like them. They are very magical."

I thanked her and went back to my room, wishing I had mustered up the confidence and strength to have talked to her about Vishnu.

The next day, we all flew back to Sydney. Lakshmi was lost in thought. She looked gray. I had never seen her look so depleted. I felt so sad for her. At last I understood what was going on. She wasn't sick. She hadn't been sick. She was heartbroken.

Chapter 15
family

Vishnu flew with Lakshmi to Singapore and then to Germany and then to Arizona while I went home alone. Apparently, Shiva had told them these stops would help Lakshmi heal from the trip, that the occult would not be able to find them if they kept moving. Vishnu called me daily as they travelled and finally told Lakshmi about us when they reached Arizona. He told me she was devastated, that she dropped to the floor and sobbed at his feet. They spent a week discussing it, fighting about it.

"At times, she handles it like an Enlightened Being," he said, "and at other times, she breaks down crying and tells me to lie to her and pretend I still love her."

I was horrified. This was the antithesis of what I had imagined. I told him we had to stop seeing each other.

"Give me more time," he said. I hung up the phone in agony. I wished I could talk to her about it, but spiritual etiquette dictated that I could not approach her; she had to approach me.

Two weeks later, my wish came true. They both flew to California. Vishnu called and said it was all arranged: Lakshmi would go for a walk on the beach with me, spend some time talking to me, give me her blessing, and then she and I would cook dinner for him at their house. *Cook dinner for him?* I thought. *Why wouldn't he and I cook dinner for* her? I hung up the phone. I was even more confused.

Lakshmi and I walked side by side down the beach. Our conversation was strained. We were both upset. I wanted to tell her how much I loved her, that I didn't want to be Vishnu's consort. But my courage to tell her anything vanished. I felt that she didn't want to hear anything I had to say. I simply walked quietly by her side. I cannot recall anything she said to me. What I *do* remember is us sitting side by side in the sand at the end of our walk, waiting for Vishnu to meet us. Each time she thought he was approaching, she would put her arm around me, only to let go of the hug as soon as she realized the man approaching was not Vishnu. I could sense she really wanted him to see her handling it well. In a sense, I was in love with her, and she was in love with him, and he was in love with me. Talk about *twisted.*

Eventually, he came strolling down the beach, hands in his pockets, smug smile on his face, a man on top of the world, a man getting everything he ever wanted. Lakshmi and I stood up, and the three of us embraced. Then, on the beach under a cliff, they presented me with a ring—the dragon ring. It was gold. I noticed then that they had both changed their own rings from their left hands to their right. Lakshmi placed the ring on my right hand as well. She explained it was a Power Ring and that I could never be separate from it. Vishnu told me when I surfed, I should keep it tied to my bikini, and when I did karate, I had to keep it tied to my *gi.* There was only one time that I could—and should—take it off: when I pooped. Somehow, it would defile the ring if I kept it on then.

"We will be one big happy family," she said. "The rings bind us together," he added. Then we walked back to their house and Lakshmi and I cooked Vishnu dinner.

After we ate, I felt sick. I walked outside for fresh air and started vomiting violently into the bushes. Lakshmi looked very concerned, and Vishnu tried to "heal" me with his hugs and by running his hands over my body in order to "pull out lines of energy." I felt afraid and unsure. I felt sad to the depths of my soul. I felt poisoned. I went home and vomited some more and cried myself to sleep.

The next morning, our life as a "family" began. I now did the shopping and errand running and cooking and cleaning for both of them. I did not sleep over; Vishnu decided it would be better to wait, to let Lakshmi get used to having me around first. I was grateful for the break. When she went back to Arizona, I would sleep over and have sex with him again. At times, he was caring and kind and I loved him; at other times he was selfish and narcissistic and treated me like a peon, and I hated him. This went on for months.

When summer rolled around again, the public events, which happened for three nights one week a month, began to take a toll on Lakshmi. According to Vishnu she broke down crying daily and begged him to stop sleeping with me, and while calling him from Arizona, she'd scream and throw the phone across the room, shattering it into pieces. Or if she were in California, she would scream and scream until Vishnu was worried the neighbors were going to call the cops. She asked him again to lie to her, to tell her he loved her.

Hearing this broke my heart. I suggested to Vishnu that I stay away from him completely. I didn't want to be sleeping with him, anyway. I complained about it often to Lakshmi, so she knew; however, during these talks she always told me that being Vishnu's consort was my Divine task, that it would make me change, make me sand down my ego, that it was right for all of us. Yet she hated us together. I would have gladly given up this task, and told him it was clearly time I resign from being his consort, but he wouldn't let me.

He insisted it was my dharma to be his consort, that Lakshmi was just under occult attack and was really fine with the idea. The two of them began to fight more often. Vishnu called me daily to tell me about their arguments and ask for advice. Then Lakshmi started to call me daily to talk to me about Vishnu. I told her I couldn't stand him. I told her I thought he was selfish and narcissistic and acted like a spoiled five-year-old. Lakshmi felt supported by this, grateful to discover he treated me badly, as well.

I was on Lakshmi's side. When Vishnu called me I disclosed everything I said about him. Surprisingly, he took it well. He started crying. He said he needed to change. He told me to please be patient with him, that he would change. So I stayed.

Meanwhile, everything was ramping up for the students. We had more tasks, more assignments. Our meditation had increased steadily; we were now meditating an hour every morning and thirty minutes every night. Our tuition increased again, radically. I began paying $1200 a month. Those who paid more would be entitled more time with Lakshmi and would be more "empowered." Vishnu continued teaching us karate.

I eventually arranged for him to teach at the dance studio where I used to teach classes. One evening, as we were getting ready for karate class, a man walked into the studio asking about dance lessons. I left Vishnu's side and spoke to the man, handing him a schedule of dance classes and explaining how to get started. When I turned around, Vishnu was fuming. He pulled me into the back room.

Then he exploded.

"Do you have *any idea* what a privilege it is to work for me?" he screamed. "Most of the students out there would *kill* to spend time with me!"

I asked him what he was talking about.

"You made a severe breach of etiquette by leaving my side to assist that man."

I explained that I did it out of respect for the owners of the studio and for the man, that as a former teacher at that studio, I could not let him walk in and leave him unattended. Then I told Vishnu that if he wanted my respect he had to earn it. I walked out to join the rest of the students.

The next day, four dozen, magnificent long-stem white roses in an exquisite vase arrived at my house. From Vishnu. In a heartfelt card, he asked for my forgiveness. He called soon afterward and asked if he could come over and apologize. When I opened the front door, he dropped to his knees, grabbed onto my legs, looked up at me, and said, "I love you fiercely. Please forgive me."

We had a long talk in my garden. I told him about my father, about how much I respected him. I told him he could not expect me to listen to him and follow him and call him a Teacher if he acted like a spoiled child. I said he had to walk the walk, not just talk the talk. At the end of the talk, we were closer, but I would never again be able to talk myself into loving him or looking up to him. It simply was not possible. I actually felt sorry for him.

November approached, and Vishnu insisted I spend Thanksgiving with him and Lakshmi in Arizona. I did not want to go.

"She won't like it," I said.

He insisted. "We're family," he said.

She called me and invited me. "We're family, " she said.

I had to go.

I flew to Phoenix, rented a car, and drove to their home. I got lost on the way and arrived tired and travel-weary. I had never been to their house before. When I knocked, Vishnu answered. I went to hug him, and he pushed me away saying, "It's patio time."

Shiva had told Lakshmi to stop meditating—the only thing in the world she loved as much as Vishnu. He told her it made her "too open" and allowed "the Dark Beings to mess with her mind." Since her break from teaching had not helped, he thought maybe a break from meditating would. So Lakshmi sat outside on her patio at sunset each day and simply watched the colors change. Vishnu, in his effort to be exactly like Lakshmi, insisted on doing the same.

I followed him out to the patio. Vishnu sat in half-lotus with his eyes closed. Lakshmi stared at the trees. I was ignored.

This was the anniversary of my father's death. I was used to spending it at home, cooking for all of my closest friends. I sat next to them on the patio and silently cried. Now I hated them both.

Once the sun set, we went inside, and I quietly excused myself, saying I was tired, and drove to my hotel. I cried all night in my hotel. I begged God and my father for guidance. No one was supposed to know I was in Arizona; I couldn't even call Lisa. The "family" and the rings and my being consort were all a huge fucking secret that was starting to kill me slowly.

The next morning, I took as long as possible to get up and get ready. I was supposed to be at the house by noon, but I was also supposed to do all the Thanksgiving shopping by myself before I got there, before I cooked for the two of them. In the grocery store parking lot I had a horrible thought about Lakshmi that bubbled up through my mind and out of my mouth. I mumbled it under my breath: *I hate you, you fat hag.*

It has to be the occult, I thought. I could never think that about her. Just then, my phone rang. It was Lakshmi. She told me to hurry up.

"I have a few more things to buy," I told her. "I will need to go to Albertsons to get them."

"I can't eat food from Albertsons," she said.

"But my recipe calls for a few ingredients I can't get at Whole Foods," I said.

"Renee, it's not all about you," she spat bitterly. It was the first time she had ever been outright mean to me, the first time I felt hate in our interaction. I put the phone back in my purse and got into my car and sat in the parking lot and cried some more. Then I told myself I was walking "The Warrior Path," that it was the hardest path there is, because you do not shut yourself in an ashram and act saintly, you live in the world and act saintly. So I pulled myself together and filled my heart with love and put the car in drive and pulled out of the parking lot . . . back on my mission.

I arrived at the house, unloaded the bags by myself, and began cooking. Vishnu sat on his ass watching TV. (We were instructed in Lakshmi's events to *never* watch TV because it linked us into the mind states of every other human watching TV.) Lakshmi stayed in her room. I thought of my dead parents and imagined them there with me. I thought of my dead God-mother and about how much she loved to cook. In fact, I was using her and my mother's recipes. Thoughts of them warmed my heart and lifted my spirits. I thought of Sri Ramakrishna washing latrines with his hair and realized this was so much easier. *I can do this,* I thought to myself and continued cooking.

Then Lakshmi came out of her room. She walked into the kitchen, opened her arms wide, drew me in for a long hug, and told me she loved me. The light was back; I could feel it flowing out of her. We giggled and laughed, and she helped me finish preparing the meal.

As the afternoon progressed, Vishnu's mood worsened. When we sat for dinner he didn't speak. He slammed plates around and jabbed at his food; like an insolent child. Suddenly, he stood up, left the table, and stormed out of the room. Lakshmi and I looked at each other and simultaneously sighed with relief. His mood had been so heavy. With him gone, we began enjoying ourselves. Giggling and chatting. Eating away.

"I need a man in my life," she blurted out. "I feel much better when that part of my life is taken care of."

I smiled, not knowing what else to do. She had spent time in almost every one of her seminars telling women that our loneliness and desire for a partner is what impedes our journey to attain Enlightenment. She had told us over and over to get good at being alone.

"I'm not very good at relationships," I said, to fill the silence. "I think I'm better on my own." I didn't know what else to say. Again, it hit me how much she loved Vishnu, he loved me, and I loved her. I wished she could see me as the solution to her loneliness, as her support. I had a sudden thought that God had sent me to her, to be her companion, to be a similar soul craving Enlightenment, but that she could not see it, because I was in the wrong form, because she insisted that love and support and companionship come in the form of a man, of a lover. And not just any man, she only wanted it from Vishnu.

It was the same way my mother couldn't be appeased with love from me, how she wanted it only from my deceased father. Utterly unable to see and accept the love that was waiting to pour into her from other sources.

As I was cleaning up the kitchen, Lakshmi offered me a tour of the house. She took me from room to room, and I noticed the house was *full*. It was as if they had kept everything they had ever owned. The garage was full of boxes and crates and shelves piled with old crap. Vishnu's room looked like a little boy's room. He still had his college baseball cap and a college sweatshirt and old photos. His furniture was old. His bed was old, with an old bedspread on it. Their house was in total disarray. I felt deflated, betrayed. I felt lied to and manipulated, duped. I thought of my Armani jacket and my baby bracelets and the beautiful photo of me surfing going up in flames.

The more time I spent with them and the closer I got, the more I noticed they practiced very little of what they taught. All of my belongings were gone. All of my friends were gone. All of the activities that made me *me* were gone. And I was sleeping with a man I could not stand. I was utterly lost. I could not go back to the life I used to live, and yet continuing with Vishnu and Lakshmi suddenly seemed outrageously wrong.

Could I trust my instincts? Or was it the occult messing with me? Could I trust Lakshmi, or did she hate me because of Vishnu? Could I trust Vishnu, or was he just using me for companionship and sex? I was so confused, I honestly did not know.

chapter 16
The Decision

Kate and I were sitting side by side on her balcony the week
after I returned from Arizona, watching the sky turn crim-
son over a calm blue ocean. Kate had left our meditation group
shortly after we all returned from Australia. She was trying to
talk me into doing the same. She thought it was a cult. She was
worried about me. She said there was too much mind control.
She said it was dangerous. I thought she was too skeptical. I
thought she lacked faith. I thought she was too locked in her
mind to follow her heart. I figured she just didn't yearn for
Enlightenment the way I did. Yes, I was doubting them, too, but
it came in flashes. Like a light going on and off. I was faithful, I
was following these guides—Lakshmi and Vishnu—and then,
with a sudden flash of clarity, I could see I was going the wrong
way, that they were leading me dangerously astray.

But I had lived life my way for thirty-five years, and it was
not working for me. I was still lost. I was still soul-sick. I still
could not figure out why I had so much sadness inside, and I felt
like I had to find my purpose if I wanted to stay on this earth. I
also saw myself getting older and couldn't bear the idea of being
in my fifties and finding joy only in surfing and dancing and

men. What would happen if I got sick? What would happen when I got really old? I had to learn to be content inside my own mind. I couldn't keep running from party to party and man to man and job to job in order to distract myself. I *had* to try something different. I simply *had* to. I had so much doubt, especially the more I got to know Vishnu, the more I got to see how he lived, yet I believed in the occult, and I believed I had a huge ego, and I saw the light coming out of Lakshmi, so I believed the problem was with me. Lakshmi had told us the path would be hard, that we would want to quit. Every time I had that flash of clarity and wanted to quit, I rethought it. I couldn't turn around and go back to life the way I had lived it before. I had to keep going forward. I had to keep trying.

"You don't understand," I told Kate. "All I care about is Enlightenment. I would give up my limbs to be free from human states of attention and to spread more light and love in this dark world."

Kate looked at me, her brow furrowed.

"And," I continued, "if it doesn't work out, I'll just write a book about the five years I spent in a cult."

"Okay," Kate said. "I'll keep working so that, if you end up crazy and homeless, you can come live on my couch."

We laughed. I looked at the sunset. She looked at me looking at the sunset. I knew she thought I was losing my mind.

————

Kate's opinion was clear: Get the fuck out ASAP. I went home that night and gave it more thought. If I wanted to win a gold medal at the Olympics, I would hire the best coach I could find, and I would do everything she told me to do. Everything. I wouldn't pick and choose which directions I wanted to follow and which ones I did not. This was the same. If I thought Lakshmi was Enlightened, then I had to commit; I couldn't pick and choose. I had to do everything she told me to. And if she told me to listen to Vishnu, I had to listen to Vishnu.

I had seen Lakshmi's flaws. I had seen her as just a damaged, confused woman, but when she was on stage in front of us, she flooded the room with gold light. I could see it! I could feel it! I saw her turn into Jesus when she spoke about Jesus.

"Do not confuse the teachings of Jesus Christ with Christianity," she would say. "Jesus' teachings were about love and acceptance. He told his students to get outside in nature, out of the churches, and to find God through meditation and within their own hearts. He taught that we *all* have direct access to God, that we do not need intermediaries, and that we are all perfect from birth." And then she would go on to explain passages in the Bible and the teachings of Jesus in the most magical and magnificent way. She told us about the *Pistis Sophia*, which mentions Jesus turning rooms gold when he meditated. The way I felt in those events was unlike anything I had ever experienced.

It has to be the Occult, I thought, as an explanation for all the times she behaved badly in my presence. I decided to go all-in, to do everything they told me to. I was going to stop arguing with Vishnu; even if it killed me, I was going to look up to him as my guru. Vishnu told me to stop dancing. He told me to not go out to eat with male friends. He told me to surf less. I did it all. As I made these changes, I got more depressed, but I believed Lakshmi when she said I was more reluctant to change than anyone else in the sangha. So each time I felt the urge to run, I told myself it was just my ego. I told myself it was the occult trying to push me off the path. I hated serving Vishnu and doing all his errands and putting up with his narcissism, but I kept doing it. I kept doing all of it.

One day, Vishnu called me from a furniture store. "I'm buying a new bed," he said, all excited. "What should I get?"

I was in his garage, sorting through old files. One of my jobs was to prepare his house each time he flew in. I had to fill the refrigerator with groceries, open all the windows, buy fresh flowers, make sure all the sheets and towels were clean, and today he had added filing away all the remaining old cards and questions from students—*years* worth of them.

After a few moments of silence, he asked, "What's wrong?"

"I think Lakshmi's bipolar," I blurted out. "And I feel like neither of you practices what you preach." I finally said it. Damn! I had just decided I was going all-in. But I couldn't stop myself. "I thought being Enlightened meant that you were free from human mind states, yet Lakshmi seems like she's in hell. She's obsessed with you, and she can't get over you. I thought tantra meant you live in the world while your mind is the ashram. Yet you don't want me to dance or surf or go out to eat with friends. I'm really upset and really confused."

He told me to go for a surf and come back to the house afterward, that we had to talk.

He greeted me at the front door with flowers. "Lakshmi just struggles with the idea of us together," he said. "And she gets hit with a lot of dark energy. The dark forces are using our relationship to really hammer on Lakshmi."

"Then why don't we stop?" I asked. "I don't understand why we don't just stop."

"Because it is not right," he said. "You are supposed to be my consort." I *hated* that word. I hated the idea of being anyone's consort. I was the family slave. I was the servant. And at times like this I felt like the family concubine, as well. I told him so, and he got on his knees again. He grabbed my legs and looked up at me. "I love you," he said. "I love you so much. We can figure this out."

———

We had one event left that year, and then I'd have a break from all of it for Christmas. Or so I thought, until Vishnu told me I would be spending Christmas with them.

"That's a bad idea," I said. "Lakshmi won't like it."

He told me I had to, that we were "family." So I flew to Arizona on Christmas Eve and spent the night alone in my hotel room.

The next morning I arrived at their house as late as possible. Lakshmi asked me to join her in her room. She showed me a painting of a Buddha emitting rays of light and told me she was one of those rays of light. Then she said, as we sat side by side on her bed, looking at the Buddha, that I could never be like her.

"I'm complete, Renee," she said. "I'm Enlightened; I've attained perfection and can no longer make mistakes. Why do you insist on sleeping with Vishnu? Why can't you just leave him alone? You have been throwing your pussy at him since the first day you saw him. You just throw that sexual energy all over the place, don't you?"

This has to be an occult attack, I thought. *This cannot be her*. I shut down, hoping that if I didn't speak, the conversation would be over faster.

Lakshmi said, "Well, maybe you're lonely. Why don't you get a dog? You don't need a man. A man will hold you back from Enlightenment."

Then she smiled and grabbed me by the hand and led me to Vishnu, who was sitting by the Christmas tree. She said in a cheerful voice, "Let's open presents!"

I couldn't stop crying. Vishnu didn't even notice. He handed me gift after gift. He had spent a fortune on me. Then Lakshmi handed me her gifts. The first was an embroidered silk tunic. It was pretty, and I thanked her between silent sobs. The second was a set of lavender sequined ballet-slipper flats. They had ribbons to tie around my ankles. For some reason, this made me cry even harder.

I felt like a child again. But I felt loved. I felt like my mother was buying me pretty ballet shoes. I was so completely unwound at this point, so utterly empty and destroyed and powerless. A thirty-five-year-old woman transformed into a very wounded child. I looked up at her with love in my eyes.

"I feel so loved," I said as I held the shoes to my chest. "I feel like I have a mother again."

She narrowed her eyes and said, "Don't you *ever* think of me as your mother."

Vishnu didn't notice. He was lost in his own thoughts, as always.

I sat in their living room, surrounded by discarded wrapping paper, and wondered how much more I could take.

Chapter 17
Threesome

By her next event, a month after Christmas, Lakshmi had gained even more weight, and she had dark circles under her eyes, but she still flooded the room with light, she still radiated with power.

"Women waste a lot of their energy getting men to notice them," she said. "Have you ever been driving down the street and suddenly whipped your head sideways when you noticed a scantily clad woman jogging?"

We all had.

"That woman was shoving her energy out, making you notice her," Lakshmi said. "Women do this all the time. Ladies, this is a *humungous* waste of your energy—energy that could be used to excel in your careers or reach higher states of mind in meditation. You spend all this time building energy in your meditations and then you throw it away when you shove it at a guy to make him check you out."

"Protect your hard-earned energy by covering your body. Wear looser clothing. Buy shirts that are long enough to cover your ass."

"Especially you, Renee," she said as she glared at me from the stage.

I sank into my seat.

Then she added, "Ladies, the men in these events, your sangha mates, are here to reach Enlightenment. I do not *ever* want to see you pushing your energy out at them to get them to notice you. This needs to be a safe place for them."

We all felt embarrassed. We cinched our jackets tighter together. Why were we suddenly in trouble?

I soon began receiving daily calls from Lakshmi; they often lasted an hour or longer. Sometimes she was kind and loving, sometimes she was hateful: "You think your pussy can pull a warrior like Vishnu off the path? It can't. You're a witch and a sorceress," she would say. Or "Don't you *ever* compare yourself to Vishnu and me. You will *never* be like us. You will *never* be as evolved as we are. You are here to serve us." Or "Why do you think Vishnu wants you over me? Am I that disgusting as a woman? I must be. Because I am Enlightened and I have attained perfection, and you are nothing, so he clearly just wants your pussy. You are a witch."

During these calls, I would slide to the floor, curl into a fetal position, and cry. I'd stay there for an hour after we hung up. I had never experienced such mental anguish before in my life. It was as if a dark curtain was pulled over my mind and I couldn't find even a crack of light. I began to not answer her calls. "I shudder to think of the karma you are creating by not answering calls from your Spiritual Teacher," she said to my voicemail. I panicked. My karma, according to her, was already bad enough. I dreaded making it worse. I answered her calls.

At this point, I hated both of them, and part of me knew it, but I wouldn't admit it to the rest of myself. And I kept replaying Lakshmi's words in my mind: "This path is the hardest path there is. You will want to quit. Only if you are doing this for others will you stick it out." And I *was* doing this for others. I was going to become an Enlightened saint to heal the world and all the suffering souls in it.

I had read about Enlightened Masters tormenting their students to test their commitment: The Tibetan saint Milarepa built a house stone by stone for his Teacher Marpa and was told to collapse it halfway through and rebuild it just a few feet away, *three different times*, as a way to erase his past karma. I figured I was erasing my past karma, and I simply refused to quit.

The next event rolled around, and the women in the sangha were noticeably frumpier. Many had gained weight. Almost all of us wore draping, loose clothing. I had bought a whole new wardrobe, my tiny body hidden under a tent of fabric. Lakshmi singled me out again while talking about past lives.

"You have had many past lives as royalty," she said to a student sitting in front of me. "Not you, Renee. You were a prostitute," she spit at me, then turned back to the student in front of me and continued.

I made excuses for this behavior. *It's the occult*, I said to myself. *The occult is really hammering her to get her to stop teaching us.* Or, *She is so pure, and she simply can't take the pressure of being in this world. She needs Vishnu by her side 24/7 to protect her.*

"We have to stop seeing each other," I would tell Vishnu. "We have to stop sleeping together." I would wail, "It's killing Lakshmi."

Finally, he agreed. We went back to the way it was before we started having sex. I spent much less time at the house, and Lakshmi pretended Vishnu still loved her. I only saw her during class weekends, and each time I did, there was so much light coming out of her that I reaffirmed to myself, *It has to be the occult. There is no other explanation. There is no way she can spread this much light and not be Enlightened.*

And then Shiva died. His two consorts called the house one night. I had just finished serving Lakshmi and Vishnu dinner. I had no place on that call. They had known Shiva for over ten years; I had only met him twice, but we all got on the phone. Vishnu and Lakshmi were devastated. As soon as we hung up I wanted to go home, to give them space to grieve, but Vishnu insisted I stay. He wanted me to sleep over, to "comfort" him.

I tried to sleep in his bed, but I couldn't. Then we heard Lakshmi screaming. Vishnu ran upstairs and was gone an hour.

When he came back, I told him I had to leave, and he said, "No. You are coming upstairs to spend the night with Lakshmi and me."

I knew that Shiva had lived with both of his consorts. I knew that when the women weren't with him, they were romantically involved with each other. I wanted *nothing* to do with a relationship like that. Was Vishnu suddenly suggesting we start one?

Timidly, I walked upstairs to Lakshmi's room. She sat on the edge of her bed and looked at me with hate in her eyes, but said nothing.

Vishnu looked at us both and said, "We are all one family, and we are going to spend the night together." He got in the middle of Lakshmi's bed. Lakshmi reluctantly crawled in next to him. I sat down on the edge of the bed, then lay back, staring at the ceiling, trying to take up as little of the bed and be as far away from Vishnu as possible. Lakshmi faced Vishnu and put her arm across his chest. Then she told me to do the same. I rolled onto my side to face Vishnu and placed my arm across his chest. My arm was now touching Lakshmi's. We lay there in awkward silence for a few minutes before Vishnu started snoring.

I am pretty sure Lakshmi and I lay awake all night. Neither of us moved. Finally, as the sky began getting lighter, I fell asleep. I awoke not much later. Vishnu was still sleeping. Lakshmi was sitting up in bed, glaring at me. Her usually blue eyes were now a deep, evil green, filled with hate. I got up and went home. I never wanted to see Lakshmi and Vishnu again.

I wasn't supposed to tell anyone about my relationship with Vishnu and Lakshmi, about how they were "behind the curtain," but I had to talk to someone before I completely lost my mind. I called Lisa on my drive home, and she invited me over for coffee. I didn't give her details, but I told her I was starting to doubt our teachers. I said I wanted to quit.

She listened and then reminded me that Lakshmi was Enlightened. She retold a tale Lakshmi had told us in a class: The *katana*, the Japanese Samurai sword, is one of the strongest blades in the world. For three days and three nights, smelters shovel up to twenty-five tons of iron-bearing river sand and charcoal into a furnace, creating a single batch of *tamahagane*, which is then fired at high temperatures but never allowed to reach a molten state. A swordsmith then heats, hammers, and folds the tamahagane repeatedly in order the blend the iron and carbon—but also, and more importantly, to draw out any remaining impurities. If impurities are allowed to remain, they will weaken the sword.

"You are just being heated up, hammered, and folded down," Lisa said. "To remove your impurities. That is going to make you sharper, right? And stronger than any other."

I smiled through my tears. She was right. This was what I had signed up for. This was The Warrior Path. I went back to work with a vengeance. I was *not* going to give up.

Chapter 18
Flip Flops

Our next Power Trip approached. This one was to the Grand Canyon. Even though I had organized the trip, while there my duties were kept to a minimum so that Lakshmi and Vishnu did not have to interact with me. I stayed in my room much of the time. In the meditation events I sat in the back. I stayed as small and as invisible as I possibly could, the way I had learned to be around my mother as a child. While at the Grand Canyon one day, I sat on the edge and contemplated jumping in.

If Lakshmi told me to jump, I would, I thought. I was that committed to her now. I honestly believed that if she told me to jump, it would blast me into Enlightenment—whatever the hell Enlightenment was. And sticking around was causing me so much pain I honestly thought jumping might be better.

When we returned to California, Vishnu became even more controlling. He said he was getting closer to Enlightenment and needed me available in case he "went through the door." Suddenly, he was too sensitive to do much of anything. Even Lakshmi began waiting on him. He wanted me to text him constantly and report on my whereabouts. He wanted me to buy more and more obscure groceries every day, and when I would call him to clarify, he wouldn't answer the phone, saying later that he had been in *somadhi* (the highest state of meditation). He took over teaching Lakshmi's classes again and ramped up our karate classes, making everyone bow to him as much as possible in both.

He wanted me to get an alarm put on my house, saying that Dark Beings would be attracted to the light coming out of my house because he had spent time there. He told me I could not trust people, that they all wanted to steal my energy. Like moths to the flame, he said, dark, broken people would seek me out and cling to me because I had been sleeping with him and his light was "flowing through me."

One night, I came home late after doing a task with Lisa for Lakshmi. I walked into my office to send Lakshmi an e-mail. My computer was gone. What the hell? I called Vishnu, afraid.

"I told you so," he said. "I told you people would break into your house. Is anything else gone?"

I was suddenly very afraid. He stayed on the phone with me while I checked everywhere in the house. My tango dresses were all gone. My tango shoes and expensive high heels were gone. My lingerie was gone, and so was my makeup and my new purse.

"Whoever broke in knew they had time and knew exactly where I kept everything," I said. "They came in through the window." I could see that the screen was bent. In the guest bedroom, where the window overlooked the street, the horizontal blinds were slightly askew in one area. Someone had been a lookout.

I had always believed I was safe in this world. Suddenly, I felt very unsafe. Vishnu was right; I should have listened. Suddenly, I doubted myself even more. Maybe I really had been incredibly naïve my whole life. I couldn't trust myself or my instincts; they were clearly leading me astray. I couldn't trust anybody; they could all be moths drawn to my flame, even my sangha mates.

I realized the only person I could trust was Vishnu. I clung to him even more, spent more time with him. We began sleeping together again. Lakshmi sensed this—or he told her. Either way, she did not handle it well.

"Get her out of my room!" she screamed. "Goddammit, Vishnu! She is killing me. Get her out of my room!"

Lakshmi had just landed at the California airport, and I was getting her room ready for her. I had washed and pressed the sheets, fluffed and folded her towels. I had put fresh flowers in her bathroom and on her dresser. I had opened the windows to let in fresh air and sunlight. I had Mozart playing on my iPod and mini speakers to raise the vibration in her room, and I was just lighting incense to clean it energetically when Vishnu walked up with the phone to his ear. I could hear her screaming through it. I was stunned.

This woman hates me, I thought.

I put down the incense. I turned off my iPod. And I walked downstairs, got into my car, and left.

After that, I avoided the house when Lakshmi was in town, but when she was gone I continued to spend a lot of my time with Vishnu. He was protecting me, I thought. With him, I felt safe. Plus, I had nobody else.

I listed my house for sale and began looking for a new one closer to Vishnu. Bruno was a real estate agent and showed me a few. When I showed up to meet him one day, he looked at me with sadness in his eyes.

"I miss you," he said.

We used to surf together, go eat together, go to movies together, laugh together. We didn't do that anymore. Vishnu wouldn't approve.

He looked me up and down and said, "You seem so sad, are you okay?"

"Of course I am okay," I answered, annoyed. I caught my reflection in my car window. It was warm out, and I was wearing a long skirt and a long-sleeved tunic, both three sizes too big for me. They looked like sacks. My shoulders were hunched over, protecting my heart. I was a specter of my old self, a shell. I was fragile and weak and broken.

I did not believe Bruno when he told me I didn't look well.

He can't see clearly, I thought. *He's addicted to the world.* I shoved him further away, stopped returning his calls the way I did with everyone else who truly loved me.

One day, I showed up to work in Vishnu's garage. After a few hours, I walked into the house and asked where my flip-flops were; I wanted to walk down to the beach. In the beginning of our relationship, he had insisted I keep some of my belongings at his house. He wanted a set of my lingerie to keep in his bedroom and he wanted me to keep a pair of my flip-flops on the shoe rack in the closet by his front door.

"They're in the garage," he said. "You shouldn't leave them in the house. When your Teacher looks at your shoes, he gets hit with your attention, and you should not be in your Teacher's attention." He was referring to himself. This man that was fucking me. This man that was letting me buy all his groceries, do his cooking, run his company, and do his errands. He *could not look at my flip-flops.* My size-six, cute, dainty, pink flowered flip-flops. Not some old ugly stinky worn sneakers or hiking shoes or slimy Tevas. Tiny pink flip-flops. This man that was *fucking* me. He could have his body inside mine but he could not look at my shoes? And they were not strewn haphazardly around the house, in the middle of the floor. They had been left neatly side-by-side on the shoe rack in the closet!

I stood there with my mouth open. I had arrived to spend another day in his garage sorting through bullshit for no pay—while *he* went to the beach.

"I can't do this anymore," I said. "I love myself too much to let you treat me like this. You have some serious problems. The only way Lakshmi can handle putting up with you is because she is an Enlightened saint. I don't care if I never become Enlightened. I simply cannot be your consort any longer." I walked out the door, got in my car, and left.

It was over.

I was finished.

He called me that night and said he didn't feel well and asked if I would come over and make him dinner. I said no but that I would order delivery for him. He didn't talk to me for days after that. I still felt an obligation to honor my commitment to Lakshmi and her company. I kept working. He ignored my phone calls and e-mails. I began to panic. Maybe I had made the wrong decision. The self-doubt set in yet again. Maybe the occult had finally pushed me off the path. I had to make amends. I e-mailed him and asked him what I needed to do to be forgiven for not making him dinner. I left him a voicemail with the same message.

He responded by e-mail: *Your ego is huge, and you are in serious jeopardy of ruining your karma forever. You must sand down your humungous ego. You can start by writing the Code of the Samurai one thousand and eighty times.*

The Code of the Samurai is about three pages long. A thousand and eighty times comes out to 3,420 pages, but I did it. It took weeks, writing every day until my hand cramped, but I fucking did it.

I submitted my one thousand and eighty writings of the Code of the Samurai in two beautiful leather-bound notebooks.

Vishnu threw them on his desk and told me that I had three days to hand over all the files I had compiled while working for them, that I had to make a document listing everything my job entailed, that I had to return my ring and the katana he had given me, and that Lakshmi had given me a "new task": to go get a full-time job at a corporation and to go back to school so I could become a computer programmer.

In a very serious voice, he said, "When you decided to become my consort, you made a bid for power. And you failed. This will ruin your karma. In the future, you will be presented with a chance to redeem yourself. You better not fail again." Then, as an afterthought he added, "I am a patient man. I can wait."

I was too numb to respond. I couldn't imagine getting a full-time job at a corporation with a background in dance; I was terrified of trying. I wished I could undo what I had done, could go back to serving them and running their company, but I knew I could not. Now I just wanted the phone call to end so I could lie down and cry.

I met Vishnu at the dojo/dance studio the next day to return the katana and the ring. Dressed in my gi, I kneeled in seiza in front of him and pulled the katana from its sheath, showing him that the blade had not been damaged in any way. I returned it to its sheath, presented it to him, and then bowed my head low to touch the ground.

As I did so, he began to yell, "If you want to become Enlightened, *change!* If you want to have love in your life, *change!* If you want to stop being egotistical and selfish and cruel and immature, *change!* If you want your life to improve, *change!*"

This man thinks he is screaming at me, but he is screaming to himself, I thought, seeing clearly how much he despised himself, seeing clearly how he was and had been projecting onto me all of *his* flaws, keeping my head low so I did not have to look at him. *My God, did I make the right decision.*

I went home and felt incredibly relieved. I felt light. I felt free. I had done the right thing, I was sure of it. I compiled the files and cleared everything I had recently built up on my new computer. I handed it all over to his new assistant and began looking for jobs. It was June 2009, and the economy had crashed. Everyone was talking about not being able to get a job. As an ex-dancer and model, I really only had the work experience I had gained working for Lakshmi and Vishnu; I barely knew how to use a PC. All my adult life, I had feared working for a corporation. That was something other people did. Not me. I was a dancer. I couldn't handle it. But Lakshmi sensed that, she sensed my fear, and she gave me the one task I dreaded.

The one task I was sure I could not do.

chapter 19
HOW it HaPPeNS

It happens so slowly. So insidiously.

At first it is like winning the lottery: You think you've finally found someone who understands you, someone who seems like she knows what you've been looking for. She sees the true you, the bigger you, the you hidden inside, the you no one else can see, the you that was meant for greatness. You sit in front of this person, and you feel so much Light; you feel God.

She showers you with love and attention, builds you up. Suddenly, you are doing things you never knew you could. You are growing and expanding. You meet like-minded people. You have a purpose, a guide. Finally, for the first time, you belong.

You're filled with new energy. Life takes on a magical quality. Every day is a new adventure. You want to tell everyone about your new Teacher, about your new friends. Many of them react strangely, not the way you had imagined they would. They react with fear, doubt, and worry.

They just don't understand, you tell yourself. *They're not wise enough to see*, you say inside your mind. *They're asleep*, you whisper to yourself.

You continue your love affair with this new group, with this new Teacher. You spend more and more of your time following the teachings, more and more time with the other group members. Your life is changing in fantastic ways and you soon find yourself not wanting to be with the old friends who don't understand this new you. You feel more comfortable with the other group members. You feel best when you're with your Teacher, the one person who truly gets you.

Your life slowly becomes filled with these new activities. There may be a long meditation practice to follow each morning, new tasks to do, books to read, movies to watch. You find yourself going on "field trips" with the group, outings with the Teacher. You stop returning calls from your old friends. Your family starts to annoy you; they ask too many questions and seem too skeptical. Your Teacher tells you that your family and your old friends don't want you to change. They want you to stay small; maybe it's best if you distance yourself from them so they don't hold you back. You agree. Your family has always seen you a certain way; they don't know this new you. Your old friends seem annoyed that you're different. It's easier just to avoid them. You change your phone number and your e-mail address, so your old friends can no longer find you. Slowly, but surely, everything that made you *you* gets dropped from your life. In your excited attempt to grow and try new things, you allow all your old favorite friends and activities to fade away. Before you know it, the group is your whole life. No one outside of it understands.

And then the Teacher starts showing you your ego, the ways you need to change. Slowly but surely, she points out all your flaws.

"Only a true Teacher will be this honest," the guru says.

The flaws get pointed out one by one. The self-doubt starts to set in. Next comes "the occult" or some sort of dark force, maybe "the devil." Anytime your intuition tells you to run, to get away from the Teacher, to get away from the group, you're told it is occult forces trying to knock you off the path, or it's the devil trying to make you fall. You start to see everyone outside the group as the enemy. Friends and family become the enemy.

You believe "they want to knock you off the path," "they don't understand," or "they are trying to steal your energy." By this point, your entire foundation is gone, your entire sense of self is gone, your intuition is gone, your life is gone. And you cling desperately to the only thing you now trust: your guru.

Chapter 20
Outcast

When Vishnu fired me, my whole world came undone. I was suddenly on my own again, and my clarity that I had done the right thing faded quickly. I began to doubt myself again, wishing I had kept my mouth shut, believing my huge ego had knocked me backward. To make things worse, Lakshmi convinced the women in the sangha that I was a witch, a sorceress, and that I was energetically manipulating all of them. They shunned me.

According to her, I was responsible for everything going wrong in everybody else's life. Lisa, my best girlfriend in the sangha, looked at me with contempt and fear. Dayna, Lisa's sister, accused me of "showing up in her attention" every time she was having sex or meditating. I still had no idea what this meant. How does one "show up in somebody's attention?" What the hell does that even mean? Was that something I could do? And why on earth would I want to? None of my female sangha mates would talk to me, and most of the men turned their eyes from me as I walked by. According to Vishnu, I was manipulating them, as well, making them all want to sleep with me.

Again I had the same decision to make: let this break me or pull myself up by the bootstraps and continue on with this crazy path. I continued on. I simply refused to quit. I opened my

computer and applied to job after job after job. I got no response.
I needed someone to talk to. I had no idea whom to trust. I
wished I hadn't pushed all of my friends out of my life. I wished
I had stayed closer with my sangha mates. I called Bruno, hoping
he would still be there for me.

"I need to talk to you," I said, crying.

"Come over," he said immediately. "Let's go for a walk in
the park."

When I got there, as we stepped out his front door toward
the park, I turned to him. "I was Vishnu's consort." I said.

After a pause, Bruno replied, "I don't know what that means."

"I was sleeping with Vishnu. I finally told him I couldn't
sleep with him anymore, so he fired me."

Bruno stopped breathing and turned bright red.

"*That man was sleeping with you?*" he screamed, outraged.
"I want to kill him."

I started to cry, and Bruno wrapped his arms around me,
pulled me into his chest, and held me.

"And," I wailed into his arms, "Lakshmi is telling everyone
I'm a witch. Lisa thinks I'm energetically fucking with her and
everyone else. Lakshmi says it's my fault that she and all the
women are gaining weight." I looked up at Bruno with tears in
my eyes. "Am I a witch?" I asked him.

"No," he laughed. "No, Renee. You are *not* a witch. Or, if
you are, you are a good one."

He laughed some more.

"Renee," he said, holding me to his chest, "you are the kind-
est, most generous, most giving person I have ever met."

He walked me into the park, and we sat in the grass.

"I hate Vishnu for sleeping with you," he continued. "I had
no idea. He is such a hypocrite. All he does is tell the security
team how we are not allowed to use our power to sleep with
women. What an asshole. And, if anyone is a witch, it's Lisa.
Come on, we need to move."

He led me further into the park, and we practiced karate
until we were exhausted. Then we walked to get pizza. We

laughed a lot. I felt a lot better. Bruno was in the group because it was fun for him. He got to be part of the security team, he flirted with the female students, he felt great when he meditated with Lakshmi, and he loved all the outings. He barely read the books and barely watched the movies. He sure as shit did not alter his life the way I had. To him, it was all a fun adventure. He could never understand why I took it all so seriously. Now, at least, he had a bit more understanding. I told him about my new task, about how much it scared me.

"If anyone can pull it off, you can," he said. "And, Renee," he added, "if you hate all of this, just quit. It's not the end of the world."

But, to me, it was.

My job search was not working. I sent my resume everywhere, but no one called me back. I was failing at my task. I was going to screw up my karma yet again. I called a temp agency. They asked me to e-mail my resume and complete an online test of Word, PowerPoint, Excel, and Outlook for Windows on a PC. I had been using a Mac for years, and I barely knew the Microsoft Office Suite. I pulled out the PC I had purchased for my Oracle class, plugged it in, and started the test. I knew none of the answers, so I googled all of them. The test was timed. I did very poorly.

The next day, I called another temp agency, and they asked me to come in. I wore an Armani suit. I was interviewed by a girl ten years younger than me. She asked me a ton of questions. The most awkward were "Why did you leave your last job?" and "What were they paying you?" *Because I was boning my narcissist boss* and *nothing* seemed like terrible answers, so I sidestepped the questions.

I said, "Because I was ready for a new challenge" and "I prefer not to answer; the going rate."

She seemed satisfied. "I need you to take a few tests," she said, "to see your Microsoft Office proficiency. It shouldn't take too long." She showed me to a small room and turned on a computer. And then she gave me the *exact* test I had taken the day before, the one I had googled the answers to. I have always had a great memory. I aced the test.

She called me back into her office and said, "I have a job you may like. It just appeared. The pay is much less than what you are used to, but you can start immediately. The woman is going on pregnancy leave." I had no idea what she thought I used to get paid, but she apparently thought I had been paid well; my expensive Armani suit had become my ally. I swelled up with pride. I had done it! I left her office with an interview the next day.

The job was actually more like four jobs. My titles were Administrative Assistant, Fleet Manager, Training Coordinator, and Claims Manager. I worked at the corporate headquarters of a national company, assisting six senior executives, managing a fleet of three hundred vehicles, dealing with insurance claims, and coordinating the training for new hires. It was a hell of a first job. I loved it. I worked my ass off, and the people loved me. I was constantly laughing because I had no idea what I was doing, but everyone was so willing to help, usually after laughing at me first.

I woke up each morning at 4:30 and meditated. Then I drove to the beach and surfed in the dark, with the moon setting and the sun rising. It was so cold I could see my breath as I waited for waves. I got home by 6:30, showered, ate breakfast, dressed, and got in my car by 7:30. I always arrived to work early and I used my one-hour lunch break and my two ten-minute daily breaks to study, cramming homemade meals into my mouth as I did so.

I left work at 5:30 and drove an hour in traffic to computer school, eating my dinner in the car on the way. I got home at 10:00 each night, *exhausted.* I ate again, showered again, and meditated again for thirty minutes. I usually went to bed around midnight. On Saturdays, I got up at 3:00 a.m. and flew out of town to put posters up for Lakshmi's events, returning Sunday evening. I did this for three months. I was on a mission.

Surprisingly, after the trauma of being so close to Vishnu and Lakshmi, these three months seemed like the happiest in my life. I was growing again in new ways. I had found and kept a corporate job, and in doing so, I was liberated from the fear that I would not be able to support myself if I couldn't dance. I couldn't thank Lakshmi enough for giving me this task, for liberating me in this way, and my infatuation with her grew stronger.

In mid-January of 2010, my temp job ended. The woman I was replacing came back from maternity leave. I decided to go to computer school full-time. We had another Power Trip coming up in March, this time to Bhutan, and I did not want to take a job that wouldn't allow me to go. The computer school I chose offered a certificate in computer information sciences; it took ten months to complete. I went every day from 9:00 to 5:00, and I loved it.

Meanwhile, Lakshmi gave us a task to break off into groups and start companies. By this time, Lisa was talking to me again, although she kept her distance and always looked at me as if I was going to pull out a wand and turn her into a frog. I formed a group with her, Paul, Matt, and another sangha mate named Leslie. We named our company Lighten Up! Enterprises and decided to build iPhone apps that made people smile. I designed them, and Paul wrote the code.

Working with the others was not easy. Lisa had grown increasingly pessimistic. She was also depressed and fat. In fact, most of the other women in the sangha continued to grow rapidly in size. More and more, they resembled the senior students in the group, the ones we first met in Egypt: fat, grumpy, mean, lethargic, and depressed. They dressed like Lakshmi had suggested, in large pants and tunics that looked like sacks.

Lakshmi insisted her mission was to empower women. She suggested we always wear makeup but that we keep our bodies covered. She told us to stay out of bars and off the Internet.

"Dating," she said, "is a tremendous waste of your energy."

She taught that sugar helped battle the occult, which gave everyone permission to binge on cookies. Her female students were growing larger by the minute, unhappier by the minute.

I began to understand more why, after twenty years on

the path, the senior students looked so forlorn. Everything that brought us joy in life was somehow off limits because it would drain our energy; the only things left were meditation, work, and food. Plus, as women, we weren't allowed to be sexy or beautiful at all. Lakshmi drilled into us the idea that if men looked at us they would put lines into us and we would lose our power, and that it was our fault if they did look at us.

The larger and bitchier the women got, the more they hated me. Lisa spoke to me when we had our company meetings, but she sat as far from me as possible and made sure to disagree with everything I said. I kept to myself. I stopped talking to the other students. The only people who did talk to me were the guys on the security team; we had grown close during our beach training, and they seemed to feel bad for me.

By the time our Bhutan trip rolled around, I was told via e-mail to sit at the back of the meditation events, even though I was already doing this. I was given a room to myself and constantly assigned to the bus that had no Teacher on it. Neither Vishnu nor Lakshmi would look at me.

To me, it was just as well. I was so happy to be in Bhutan and completely overjoyed to be in a room by myself. The country was magnificent: lush green forests against snow-capped, jagged mountain peaks; bright, clear rivers rushing between towns; exquisite temples, precariously perched in mountain caves thousands of feet above ground. Many of the caves were said to be created by the energy blasting off the back of the Indian tantric master Padmashambhava as he meditated for months high above the villages on mountain ledges, flooding the country with his light. I could feel his energy permeating the land.

I spent most of my time meditating in my room or walking around in the gardens. I ate alone. I went to the events alone. I felt so close to God in those amazing mountains that nothing was going to upset me. I often chatted with the Bhutanese staff, listening cheerfully as they told me what it was like to live in Bhutan, about how they revered their king, who had abdicated the throne in order to go off into the mountains to meditate, but not before he provided free schooling and healthcare for everyone in the country and established something called *gross national happiness* as a way to measure the success of his country, instead of GDP.

One day, Vishnu noticed our guide sitting with me for lunch. It was the first time someone had joined me. Afterward, at a temple, one of our drivers came up to me and spoke to me as if I were in charge of the group. He covered his mouth while talking to me and asked how long I planned to stay and when I would want the bus ready to depart. He backed away as he left.

Vishnu noticed this, as well. He came up to me and said sternly, "It is *my* light flowing through you. Stop using my light to get attention. These men should not be talking to you. I do not want to see this happen again. You are blowing my light through your pussy. You need to shut it down." He walked away.

It was the first time he had spoken to me since our phone call seven months ago. I closed my eyes, took a deep breath, and asked God to please guide me. I turned around and walked to a boulder outside. I sat down and looked up at the mountains. How on earth was I doing anything with my pussy? Lakshmi and Vishnu kept coming back to that. "Blowing light through your pussy"—what the hell did that even mean? I was dressing like an old fat lady. I barely left my hotel room. I had not dated or flirted for close to a year. The only way my pussy could be more shut down was if it was sewn up or removed completely.

I breathed in the fresh air and closed my eyes. I felt at peace. I would be okay. I wasn't sure how, but I knew I would somehow be okay. I turned my light down even lower, became that much more invisible, just as I had around my mother. If I could utterly disappear, I wouldn't upset these people so much. Me just being me clearly enraged them. I spent even more time in my hotel room. I arrived to events at the very last minute. I spoke to no one.

Toward the end of the trip, we had a very special meditation event. The hotel Lakshmi chose was exquisite. Halfway through the event, she explained that it had come to her attention that some of us may want to be ordained as monks. An ordained monk herself and apparently given the authority to ordain others, she stood from her chair.

"I have decided to ordain you tonight," she said. "You made it all the way to Bhutan. If you are in this room you are dedicated."

We gasped.

"Those of you who would like to be ordained, please stand and approach the stage."

I stood at once. I walked to the end of my aisle, and then, when it was my turn, I approached the stage. I had wanted to be ordained since the first day I heard the term "ordained monk." I walked to the front of the room and bowed low in front Lakshmi. She dipped her head slightly to acknowledge my bow. I raised my face toward her. I couldn't help myself; I loved this woman with all my heart. Even with all the wicked things she had said to me and about me, I still loved her. I believed she was my Teacher and that she was helping to liberate me. I believed her when she said I misused my energy. I was going to learn how to control it, no matter what it took to do so. I believed that she was sanding down my ego.

With her finger, she dabbed a drop of oil on the space between and slightly above my eyebrows, my third eye. She chanted something I could not hear. As she touched me, I felt my entire world change, as if I had just been blasted into a different realm. I bowed low before her, backed away from her, and then sat back down in my seat, trembling. I was crying and shaking. I had just instantly and radically changed my future.

Twenty-two years after starting my spiritual journey, I had just taken the step that, in my mind, dedicated my entire life to God, to Enlightenment, to upholding Truth. My life had now officially become an offering to the Divine.

I will do whatever it takes, I thought. *I do not need to surf anymore. I do not need to dance or travel. I do not need my family or a man. I do not need to date. I will be celibate. I can be celibate. Unless I find a similar Being, someone else walking a spiritual path and dedicated to Enlightenment, I will be celibate. My life can be work and meditation and karate.*

I wanted so badly to be like the saints I had read about, to spread peace and light and love. By the end of this trip, I was sure I wanted to spend the rest of my life alone and in the service of God.

I had sold my little house and bought a larger house that I was remodeling. I was building my dream home, and without even realizing it, I had been remodeling it to resemble an ashram. In the back of my mind, I was building it as an offering to my Teachers, imagining that they may some day forgive me and want to live there with me. I designed the living room to be a dojo for Vishnu. I had a heavy punching bag in a closet that rolled out into the middle of the room on a track. I designed the master bedroom with Lakshmi in mind. I built her a steam shower, with a huge bathtub. I built her a meditation nook. I figured I could live in the guest bedroom at the back of the house.

I took my ordination seriously and truly considered myself a monk. In further self-denial, I forced myself to believe I was changed, radically this time. I was now utterly dedicated to God and solitude. I wished I could start over in life. I wanted to erase everything. The saddest part is, I wanted to erase myself. I was so sure I was all wrong the way I was.

I imagined being left behind in Bhutan, to meditate in a cave for the rest of my life. Or being dropped off in Asia, nameless, with no documents and no one who knew me. That is the only way I could see me not being me anymore—not being so flawed, with so much darkness, so . . . human. I returned to California. I rewrote my will, leaving the house and seventy percent of my inheritance to Vishnu and Lakshmi.

A few weeks later, I moved into my new house, before it was finished. And then, before I had even unpacked boxes, I flew to Florida for the weekend. When I returned Sunday night, I pulled into my driveway and noticed the garage door was up. I also noticed the door from the garage into the house was open.

I was pissed. The workmen must have left it open.

I pulled into the garage, and then I immediately locked my car doors, reversed into the street, and called 911. First, I said, "This is a non-emergency." Then I said, "I think my house was broken into," and explained the situation.

The woman told me to stay in my car with the doors locked and wait for the police to arrive. Two officers arrived. They told me to stay in the car while they walked around the side of the house. They were gone close to ten minutes. When they reappeared, the one who approached my car had a horrible look on his face.

"Please tell me you just moved in," he said.

"I did."

"Please tell me you did not move any of your belongings in yet," he said.

"No," I told him, "everything I own is in there."

"Was," he said. "I'm so sorry, it's *all* gone."

I walked inside with him. It was all gone, just like he said. It was like a scene out of *How the Grinch Stole Christmas*. Not only were my computer monitor and keyboard gone, but all the cables were gone. Everything in my bathroom was gone: the toilet paper and electric toothbrush, the tampons under the sink and the towels. My pillows were gone, sheets gone, bedspread gone. All of my boxes of files were gone. The wall art was gone. There was a lone empty hanger in my closet.

And there was a big pile of shit, in the middle of the living room.

The police wouldn't leave me there alone. They were going to fill out a report and wait until I had company.

I called Bruno; he didn't answer. I called again; no answer. I called again; no answer. On my fourth try, he answered and, in a very exasperated voice, said "Renee, I'm on a date. I will call you later."

"No!" I cried. "Please, I need you! My house has been broken into, and everything I have is gone. The police are here. I don't know what to do. Please come."

When he arrived ten minutes later, he hugged me. He talked to the police, and then he sat next to me on the curb, under a huge Torrey pine tree, as we waited for the police to finish the report.

"This is Divine Intervention," I said to Bruno. "I prayed for this. I wished that I could start all over. After I got ordained, I wished that everything I owned would go away."

He looked at me like I was crazy. "I have no idea how you are handling this so well."

"It's so insane. It's so over the top. It has to be Divine Intervention," I said.

"I can't sleep here," I blurted out next.

"First of all," Bruno said, "I'm cleaning up the pile of shit." He went inside and came out a few minutes later.

The police left, and Bruno and I walked through the house. We locked all the doors, turned on all the lights. He invited me to stay with him, but Lakshmi and Vishnu had taught us to not stay with other people so I refused. I checked into a hotel for the night instead.

I went back home the next day and called the insurance company. I cleaned up the house; the floors were filthy. And then I took a long, hot shower. What was I going to do? While in the shower, I had a vision. It was of New York. And I suddenly thought, *What if my life abruptly changed and I had to move to New York? Wouldn't that make this all so much easier? Wouldn't that be fun? What if I could start all over in a huge city where no one knew me? I could be anonymous. I could be free.*

Chapter 21
Karate

"**I** do not want to fuck any of you, so stop trying!" Vishnu screamed at the women in his karate class. "If I see your tits or your pussy in my attention one more time, I am going to kick you out of the sangha!"

We were all kneeling in seiza, getting ready to bow out at the end of his class, when he had suddenly started yelling. He said students were being inappropriate with their energy. And then he screamed, "Renee, you are the *worst*!"

My spirit crumbled. My heart broke. I felt humiliated. From my knees, I responded "Osu, Sensei."

He continued, "Stop pretending like everything is fine and you are happy. You think you are so great. You think you are so evolved. You have been shoving yourself into everyone's attention. You want everyone to want to fuck you. The only reason you have light is because of me. That is my light flowing through you. You are *this close* to being thrown out of the sangha!"

I replied "Osu, Sensei."

I was meditating almost two hours a day and in computer school full-time. I was still remodeling my house because it had been stripped to almost nothing and had to be finished in order to comply with the building code. I was on the board of directors of a nonprofit and working at a tech start-up company and co-creating Lighten Up! Enterprises. How on earth did I have the time to shove myself into anyone's attention?

I sat there, kneeling on that hard wooden floor, in the dance studio I had worked in for close to ten years, my hands in fists at my waist, my back straight, my heart breaking, saying, "Osu, Sensei" over and over as he yelled at me in front of everyone. As soon as we were dismissed, I ran to my car and drove home, to my empty house with the dojo I had built for him.

We had karate class the next night. I dreaded going, but I knew I had to. Some part of me knew I had to show up. I ironed my gi, combed and gelled my hair, and drove to the dance studio. I stood in line with the other students until we were admitted in. No one spoke to me. And then I went to the back corner of the studio and quietly started stretching on the floor, wondering how I would ever make it through the three-hour class. I bent over my outstretched legs and silently sobbed, feeling so out of place and so hated.

Suddenly, I heard a timid voice asking, "Renee, would you help me with a kata?"

I looked up, startled. A senior student was standing over me. She had so much kindness in her eyes.

"Yes," I said. "Of course."

I stood up and dried my eyes. We began the kata side by side. Quickly, another senior student approached.

"May I join?" she asked.

"Yes, of course," I said.

Then another and another and another asked to join. Soon, the junior female students walked over. Quietly, they joined in, as well. These women were backing me. Quietly, and in their own way, I could feel their support. I could feel them holding me up, like they were saying, *We're so sorry. We have no idea what is going on, but it is not true and it is not fair.* In unison, side-by-side, as one entity, as woman supporting woman, we all performed an ancient dance of power. We bowed at the end of it.

I turned to face them. They smiled at me, with love in their eyes; I smiled back with love in mine. And then Vishnu started class. It was the last karate class I ever took with them. I got thrown out of the sangha the following month.

part 3
CRUCIBLE

"It is in the nature of things to be drawn to the very experiences that will spoil our innocence, transform our lives, and give us necessary complexity and depth."

—Thomas Moore

Chapter 22
The Task

It was August 17, 2010, a month after Vishnu screamed at me in karate class. I had decided I was going to love my life as a computer programmer and throw all my energy from meditation into building an exciting new career. I was almost finished with my CIS certificate and was enjoying my internship at the tech start-up. I was really proud of the apps I had designed for Lighten Up! Enterprises. I had recovered from the humiliating karate class. My sangha mates had suddenly befriended me again after that, and I was in the process of replacing the furniture and clothing that had been stolen. I was leaving Office Depot with a new laptop PC when my cell phone rang. It was a private number.

"Hello, Renee. It's Lakshmi," she said.

My heart began to pound. "Hello," I replied. I immediately pulled over into the parking lot of a Pancake House. I held my breath.

"I have a new task for you," she said.

My body began to tremble. This woman, my Spiritual Teacher, my guru, had blatantly ignored me for over a year and now, all of the sudden, a phone call. Adrenaline flooded my body. I was terrified. Another task? What next?

"You need to go get an MBA," she stated. "Not just from any school, from a really impressive school with an accelerated program. And you need to start in January."

I was still holding my breath.

She continued, "But, this is not the task . . . this is something you must do in order to start the task. The task is to start a company, any company you want, and make $10 million dollars net—profit *after* taxes. Once you do that, you will be able to do anything there is to do in life, including attain Enlightenment. Do you have any questions?"

The first thing that came to mind was my sangha, all my friends in the meditation group.

"Can I still attend the monthly meetings?" I asked.

"No," she responded. "In fact, you have forty-eight hours to say good-bye to all of them. You cannot contact any of them after that. This program, Renee, is too coddling for you. You need to apply these teachings in real life. You need to learn to draw from the Source. Anyone who knew you five minutes ago will hold you back."

"What about the company I started? Can I still be a part of it?" I asked.

"No," she said. "You have to leave it. You have forty-eight hours to turn it over to your partners."

"Can I still send you tuition?" I asked.

"No," she responded. "It is no longer appropriate."

"Can I ever be a part of the program again?" I questioned.

"Once you have made $10 million after taxes, you may contact us again," she replied.

"How will I know where to find you?" I asked.

"You'll be able to," she said. She made some comment about remembering who it was that had empowered me to do this task and something about sharing some of the money. Then she said, "Vishnu is also on the line. Vishnu, do you have anything to add?"

"Hello, Renee." He sounded defeated, dejected, as if he didn't want to be part of a phone call that was sending me away from the group. "No, I have nothing to add."

Then, suddenly, he said, "You should still practice karate. You are very good at it. Find a dojo wherever you go."

He sounded like he was going to cry. Then, quickly, with a saccharine and poisonous "Welcome to your new life," Lakshmi hung up the phone.

I sat there in the parking lot, dazed. And then I started to cry. My life, as I knew it, was over.

This wasn't really a "task." This was her way of throwing me out of the sangha. But I couldn't bear to see it this way, not yet. If I was going to survive, I had to see it as a quest, as part of my path to Enlightenment. And I had to believe I would be assisted by my Enlightened lineage, that I was taken care of.

I called Bruno and asked him if he would meet me at my house. I was crying again. He could barely understand me.

When I got home, he was already in the driveway, sitting on the curb. I got out of my car and sat next to him. I told him about the phone call; that I was leaving. We both started to cry. "You have to leave?" he asked me. "You're not allowed to even stay in contact with me?" he cried.

"Yes, Bruno, I have to do what she says," I replied. "I'm so unhappy. I have everything—*everything*—and I'm in hell. I can't bear to live in these mind states any longer. I'll do anything to transcend my ego."

The next day, I quit my job. I quit computer school, where I was nearly finished. I said good-bye to my few close friends in the sangha, not able to tell them anything besides "Lakshmi gave me a new task so I am going to disappear." I wrapped up and handed over my role in Lighten Up! Enterprises. And then I listed my dream house, the one I had just moved into, the one I had imagined building my whole adult life, for sale. I booked a plane ticket to the Northeast and I left two days later.

———

I started in Boston—my roots, where I was born. I visited Harvard and MIT. Next, I went to New Haven, to see Yale. I cried my guts out there, trying to meditate on the floor of my hotel room. I couldn't imagine spending two years there with a bunch of twenty-something-year-old kids. But I was going to do it. If God wanted me there, I was going to stay. I finished crying and started to meditate. I vowed that if God had New Haven in my plan, I'd spread as much light as possible in New Haven.

But when I finished meditating, New York was in my mind. I googled hotels in New York, and a great deal at the Four Seasons popped up. I reserved my room, then I bought a train ticket for 6:00 the following morning. I immediately felt better. I remembered my vision. I could handle New York. Suddenly, it all felt right.

I arrived at the Four Seasons and got upgraded to a suite—no charge. It was gorgeous!

"This is not the poverty path," I remembered Lakshmi saying. "Everything is vibration, and the more you surround yourself with highly vibrating energy, the better you will be able to meditate."

I went down to the restaurant for breakfast. The hostess' last name was Rama (a Hindu deity and an incarnation of Vishnu). Another sign. I felt so supported. My heart glowed. I was headed in the right direction. The signs were there. I ate a delicious breakfast, and I cried again, but this time tears of joy.

"It does not have to be hard anymore," I reminded myself. "I do not have to suffer to find God."

After breakfast, I took a taxi to Columbia University. The campus was in full bloom. I found the business school, and as I approached the door, a hawk—glorious, huge, fierce, and mighty—landed in front of me on the statue in front of the school. I dropped to my knees in the grass and cried with gratitude. If this wasn't a sign, I did not know what was.

I watched students come and go; I listened to the sparrows chirping in the bushes. I knew I had found my school. Next, I meandered through the pathways and read plaques that held sayings like *God and wisdom united* or some such spiritual talk of combining education and spirituality. It all added to my belief that I had found the perfect school for me. Plus, Columbia had an MBA program starting in January.

Next, I found an apartment. Within thirty minutes, I had signed a year's lease and paid a security deposit and first month's rent. Now I had to get into Columbia.

———

I flew back to California, ready to get my ass into Columbia's MBA program. I had no idea how difficult that would be. I wrote the worst application possible. I took the GMAT multiple times and never got a grade good enough for Columbia to even look at me. Plus, I wrote the truth on my application essays: That I was thirty-seven years old and had no idea who I was, that I was searching and I was asking them to please teach me. I had traveled to over fifty countries, I had started five businesses, I spoke two languages fluently, I graduated Magna Cum Laude with a double degree, I had been a professional dancer and an entrepreneur and a published author, and I had sponsored charity events and humanitarian projects all over the world. But, no I was not an automaton. And, no I was not a finance person. And, no, I did not fit in a box.

I mailed off the application and called a moving company, sold my car and bought a plane ticket. I arrived in New York twelve days later.

When I got to my new apartment, I had two e-mails waiting in my inbox. The first was from the moving company:

> *Your stuff will arrive tomorrow between 9:00 a.m. and noon. Please make sure you have an elevator available.*

The second was from Columbia:

> *Thank you, but we have no interest in a lost thirty-seven-year-old dancer searching for Truth.*

They didn't really say that, but it's what I read. I had been rejected.

What the fuck do I do now? I asked myself on the floor of my empty apartment.

Days went by. I got sick. I stayed in bed and threw up a lot. And cried and cried and cried. And then I called Andre, my hairdresser and my one remaining friend. He was the only person I had not pushed from my life, because he had not been in the sangha, and I saw him so rarely that he never fit the "old friends will hold you back paradigm." Andre was the only person who knew where I was and what I was doing. I hadn't even told my brother, Gary.

Andre said, "You can always come home. But since you're there, why not take that test again and take your time and fill out a good application? Don't rush it and do it all shitty; take your time and do it correctly. Oh, and go find a yoga studio immediately."

He was right. I found a yoga studio the next day and took a class and instantly felt better. I signed up for a GMAT prep course. I began going to prep classes two nights a week and hauled myself out of bed at 5:00 a.m. every single Saturday to traipse through freezing rain and snow and ice to the testing center where I took the four-hour practice GMAT, *every single Saturday*, with people sitting next to me, moaning while rocking back and forth and pulling their hair out. And I studied. I studied my ass off. I found a karate dojo and started taking classes five days a week. I was back. Working towards my black belt, working towards my MBA, walking my path to Enlightenment in New York City, Baby!

Two months later, I took the GMAT again. And I got the same fucking score as the first time.

I cried some more and almost gave up. It was almost January. I was failing my task. I was ruining my karma. And then I heard about Columbia's School of Continuing Education and their Business Certificate Program. I thought, *If I can get my foot in the door at Columbia and do well in some business classes there, maybe I can get into their MBA program.* And so I applied . . .

chapter 23
Determined

I got in. To Columbia University, one of the most prestigious schools in the world—at thirty-seven years old and with a background in dance. *This path seriously rocks,* I thought to myself as I read my acceptance e-mail. I set off on the first day of school, with my new backpack and all my books. The forecast called for freezing rain and ice pellets. I didn't even know what that was. I dressed warm and carried an umbrella, but the second I stepped outside my umbrella got blown inside out and broke. By the time I got to campus, I was soaked. When I opened the door to the building, I could hardly move my arms because I was so cold and my clothes were so wet and heavy; I got stuck in the door, heaving it open only to have it swing closed on my back pack and pin me, obstructing the traffic of all the young, cool students rushing to their next class. I held back the tears as the kids pried me out of the doorway so they could get by. And then I sat through a ninety-minute Calculus class, not understanding any of it, shivering in my wet clothes, with students half my age.

Over the next few months, I scratched and clawed my way to an A in calculus and a B+ in statistics and economics. It was the hardest thing I had ever done. I studied my ass off and went to after-school tutoring. I had not taken a math class in twenty years and had never taken a business class in my life. I took trains from New York to Pennsylvania and Boston to visit Wharton and Babson. I hired consultants to help me fill out my MBA applications. The first consultant told me no top business school would want a thirty-seven-year-old dancer from Jacksonville University and to just give up. The second helped me write terribly juvenile essays about my most embarrassing moment and a time I faced my fears. He also told me I really had no chance. A month later, my rejections from the MBA programs at Wharton and Yale proved him correct. He told me he could not help after that. I cried some more and almost gave up.

But one morning, I woke up angry.

"Those motherfuckers! They have no idea who I am!" I yelled to my quiet apartment.

I got out of bed, showered, and sat down to meditate. As I quieted my mind, *NYU* popped into my attention. I stomped over to my computer. I was fuming. I re-read my resume, and introduction letter. I realized I had short-changed myself. I had come across as timid and shy, with nothing to offer. I realized *I* was the one who did not realize who I was. *I* was the one who did not think I was good enough for these schools. Subconsciously, I was telling them I was not a good fit—not smart enough, too old—because I was scared.

So I changed.

I wrote a new kick-ass resume and letter to introduce myself. I decided I didn't want to go to an MBA program with a bunch of kids fifteen years younger than I was; I wanted to be with people my age. And I didn't want to live in Boston or Pennsylvania or New Haven; I wanted to stay in New York. So I applied to NYU's Executive MBA program.

I hit "send" on the application.

"I'll show you!" I screamed to my apartment.

I made breakfast and coffee, and then my cell phone rang. It was NYU, calling for an interview. My appointment was set for the following week.

As my interview approached, I grew increasingly nervous. I was going because Lakshmi had given me the task, but I couldn't tell them, "My guru sent me," when they asked me why I wanted to get an MBA, so I was going to have to make something up.

I was additionally stressed about what to wear. Lakshmi had told me to keep my butt covered up. The problem, of course, was that the fashions had changed since she was in the corporate world, and it was now nearly impossible to find a suit with a jacket long enough to cover my round bottom. So I bought a beautiful navy wool Armani coat.

It could look like a jacket, I told myself.

I decided I would wear long black Armani pants, five-inch stiletto Italian leather mock boots, the new coat, and "to feel comfortable" an old black well-worn waffle long-underwear style shirt.

No one will see it, I told myself about the shirt.

I put the navy coat on over the black shirt and finished the look with a lavender silk scarf.

The outfit was great, in my mind. The problems, and there were many, started with a freak heat wave on the day of the interview; instead of being 50 degrees out, it was 103. And I had no back-up outfit. So I stayed with what I had picked out.

It will be air conditioned, I reasoned.

Problem number two: the shoes. I had never looked at my outfit sitting down. While sitting, with one leg crossed over the other, I noticed you could see my full shoe—not just the slim sleek black heel peeking out below my elegant and sophisticated pants, but the entire shoe: a mock boot with a borderline-sleazy, thick, silver zipper. The shoes were terribly wrong, and sitting down, I could not hide them. I swear, each person who walked through that room looked at me, looked down at my shoes, and then looked back at me with a funny expression. I fidgeted, trying to make my pants longer, trying to cover my shoes. It was impossible. I gave up trying.

When I got called in for the interview, the first thing my interviewer said to me was, "Do you want to take off your coat?" She was in a tank top and skirt and sweating. It was *so hot* in there!

But I couldn't take off my coat. The only thing I had under it was that old, worn-out black waffle thermal long-underwear shirt. What the hell had I been thinking? Why didn't I wear a blouse? I mean, come on!

So I said politely, "No, thank you." Then I lied, "I've been in air conditioning all day, and I'm just chilled to the bone," as sweat beaded up and dripped from my temple.

Scarf. Thermal shirt. Wool coat. She knew it wasn't a suit jacket. Just as the adorable salesman had told me when I bought it at the store, "Honey, this is a coat, not a suit jacket." I'm from California. We don't wear coats. I didn't know!

So I was sweating my ass off in this interview and trying to come up with some reason besides "my Spiritual Teacher sent me" to explain why, all of a sudden, at age thirty-seven, I had decided I wanted to get an MBA.

Somehow, I did it: I made it through the interview. And then I was out in the street, in the sweltering heat. I was still relatively new to New York, with no idea how to get back to my apartment. My heels were un-walkable, and I was sweating buckets.

I took off the heels, going barefoot in downtown New York. *Disgusting!* My expensive Armani pants were dragging on the dirty street, so I rolled them up. The only way they would stay rolled was if I rolled them up to the top of my thighs. Then I took off the coat and the scarf and rolled up my sleeves. Oh, and I had a briefcase. So I was shoeless in downtown New York with pants rolled up to my crotch and a tight long-underwear shirt on in blazing-sun-heat with a wool coat and a silk scarf slung over my arm and my slutty high-heel mock boots dangling from my hand.

I walked . . . and walked . . . and walked, until I found a cab. I finally got to my apartment, wilted. Sweating. Dirty feet. And it was then that I realized the following: Four is my favorite number. I had just had an interview on 4/4, at 4:00 p.m., on the fourth floor of 44 West Fourth Street! My interview had ended at 4:44.

Chapter 24
Hiroto

Meanwhile, I had met a man. I met him at the dojo a month after I moved to New York. Tall, handsome, powerful, strong, gorgeous, in a bright white gi. He was a fifth-degree black belt. We noticed each other immediately. He was ending his color-belt class as I kneeled down to bow into a white-belt class that was starting beside his. His head turned to look at me, and our eyes met. We both flushed red. He taught on Wednesday nights, and as I approached the studio, I could hear him yelling from half a block down the street. His students yelled back; his energy was infectious. He was intense. And his karate technique was so beautiful. He was so flexible, and so fast, and so strong, it was awesome just to watch him. I could not wait until I was a color-belt so I could take his class, too.

Determined to complete the tasks Lakshmi had given me, I began looking for dojos as soon as I arrived to New York. However, finding a school I wanted to be a part of was harder than I'd imagined. The first dojo I found was in the basement of a church. The room was tiny, and the men training there looked unhappy and lethargic. I stayed for five minutes and left. The second dojo was also all wrong. The men wore black gis; I left immediately.

The third dojo was worse—mixed martial arts. I felt like I'd get my head split in half there. The fourth dojo was in somebody's apartment, and on it went.

I wanted to find a traditional Japanese dojo. I wanted to see a clean space and formal Japanese etiquette. I was about to give up.

Maybe I'm not supposed to continue karate in New York, I thought to myself. *Maybe I was only supposed to train under Vishnu.*

For as much as I had struggled with my relationship with Vishnu, I had to admit I was grateful for the karate he taught me. He insisted we iron our gis before each class, that they stay crisp and bright white. He insisted we bow each time we entered the dojo and each time we passed a senior student. He insisted we tie our belts perfectly. And he pushed us to our limits. We had to do 108 push-ups on our knuckles in three minutes to pass our first promotion, from white belt. We had to break a board in order to advance to green belt. He made us learn the Japanese terms for everything. And he trained us to exhaustion every class. He had even given the security team and me katanas and had trained us how to use them.

As a ballet dancer, I am drawn to discipline, and I knew, as a small woman, that the only way I could ever be effective in karate was with perfect technique and impeccable timing. I wanted to continue learning about Japanese custom as much as I wanted to continue learning to fight. I did not want to join a dojo where a bunch of men came to beat each other up.

One night, while sitting in a bubble bath and thinking about karate, I suddenly had the urge to alter my Google search; instead of "karate dojo NYC" I entered "traditional Japanese karate NYC." I discovered a dojo I had not seen previously. I went the next morning and knew immediately I had found *my* dojo. The space was beautiful. It had polished wooden floors and huge floor-to-ceiling windows. The class I observed was small, but I could tell by the way the students stood and by the way they were dressed that they were being trained well. The instructor looked kind, and when he demonstrated a move, I instantly saw how talented he was. His gi was crisp and white and perfectly pressed. His black belt was tied neatly. I signed up immediately and returned that evening for my first class.

It wasn't long before I fell in love with the dojo and, because of my training with Vishnu, it wasn't long before I was promoted to Hiroto's Wednesday night class, and fell in love with him, as well.

I woke up every Wednesday morning excited about karate that night. My heart would beat fast as class time approached; as I climbed the stairs to the dojo, I'd get filled with nervous energy and high-school girl giggles.

"I love him," I would tell anyone in the locker room who would listen, referring to Hiroto. I loved his thick New York accent. I loved the way his gi opened and showed off his muscular chest. I loved how strong his hands were and how great his karate technique was. I loved watching him walk up and down the rows of students, yelling at them, encouraging them, infusing them with energy, pushing them to their limits.

After the nightmare of dating Vishnu, I was really, for the first time in my life, ready to love a man, with all his faults and flaws and imperfections. I had been dating that snowboarder when I began the University of Mysticism, but I had realized that even though he was an amazing man, I still tore him apart in my mind, the way I did with every guy I dated. It suddenly dawned on me that if I could do that with him, the problem was not with the guys I was dating, the problem was within myself; there was something lacking within me. If I ever wanted to be able to have a real partnership, if I ever wanted to be able to truly love another, I had to fix what was broken within me.

Now I was an ordained monk; I felt like it was my duty to love. That's what saints and monks did. And I felt like I could love anybody. Nobody could be as bad as Vishnu. Dating him had been great training ground; anyone would be an improvement after that experience. Plus, I was now in school at Columbia University. I felt much more secure about who I was and in which direction I was headed. I was ready to start the next chapter in my life. My heart was wide open. I was ready for a new adventure.

And I felt like falling in love with someone in New York would help me settle in to my life there. Plus, I was so lonely. I had not been hugged for months. I was ready to be close to someone and I wanted that someone to be Hiroto.

One day, I was walking toward the dojo when I noticed him a few feet ahead of me. My heart started beating wildly. Something in a store window caught his eye and he turned left, toward the store, before continuing on. That delay was long enough to put us side by side just as he opened the dojo door.

"Hi," he said.

"Hi," I replied.

We started to climb the stairs together, him in front, me behind; I had let him go first since he was much senior in ranking. He turned to look at me as he was climbing the stairs.

"You obviously have some movement training," he said, referring, I assumed, to the way I moved in his classes.

"Yes, I'm a dancer," I replied.

His eyes lit up.

"That's why your kicks are so good," he said.

"My name is Hiroto."

"I know. I'm Renee," I answered.

My heart was fluttering. I smiled, he smiled, we both checked ourselves in to the dojo, and then he went to change.

As he walked from the lobby onto the dojo floor, everyone stopped stretching, stood up, turned to him, and bowed. My heart raced. That night, he made sure to say my name in class, to compliment me, and to help me with some of my technique. When helping me with a kick, he kept his hands on my hips a little longer than necessary. As he did, his eyes sparkled. Electricity flowed between us. I thought I was going to melt.

A few weeks later, I entered myself into the dojo tournament kata competition. When I showed up to perform my kata, I discovered to my horror and amazement that Hiroto was one of the judges. I had been nervous before, but now, with him in front of me, judging me, I could barely breathe. I got called to go first, to open the kata competition, and I ended up getting second place.

Hiroto came up to me in class the next week, put his hand on my back, and said, "Nice kata." He left his hand there a moment longer, his touch filled me with warmth. I smiled from my toes to my ponytail.

That night, I stayed for a later class, and he was the substitute teacher. The class was smaller, so we each got a lot more individual attention. We got to see him break down each kick and punch. He had so much knowledge; he had studied karate for close to thirty years. He was a Master. Each move was flawless, executed with precision, delivering what would be a crushing blow at the end.

After class, as we were all sitting in the lobby of the dojo (in front of a large framed photo on the wall of a younger Hiroto breaking a stack of cinder blocks with the side of his hand, dust flying everywhere, gi open, muscles bulging), he loudly proclaimed, "I'm having a party at my exercise studio at the end of the month. Everyone from the dojo is invited." His eyes lingered on mine as he finished his sentence.

A few weeks later I went to the party with some other students from the dojo. His small studio was crowded, but he noticed us as soon as we entered the front door and came toward us, tall and powerful and handsome, with a huge smile on his face.

"I'm so glad you came," he said. I flushed red and smiled back. He showed us around his studio and introduced us to some of his staff, who informed me that, in the style of exercise Hiroto taught, he was one of only eighteen Master Trainers in the world. I let this information sink in as he sat down in front of a large drum and began drumming. He was amazing. Everyone began dancing. Not only was he a fifth-degree black belt, and one of only eighteen Master Trainers, but he was clearly an expert drummer, as well.

This guy is great at everything he does, I thought to myself.

Not just great—he seemed to *master* everything he did. Talk about somebody focused on every detail. Talk about somebody bringing the best of himself to everything he did. He was clearly walking some sort of spiritual path. This guy had to be my soul mate. I was now even more in love with him, if that was possible.

I had a great time at the party; we all did. As I was leaving, he ran outside, chased me down the street, and said, "Hey, Renee, I teach tomorrow at 1:00. Come to my class, as my guest."

I smiled all the way home.

The next day, I schlepped from the Upper West Side to his fitness studio downtown. It took close to an hour. Class was great. The sheer power coming off of him was electrifying. He seemed too big for the machines, as if he had an energetic wingspan that was too large for the room. His thighs were massive, and I could see them straining against his sweat pants. I had to keep looking away. The muscles in his arms rippled as he demonstrated movement on the machines. It was all I could do to not imagine him naked.

When class ended, I felt euphoric. As I was putting my shoes on by the front door, I overheard Hiroto whispering about pay to the girl at the front desk. She whispered back, "I'll take care of it," and then said politely, "Renee, it will be $20 for the class."

I was shocked. He had invited me as his *guest*. In my mind, *guest* meant *free*. But I paid the $20; I wasn't sure what else to do. Maybe I was wrong. Maybe I misheard. Maybe he had been drunk last night and forgot this morning. Again, I doubted myself. I must have misheard. I went home and called Andre.

"Well, I think Hiroto is a jerk," I said.

"So, you're not in love anymore?" he asked.

I thought about it. "No, I still love him," I said.

Andre laughed.

But it was true: I still loved him. I still dreamed about seeing him. In every karate class, he talked about the importance of a meditation practice and about focusing our minds. He spoke about integrity and drive and about bringing the best of oneself to each moment. He was right on board with everything I believed. I was a monk for crying out loud! A monk that practiced karate. This was my *man*.

And by this point, I had been ignoring my instincts for close to four years. I had been taught to believe my intuition was "the occult" trying to push me away from everything that would lead me to Enlightenment. So I excused the *guest* mix-up, telling myself it must have been somehow my fault, and signed up to take private sessions at his studio.

One night, as I was finishing a private session, he smiled at me and said, "A group of us from the dojo are getting together this weekend. Would you like to go? Maybe we could have dinner beforehand?"

"I'd love to," I responded, my face glowing.

"Great," he said and got my phone number so he could contact me.

The next day he texted to tell me where and when to meet him.

He didn't offer to pick me up. I was new to New York, so I wasn't sure if men usually offered to cross town in order to pick someone up, but a part of me felt disappointed. I ignored it, decided it made more sense for me to just meet him at the restaurant.

That night, I got home and checked my e-mail. I had been accepted to NYU Stern. The timing was magical. My life was finally falling into place. I had been in New York eight months. I had endured calculus at Columbia and countless GMAT practice tests and commuting through freezing rain and ice pellets. I had endured living in a huge city with no social support structure. And I had made it! I was working my way toward black belt in karate, I had gotten accepted into a top MBA program, and I had a date with a *major* hunk. Holy Crap! The only thing left I had to do was start the business that made ten million dollars after taxes.

Chapter 25
Bodhisattva

I took a cab in the rain to the restaurant to meet Hiroto for our first date. I was beyond excited. I was going on a date with a fifth-degree black belt. He was *so* New York: so tough, so masculine. When I got to the restaurant he was waiting for me inside by the front door. He was huge. He took up the whole window. And he looked so incredibly handsome. His eyes sparkled when he saw me. Mischievous and adoring and sexy. I really loved him.

At dinner, he pulled out a chair for me when we sat down. He ordered for me. He even did the half-stand-up each time I left the table (which I did three times to make sure I didn't have food in my teeth, even though I barely ate because I was so nervous). Each time I came back to the table, he had his phone out and quickly put it away. He told me he didn't eat meat and only ate shrimp. I thought that was an odd distinction, especially for someone so large, but I brushed it aside.

From dinner, we stopped by the dojo party and then headed to a cozy little Flamenco restaurant in the East Village. Hiroto rode a motorcycle. I had always thought men who rode bikes were immature, more interested in looking cool than being safe with their bodies. But Hiroto explained that he only rode one in order to navigate traffic in Manhattan. Still I hesitated to get on his motorcycle; they scare me. But something inside of me said, *Do it. Go ahead; you'll be safe.* So I jumped on the back, put on his extra helmet, and wrapped my arms around him. I had been dying to hug him, and this was my first chance. I loved the way he felt.

He started the bike, and we took off down the block. I quickly turned my head to the left and saw a five-story mural of Padmasambhava, my favorite Buddhist tantric master, painted on the side of an art museum. Almost the same painting I had hanging on my bedroom wall in a thangka. To me it was a sign: *This man is a part of your path.*

In the Flamenco restaurant we sat side by side at the bar, and he told me he had been given a spiritual name when he completed his yoga certification: Varutra—a Hindu name meaning "Protector."

My heart sang. I loved him even more. For twenty-three years, I had dreamed of having a man back in my life that protected me. This was my man, the Being I had dreamed about meeting ever since my father died. I was sure of it; everything about him fit me. I watched with joy as the older female dancer stomped her heart out on the dance floor. I could feel Hiroto's eyes on me as I watched her dance. I could feel him adoring me, loving me. He was so sensitive underneath that tough exterior. I wanted to let him wrap me in his arms and hold me forever. It was close to midnight when we left the bar, and he was leaving for Japan in the morning, so we said good-bye, and I got into a cab to go home. The twelve days he was in Japan seemed like the longest days of my life.

I created a Facebook account to be in communication with Hiroto while he was away; he loved to communicate by Facebook. A few days into his trip he messaged me and told me how much he missed me, and how he couldn't wait to get back and see me. He said he had never met anyone like me and that he felt "so much light" in my presence. "You radiate with light," he said. "I feel so much love around you. You are an angel."

This man can feel me, I thought. *He gets it.*

I could not believe how easily and perfectly he had just appeared in my life. He returned on a Friday and we made plans to have dinner together that Saturday. I couldn't figure out why he didn't want to see me Friday, but as with everything else that seemed a little odd, I brushed it aside. Waiting one extra night to see him, however, felt like an eternity.

Saturday night, we met on the corner outside a sushi restaurant at the end of his block, almost an hour from my apartment. Again, I took a cab. Again, I ignored the fact that he chose a spot in his neighborhood and I had to travel. As we waited outside for a table, I noticed he was in a foul mood—irritable and anxious. He was criticizing everything, pacing back and forth, complaining about the dojo.

I tried to lighten the mood, to get him focused on something he loved, so I asked him about a kicking technique. Then he started criticizing *me*. Rudely, he said I was doing the kick all-wrong, but he didn't show me the correct form, insinuating I wouldn't be able to do it.

I suddenly felt really sad, like a little kid being scolded by my mother. I felt stupid, like I was too dressed up and had on too much makeup. I felt vulnerable and small.

If I were in my right mind, I would have left and never gone out with him again. But I was not in my right mind. I had turned the volume to zero on my intuition and had gotten used to being surrounded by bipolar, narcissistic people. So standing outside a sushi restaurant being criticized by a man I hardly knew fit right into my idea of "normal" at this stage in my life.

After struggling through small talk and awkward silence for ten minutes, I suggested we go someplace else. He proposed the restaurant next door and walked in ahead of me, letting the door swing back and almost hit me in the face.

I felt sick the second we walked in. The energy of the place felt *off*, as if the restaurant was a front for something sordid. It was straight out of a *Godfather* movie—very dark inside, old furniture, low ceiling, stale air, and a waitstaff that looked as if they could double as hit men. There was only one other pair of patrons, at a table in the corner.

Hiroto was right at home; the entire staff knew him. He sat down and ordered his "usual" before I had a chance to look at the menu. When his food came, he shoveled it into his mouth as if I was not even there. He was nervous and fidgety and had trouble holding eye contact with me.

Suddenly, with a mouth full of food, he looked up and declared that he had a problem with women. "My cousin says I love women so much that I'm a lesbian," he said and laughed, a dark heavy forced laugh.

I still have no idea what that means.

He told me that anytime he really liked a woman, he pushed her away. He said a few more things that should have made me run in the opposite direction, that were intended to make me run in the opposite direction.

Maya Angelou and Oprah Winfrey once had a conversation about bad relationships; the key takeaway was: *When people show you who they are, believe them.* I once attended an Al-Anon meeting and was told that people tell you everything you need to know about them in the first two minutes you meet them, but most of us don't pay attention to the red flags.

Hiroto was showing me who he was, waving bright red flags, but I wanted to see something else. I wanted to see a Magnificent Being that I had known and loved in past lives. I *saw* a Magnificent Being that I had known and loved in past lives. I refused to see the Truth even though he kept showing me. Denial is so powerful.

Lakshmi had taught us that we were Bodhisattvas, that it was our duty to save people, to pull them out of hell. I sat across the table, listening to him tell me about his sordid past and his problems with women, about how he was not really loved or wanted as a child. I saw it as my Bodhisattva duty to save him with my love, pull him out of the dark and up into the light. In my mind, he was magnificent; he had just forgotten. All I had to do was believe in him and love him.

As if reading my mind he said, "I really like you. I can tell you would be really good for me. I'm worried I'm going to freak out and push you away. I don't want to do that. I've been seeing someone, but that has been winding its way down. We're moving in opposite directions. I want to be with you. I'm just worried I'm going to blow it."

I grabbed his hand, looked into his eyes, and said, "I believe you are perfect. You are not going to blow it."

He glanced around at the waitstaff and nervously pulled his hand away.

I felt strangely elated. I felt that, if anyone could handle this man, because of my spiritual practice, I could. I could love him with all his flaws. I could tame him with my love. I was the answer. I could heal him, save him.

After dinner, we walked to the corner of the street, and I turned to hug him good-bye and said, "I'm not going anywhere; I can wait. Work things out with the woman you have been dating. I'll see you at the dojo," and I turned to hail a cab.

But he held on to me and said, "I don't want you to go home." It felt so good to have a man's arms around me, to have human contact and to be held so close. "I want you to come over," he said.

So I did.

chapter 26
spirit guides

His apartment was great. It was large with a nice balcony, on a beautiful tree-lined street, directly above his fitness studio. It was sparsely furnished and very masculine, but warm. I felt immediately at home.

We sat side by side on the sofa, making awkward small talk. I was tense. It had been so long since I had been touched or kissed by a man and I was very nervous.

Suddenly I blurted out, "I haven't dated in close to two years. I got ordained as a monk; I was planning to be celibate for the rest of my life if I had to. I'm really nervous."

He did not respond. Instead, he leaned over and kissed me. A warm, tender, soft, loving, gentle kiss. I melted. He let his lips linger on mine, then he pulled away and stood up. He looked at me adoringly, smiled, and picked me up and carried me into his bedroom—*very* romantic. I wasn't sure having sex with him was a good idea, but I was desperate to hit the "reset button" after Vishnu. I had to wash away the residue from "consort" and "family slave" and "witch." I had been living in ugly, baggy clothing for close to four years, and I was dying to feel sexy again, to use my body in a sexual way.

As we entered his room, I looked around. He had an altar, just like mine. He had a meditation cushion and statues of Hindu deities. He had paintings of Buddhas on his walls. His bedroom looked like mine. This man was everything. He was strong and fierce and mighty, and he was soft and spiritual and searching. We made love, and it was making love. He was a very attentive lover. As we drifted off to sleep, with me nestled in his arms, he whispered in my ear, "Renee, I have never felt that much love in my entire life. I love you."

"I love you, too," I responded, a huge smile across my face.

———

His alarm woke me up at 7:00 a.m. He jumped out of bed and said he had to be at the dojo, which surprised me; he hadn't mentioned anything the night before about having to be someplace early. He got in the shower and dressed quickly.

"You can stay here and sleep as long as you want, I will be gone all day," he said. Then he left. My plans to make love and have breakfast and spend the day together were dashed. I went home a bit disappointed and slept all day, calling that night to check in and tell him what a great time I had, but he did not answer. Instead he sent me a message through Facebook saying he had a great time with me too and was looking forward to seeing me Wednesday at the dojo.

When I saw him Wednesday night, he was distant. I called him after class to ask about it, and he did not answer. I thought about him saying, "I have never felt that much love in my entire life" after we made love. I wondered if maybe he was afraid. Then I got another message through Facebook: *I have spoken to my spirit guides and they tell me I need to take a break from women for forty days. Please help me with this. Please understand.*

Of course I understand, I wrote back. After all my time with Vishnu and Lakshmi, it made perfect sense to me. *There is a lot of light between us and the occult will try to keep us away from each other*, I wrote, believing it to be true.

And so we began a pattern—a relationship of sorts. We

would sleep together, and he would tell me how much he loved me and how he had never met anybody like me. Then he would request a forty-day break. Twenty to thirty days into his break, he would contact me, tell me he missed me, and invite me to dinner near his apartment. I'd spend the night, he'd hold me and say, "I love you, Renee," and then his "spirit guides" would tell him he needed to take a break.

The breaks broke my heart. I yearned to see him and some-times I got to, but just as friends. I travelled around Manhattan with a toothbrush and an extra pair of panties in my purse just in case he called and invited me to spend the night. I was per-manently on call.

I made excuses to myself for his behavior. I told myself it was okay, that I was a monk and my mind was the ashram and that this was perfect training ground, that I could not control him or his actions, but I could control the way I felt about him and his actions—and he was perfect just the way he was. I told myself he was my soul mate and the occult was trying to keep us apart. One night he called and asked me to come over. I had just finished class at the dojo. It was raining and I could not get a cab so I walked, in pouring rain, half an hour to his apartment. Soul mates—I was convinced we were soul mates, and I was willing to do anything to be with him.

Throughout the summer and the off and on of our "rela-tionship," we began planning to build a business together. He had a vision of a huge studio with enough space and enough machines to have large group classes. He envisioned twenty people on machines moving as one. His eyes lit up as he spoke about it. I began envisioning a franchise of studios, building our first studio in my mind. I saw "wombs of light" in which people— mostly women—would nurture their bodies, minds, and spirits. I imagined pitching his system as the best-kept secret in exercise, premium branding and a premium spa. And I began fantasizing about the start of my final task: to build a company that made $10 million profit after taxes. I was afraid to do it on my own, but I thought with Hiroto by my side, we could pull it off. And, the truth is, I thought if he and I were business partners, he would eventually fall in love with and commit romantically to me. He had massive potential. I figured I would heal him with my love, and together, we would take on the world. I imagined him meditating downtown and me meditating in the Upper West Side and the two of us flooding Manhattan with gold light.

We began looking for studio spaces. I would sit on the back of his motorcycle, my arms lovingly wrapped around him, and we would cruise up and down the streets of Manhattan looking for *For Lease* signs. We saw space after space. We ran around like little kids inside them, eyes sparkling, imagining our studio.

While on the back of his bike, I watched his head turn to look at every woman we passed, and I felt, every single time, as if I was being stabbed in the heart. But I ignored it, shoved the feelings deep down inside—telling myself I was a monk and it did not matter.

One morning in August, I woke up panicked. How could I go into business with a guy I just met that I was in love with that was not in love with me? He said he loved me, yes, but he clearly could not commit. Something else was going on, something he did not want to tell me. Going into business with this guy was asinine.

I called him immediately. "I can't do this," I said. "I'm in love with you. I can't go into business with you. It's a horrible idea."

He was crushed. He said he understood, although he sounded bitter, and hung up the phone.

During class that Wednesday, he was so powerful, so dedicated to his teaching and students, that I was reminded of what a master he was in all that he did, what a powerful asset as a business partner he would be. I approached him after class and told him I was wrong. We could build a wonderful business together; we would find a way to make it work.

He smiled and hugged me. "I love you," he said. "I know I can't be a good boyfriend right now, but I do love you. I think we could be great together in the future. No one has ever believed in me the way you do. I will not let you down."

Those words were all I needed to keep my dream alive.

chapter 27
MONSter

Meanwhile, I was about to start the executive MBA program at NYU Stern and was incredibly nervous to start school; I did not believe I would fit in. I knew I wouldn't be able to talk about my spiritual path and my guru sending me to get my MBA. I was going to have to lie some more.

I hated lying, but Vishnu and Lakshmi had stressed the importance of inaccessibility, so people couldn't pin us down with their thoughts. According to them, that meant we had to lie—we had to lie a *lot*.

My first week at Stern was an orientation—held off campus at a resort in Westchester. I arrived early in the morning and checked into my room. I dressed in a black suit with an oxblood silk shirt and high heels and sat in the lobby, anxiously awaiting the arrival of the other students.

Hiroto called. I was so happy to hear from him.

"I'm so proud of you," he said. "You are going to do just fine. You are amazing."

I glowed. He was giving me the support I needed. It was such a godsend to have a man in my life again, someone to stand by my side. The first week of school empowered me. It was incredibly intense. We had so much work to do and so little time to do it. By the end of the week, we were completely broken down, bonded. There was no energy left for ego or façade. We had become a team. My sense of self rose. My power rose. And I suddenly questioned what the hell I was doing with Hiroto.

The week away from him helped me see the situation clearly: This man was not right for me; I deserved someone more emotionally available, someone who wanted to be with me all the time. I vowed to distance myself from him when I returned.

And then, as if he felt my change of mind, my strengthening, he called again and was kinder and warmer than he'd ever been.

"I miss you," he said. "I really want to see you. "Will you come straight to my place and spend the night, let me take you to dinner?"

My resolve from moments before broke. I swooned. Of course I would. I paid $100 for a car to take me back to the city. A hurricane was on its way to Manhattan and even though I was safe in Westchester, I went back. "I'll protect you," Hiroto told me.

He met me at the door with open arms.

"Welcome home," he said as he held me close. "Let's go eat."

While hugging him, I glanced at the sink. Two wine glasses rested upside down in his dish rack. He did not usually drink. A vision of a young blonde flashed through my mind. I ignored it. I went to dinner with him. I slept over. And then I allowed him to send me home in the morning—to my apartment on the thirty-seventh floor of an all-glass building—alone, with the hurricane approaching. I hunkered down in the bathroom as he ignored my calls for the next two days.

Another month rolled by, and Hiroto's birthday approached. He wanted to spend it at an ashram in the Bahamas and was hinting to me about joining him. However, he never invited me. Instead, he went with someone else; I couldn't bear to ask him who. The day before he left, he asked me to lunch near his apartment. After the meal, he invited me over "for a nap."

I noticed he was lost in his thoughts. His eyes were closed, and I could tell he was not present. I had no idea where he was, but it was not with me. He fell asleep, and I left. I didn't hear from him while he was gone.

When he returned, he texted simply, *I'm back.*

I replied, *Welcome home! Let's go to dinner tonight, to celebrate your birthday.*

I'm really tired, he wrote back. *Not sure it's a good idea.*

I was crushed. I went to his class that night anyway.

After class, he ran up to me and said, "Your energy was so great tonight. I really missed you. I'd love to go to dinner with you; I changed my mind."

"I made other plans," I responded. I walked out to the street, and he followed me.

"I really missed you," he said again.

I hailed a cab and jumped in. When I got home, I called him. "I don't think we should sleep together anymore," I said.

"Why not?" he asked.

"I just think it's a bad idea, especially if we're going to be business partners." I knew the sleeping together had to end. But I still loved him and I still wanted to go into business with him and I still hoped that one day we could be together as boyfriend and girlfriend.

In November, we found a new studio space. Just as we were about to finalize the contract for the lease, Hiroto called me. He said he was panicked. He said the space was too big and the lease cost too much. He suggested I become his partner in his existing business, the one he had owned for twelve years.

It was a horrible idea. His studio was run-down. His equipment was old and broken. His books were a mess. But, I went ahead and asked my CPA to value the business. One morning, I was sitting in a coffee shop struggling with this decision. My instincts told me to run, that buying into Hiroto's business was a terrible idea. But I didn't trust my instincts anymore. I seriously thought my intuition was the occult trying to prevent me from becoming Enlightened.

I opened a book of poetry written by Lakshmi, randomly letting it fall open where it would. The book opened to a poem about a wasp trapped in her house. She explained how it kept tracing the same path along the ceiling and the closed window, refusing to make the simple change necessary to fly out the open door to freedom. I was still so desperate to change, to evolve, to become Enlightened. I was still so sure I had to change completely to do so. I thought maybe this was the way; never even noticing the same path I kept tracing was the path of not believing in myself, the path of allowing others to take advantage of me, the path of not standing up for myself. I believed going into business with Hiroto would change me radically. I closed the book and paid my bill and walked to his studio.

"I'll do it," I said. "I will be your partner."

My CPA had determined that Hiroto's business was worth $500,000. I became a 50 percent partner by paying him $250,000.

We were going to need a full remodel, a full rebrand, software upgrades, and all new machines, so I got a $500,000 line of credit in my name. And then I worked myself to exhaustion building him the business of his dreams. I picked out paint and tiles and grout and doorknobs and toilet paper holders and lockers. I picked out furniture and toilets and sinks and faucets. I interviewed graphic artists and web designers and with them designed the website and business cards and pamphlets and advertising and logos and wall art. I planned classes and schedules. I hired a PR firm and planned a launch party. I organized his accounting and upgraded his software. I ordered all new equipment: machines, yoga mats, yoga blocks, pillows and towels. I designed company T-shirts and water bottles and bags. I interviewed photographers and had photos taken of the studio and all the staff. I found a beautiful photo of a lotus, located the photographer and got permission to blow it up seven feet wide for our back wall. I found a photo studio to print it. I rewrote the website. I created countless spreadsheets. I turned our downstairs into a staff lounge and made the trainers employees instead of independent contractors; I started looking for health insurance for them. And I oversaw every aspect of the construction. I did all of this in a month.

The weekend before our opening, Hiroto freaked out. He was barely there. I stayed late into the night cleaning and organizing, filling paper towel holders and soap dispensers, assembling furniture and breaking down boxes, all alone. I was exhausted. And I was furious that I was doing it alone. He was shaky and distracted when we opened. He wanted to go back to business as usual for him, but everything was different. He had scheduled a teacher training during the opening week, so he spent most of each day teaching a small group of teachers in the back of the studio. Overtired and trembling, I worked out the kinks at the front desk.

Halfway through our opening week, Veronica, a young girl from the dojo, walked in. She had a huge smile on her face. She said Hiroto had invited her to his class. She did not pay. And then she ran up to him with love in her eyes and threw herself into his arms. It broke my heart. She was adorable, voluptuous, with a beautiful smile, and easily twenty years younger than he. The image of the upside down wine glasses flashed through my mind.

Oh my God, I thought.

I grabbed my coat, walked out of the studio, and went home. I cried my eyes out. I instantly knew they were lovers, that they must have been for a while, and I was crushed that he invited her to our studio for opening week when he knew I was in love with him.

He called me. "Are you okay?" he asked.

"No," I responded. "I'm going to work from home from now on. That was our deal, anyway. I do the back end; you run the shop."

Maybe if I never saw him, it would be easier for me.

He said, "Okay, that is probably best."

But, he was not ready to hang up the phone.

"Also," he said, "I've been meaning to talk to you. I am used to getting paid weekly from the studio. This is not happening now, so I have nothing to live off of."

What about the $250,000? I thought.

"Could I get paid a salary in advance?" he continued.

Too worried about alienating him, I never suggested he live off of the $250,000. He asked for $58,000. I gave it to him the following day in one lump sum from the line of credit.

"Also," he said, "when I teach private lessons and teacher trainings, I'm going to keep the money, okay?"

"Sure," I responded.

He now had $250,000 plus $58,000 in cash, plus a weekly income from private lessons. Not only did I get no pay, but I also honored all the classes that students had purchased before I came on board; that money was long gone, but I still had to pay the instructors. Naïve, insecure, afraid of confrontation, and trusting, I kept using the money from our line of credit.

Within a week of receiving his salary, he stopped showing up to the studio completely, even though he lived above it. The staff began to feel like Hiroto and I didn't care, so why should they? I was never there (they did not know I was running everything from home), and now he was never there. They started slacking off. I would walk in and find a vase of dead flowers on the front table, bathrooms with no paper towels or toilet paper, yoga mats and pillows all over the floor and weird music playing. The trainers would be sitting on the machines eating lunch and gossiping. It was a disaster.

I called a meeting with some of the trainers. They told me stories that made me cringe. It became clear how many of them detested Hiroto, how much disrespect they had for him. I had never noticed before. Utterly in love with Hiroto, I had never thought to interview the entire staff before I bought into the business; I had just hung on the words of the few I met during his party, the few that adored him. I had messages from clients who left the studio. I met with them and heard more stories about Hiroto and his interactions with them that were appalling. I had gone into business with a monster.

The signs had always been there; I had just refused to see them. Denial is powerful, and I simply did not want to believe this man was anything but my soul mate, no matter how many different ways he showed me. But with these crying women in front of me, telling me tales I did not want to hear, I could no longer ignore the obvious.

Meanwhile, I had asked Hiroto to get rid of all our coupon deals because once we upgraded the space and the machines, discount first-timers were not our target market; when he did, the studio emptied out. I had no idea the group classes were filled with first timers. Suddenly, we had no business.

I was falling apart. I was still trying to make it through the program at Stern. Still trying to get my black belt in karate. Still meditating two hours a day. I had listed my California house for rent because it was not selling, so I was dealing with tenants and being a landlord. I was still on the Board of Directors of the nonprofit. And I was spending close to twelve hours a day building our new business. I was exhausted. I was not eating enough, not sleeping enough. I had lost weight and was close to ninety pounds. And now I had to admit my business partner was not at all who I thought he was. I had made a *huge* mistake.

I pulled Hiroto aside. "I want answers," I said. I began telling him what I had heard.

He looked at me with contempt in his eyes and said, "I am not who you think I am. I have been trying to tell you this since we met. I cannot change. I will not change. You keep trying to change me, and it will never happen."

Defeated, I decided I would let him run the studio his way. I would retreat.

His way was to scrap my idea of our target market and go back to filling the studio with coupon users, to heavily discount our lessons. Each group class was taught randomly, with no plan and no progression for the clients. He paid our employees less and not at all if their classes were empty. He treated them as independent contractors so we did not have to offer benefits. He wanted to show up whenever he felt like it and to not be around when he didn't. He wanted to treat customers poorly if he was in a bad mood. And he didn't want me there at all, *ever*. I figured, if he went back to the way he was used to, he'd show up to work more; he'd be happier.

But he didn't show up to work more. He wasn't happier.

I went to his karate class one night and listened to him give his usual speech about integrity and honor at the end. I watched the students look up to him with admiration, buying his act hook, line, and sinker, as I had done. As we all stood in line to bow to him at the end of class, I was disgusted and heartbroken and afraid.

What the hell had I been thinking? What the hell was I doing intertwining my life with this person? He was a total stranger. I was in deep trouble. It took a long time coming, but suddenly it was crystal clear: the reason it hadn't been working wasn't because I was defective and not trying hard enough. The reason it hadn't been working was because this man was a monster.

I called Hiroto after class that night and told him I wanted out. I could not be his business partner anymore. I said I would give him the studio, pay off half the money we had taken from the line of credit minus his $58,000 salary, and that he could take two years to pay off the other half. All I wanted was my initial investment back—the $250,000 I had given him just three months before, and I wanted the studio out of my name. I had to leave for Chile and Argentina that week, for a study tour with NYU, and I told him we could work out all the details of my leaving when I returned.

He agreed that I should leave the business. "You have been blocking me. I feel like I cannot be who I truly am when you are around. I agree it's for the best."

It was decided. I was out. Thank God. Hallelujah. Amen.

While I was in Chile, Hiroto and I were in contact through e-mail. He seemed a lot happier. His e-mails were light and jovial and full of energy, reminding me of the Hiroto I first met, but eventually our e-mails grew angrier. When I got to my apartment immediately after returning to New York, after traveling for close to twenty-four hours, I checked my e-mail to see what had come in while I was en route. Hiroto had e-mailed to say I was irresponsible for not checking my e-mail in the last twenty-four hours, for having an autoresponder that said I was out of the office, and that he had never been unavailable in the twelve years he had run the studio. Then he added that he would not return *any* of my money.

Not return my money? How was that possible? I was giving him back the studio. Why would he keep the $250,000? It made no sense. Without even changing clothes or brushing my teeth, I jumped in a cab and travelled an hour in rush hour traffic to our studio. I had to see him. I had to talk to him face to face. He was walking down the street toward the front door as I got out of the taxi.

"Hiroto," I said. He looked at me. He opened the door to walk into the studio. "Stop," I said. He stopped. "What is going on?" I asked.

"I don't have time for this; I have to teach," he said. He would not look into my eyes. He looked down at the sidewalk.

"Are you really not going to return any of my money?" I asked him. "Do you really think that is fair?"

"I don't have time to talk right now," he repeated. "I have to go teach."

"I need you to look in my eyes and tell me you really won't return my money," I said.

No response.

"I don't understand. I have given you everything. What more do you want from me?"

He looked up at me. His eyes were the same color Lakshmi's had been the morning after Shiva died—an evil green, filled with hate. He said, "I need another $100,000. To make this work, to get this studio back to how it was before you ruined it, I need more money." Then he walked into the studio and shut the door in my face.

By this point, we had pulled $290,000 from my line of credit—$58,000 for his salary and $232,000 for the remodel, $100,000 of which went toward new equipment. Even if he returned my $250,000, he still had $58,000 in cash plus a brand-new studio, a brand-new website, and a PR launch party on the way. The founder of the exercise method had been so impressed with our new studio that he scheduled to teach a workshop there, his first workshop in the US for *years*. I had paid all the outstanding bills and had put money aside for payroll for two more months. How could he possibly need more money?

I hailed a cab home. I was dumbfounded. *We'll work this out*, I thought to myself. *It's a mess, but we'll work it out. I'll be fair. I'll give him the business, and I'll pay off half of the loan. That's more than fair. We'll find an amicable way to sort this out. He's just not thinking clearly.* I walked into my apartment. I took a long hot shower. I made breakfast and put on Mozart. I sat on my sofa and the phone rang.

Chapter 28
Shattered

"THAT MONEY IS GONE, JACK!" he screams into the phone, his thick New York accent venomous with rage. "THAT MONEY IS GONE, JACK!" he yells. "I SPENT IT!" he screams. "I SPENT IT AND YOU CAN'T EVEN ASK ME WHAT I SPENT IT ON! THAT MONEY IS GONE, JACK!" Over and over he yells the same thing. Like a CD with a scratch repeating a phrase indefinitely.

The afternoon sun is streaming into my apartment, filling the space around me with gold light. Mozart plays quietly in the background. I close my eyes and hold love in my heart. It is all I can think to do as my world crumbles around me.

What a bizarre dichotomy, I think, as time appears to stand still. *There is so much light, so much peace, so much stillness, and yet the man I loved and trusted and gave close to $300,000 dollars to has, in less than twenty-four hours, turned into a psychopath.*

I let him scream for a while, knowing that interrupting him would be futile. Then his story changes: "I GAVE IT TO SOMEONE TO HIDE AND COULDN'T GET IT BACK EVEN IF I WANTED TO!" he yells. "YOU RUINED MY LIFE! YOU TRIED TO BUY MY LOVE! YOU USED ME!" he shouts. "THAT MONEY IS GONE, JACK!"

I still did not say anything. I waited until he wore himself out, wondering why on earth he kept calling me Jack. And then, once he paused, I said calmly, "Hiroto, you're not showing up for work. You're never there. I'm doing everything. That was not part of our deal. Are you really surprised that I want to leave?"

"Did you expect me to do as much work as I did before, now that I have a partner?" he asked me.

"Yes!" I responded. "I was expecting you to do more. That's what starting a new business entails. In the beginning, it is *a lot* of work."

He had no response.

I continued, "Do you really think it's fair that I'm doing all the work, putting in all the money, that I'm going to give you the studio and pay off half the remodel loan, and I still don't get my investment back? Does that seem fair to you?"

He was quiet. And then, "THAT MONEY IS GONE, JACK! YOU'RE TRYING TO GET BLOOD FROM A STONE. THAT MONEY IS GONE, JACK!"

I hung up the phone and called my lawyer. I explained everything to him. I knew I could never talk to or see Hiroto again. If I did, my heart would open up, I would forgive him, and be sucked back into the drama.

As spring turned to summer, I realized I was never going to get my money back. Hiroto was not going to budge. I had a decision to make: walk away and lose everything or sue him and hope he would settle. I didn't want to sue him. I wanted to just walk away. But everyone I spoke to told me I had to sue him, that I couldn't let him get away with this. I felt like maybe I really did have to fight, like I had to at least *try* to get my money back. So, after four months of attempting to negotiate through my lawyer, I hired a litigator and sued him.

As soon as we filed our lawsuit, reporters started calling. My lawyer advised me to not answer my phone, so I let it ring all day long. Reporters must have been calling Hiroto, as well. I got a text from him that said, *I have $200,000; I can get you the rest. Please don't do this. Think about the trainers.* Then he called my lawyer and left a message saying the same thing. It was too late. I could not call off the reporters. I had not called them in the first place.

The next day, as I was making breakfast, I got a text from a friend at 8:00 a.m.: *Good morning. Are you okay? Have you seen the paper?*

I had not. Immediately after, I got a phone call from a classmate. I didn't answer because I did not recognize the number. He left a voicemail: "Renee, are you okay? Is there anything I can do for you?"

Worried, I got online and googled my name.

Oh. My. God.

The lawsuit was all over the Internet. The *New York Post* popped up first. Then the *New York Daily News*. I read those two articles and called my lawyer. Meanwhile, it went viral: the UK's *Daily Post*; the UK's *Daily Mail*, the *Gothamist*; *InsideCounsel. com* with the title "8 of the Strangest Lawsuits Making Headlines." I was afraid to go outside. I was embarrassed to see my doormen. My phone kept ringing: unknown numbers, reporters; I didn't answer. I called my lawyer again. I was horrified, but I couldn't stop laughing. The articles were priceless:

> "There's no heavy lifting at one Manhattan fitness studio that offers low-impact workouts—but apparently, there is a lot of grunting."

> "Is it possible that the steamiest establishment on Tenth Street isn't the Russian Bath House?"

I was doubled over in laughter; it was surreal. Yes, I was being slaughtered along with Hiroto, but I didn't care. I had suffered so long because of him and lost so much. It felt so good to finally laugh.

The laughter didn't last long, however. He created a counterclaim and attached edited versions of my most personal e-mails. It was a blow that brought me to my knees. Somehow, through everything we had been through, I still believed deep down he was a good guy; that he was damaged and just needed love and therapy. But when I saw my most personal e-mails in print, when I saw a counterclaim filled with lies, my world shattered. I knew what horrible things people did to other people, but I never imagined someone I knew, someone I had slept next to and made love with, someone I had believed so strongly in and given so much to would want to tear me apart like this; could lie so blatantly; would use the e-mails I wrote, the e-mails that said he was a Magnificent Being, as evidence that I was obsessed with him and thought he was God and had lost my mind. And I could not *believe* I was really going to lose all that money. I had been ordained as a monk. I had dedicated my life to God and spreading love and light and peace. Something like this was not supposed to happen to someone like me. Everything I believed about the world, everything I believed about people, unraveled. I became undone.

Chapter 29
oatmeal

I lie on the floor of my apartment. I have to get up. I know I have to get up. Eat. I have to eat.

Just make it through a bowl of oatmeal, I tell myself. *That is all you have to do today. Just make it through a bowl of oatmeal. You can do this.*

I drag myself into the kitchen. I stumble, fall into the wall. I start to cry and start to slide down the wall to the floor again.

"NO!" I scream to myself. "Get up!"

I think of Trinity in the first *Matrix* movie.

"Get up, Trinity. Just . . . get . . . up," she tells herself.

I make myself get up. I make myself cook oatmeal. I make myself sit down and conquer one spoonful at a time, until it is all gone. I cannot let my mind move forward or back. If it drifts to the past, I start to die. If it drifts to the future, I start to panic.

"Stay here," I tell myself. "Stay here now."

To get each bite down, to make it stay down, I must keep my mind—hold my mind—in the present. It is the only way.

chapter 30
opt out

I was trying so hard to be a monk, my idea of what an Enlightened monk was. I was trying so hard to live in hell but have my mind be in heaven, like a lotus flower growing in mud. I had been sure, as my time working with Hiroto grew more and more difficult, that it was my Bodhisattva training ground, that opening a business with him was my Divine task. Now, all of that was gone. As was my reputation and the business I had built and all the money.

No one besides Lakshmi would understand. I prayed for her to show up back in my life. I had tried everything, I had tried changing myself in every way possible, and *nothing* I was doing was working. Everything was blowing up in my face. *Maybe,* I thought to myself, *maybe I need to give up meditating. It is the only change I have not made.* I quit meditating that day. After never missing a day for six years, I quit cold turkey. Within 24 hours I noticed a difference in my face. It looked grey; I had worry lines in my forehead. I felt heavier. I felt *worse. Lakshmi,* I thought, *please show back up in my life. I need you. I am so lost.*

A few days later I was in a coffee shop near NYU and saw one of her flyers. For one night only, the University of Mysticism would be in New York.

Are you fucking kidding me? I needed her so badly. I needed to see my sangha mates, my tribe. I needed to believe again in magic and miracles and mysticism, and she was going to be in New York! I began to see her posters all over town. There was one in the window of the store in the lobby of my apartment building!

I showed up early to the event. I was uneasy. Was it okay that I was there? Some part of me believed she was in New York because of me, because she knew I needed her. I entered the ballroom with the rest of the people, and I timidly asked Leslie, who had been one of my partners in Lighten Up! Enterprises and was clearly the new event manager, if it was okay that I was there.

"It's a public event," she said, not outright mean, but definitely not welcoming.

In the two years I had been gone, her hair had turned completely grey.

I saw some of my favorite sangha mates. I bowed to them with so much love in my heart, and they bowed back. I saw Jessica.

"I love you," I whispered as I walked by her.

"I love you, too," she whispered back.

I sat in the back row and kept my head low. Jessica sat next to me and smiled. It felt so good to be back beside her; she and I had been friends for close to twenty years.

Lakshmi walked on stage, escorted by Vishnu. She looked fit and strong and fierce again. Lisa was a few rows ahead of me. She turned around and looked at me with fear in her eyes. She said nothing and turned back around. Her hair was now long, like Lakshmi's, and she had gained even more weight.

During the break, some of the remaining senior students approached me and started asking questions: Was I living in New York? Was I still part of the group? I answered vaguely, but with so much joy to be speaking with them. I was thrilled to be back among them. Paul, who had relocated to San Diego just to be a part of the group with me, looked happy to see me but afraid to be caught talking to me. He kept it short and walked away.

I did not feel the same light. I was now able to meditate much better on my own than I was in this seminar. However, I left that night filled up again, fortified, knowing I was taken care of, that Lakshmi would always be there for me. She had arrived to New York exactly when I needed her. She was, and always would be, my Teacher.

———

As the lawsuit wore on and Hiroto's attacks through his lawyer became more vicious, I dipped back into periods of deep despair. I was still going to the dojo, determined to finish my task of getting a black belt and unwilling to let the rumors and gossip keep me away. It wasn't easy. I had to deal with almost all of the advanced black belts looking at me like I was the devil. Hiroto had gotten fired, and they thought it was my fault. They had no idea what I had invested or what my side of the story was. To them, I was just a jealous woman that left Hiroto and sued him.

I was struggling to make it through school. I slept a lot, cried a lot. I wanted my guides back. With Lakshmi and the sangha in New York, I felt strong, but as soon as they left, I fell apart. I spent a lot of time meditating. Only in meditation could I find peace. I touched those pristine mind states, light and love and quiet and bliss, and I didn't want to stop meditating. I didn't want to return to the world.

Suddenly, I understood suicide. I had always thought people that did it were selfish and weak; now I saw them as simply wanting the pain to end and being willing to do whatever it took to make that happen. No one understood me; no one ever would. What was the point to even being alive? I had arrived to New York as a newly ordained monk, eager and wanting to spread light and love as far and as wide as I possibly could, and instead, I got creamed.

I imagined different options for killing myself: jumping off a building, turning on a car in a closed garage, taking sleeping pills. Fortunately, I didn't have the energy for suicide. I figured that if I tried, I'd fail and end up maimed or mentally impaired. This depressed me more.

I was broken. I had no idea just how broken. I was still loyal to Vishnu and Lakshmi and the sangha. I still believed their Teachings. I was not ready to give that up, because if I did, I would truly have nothing. Having something broken and twisted, at this point, was better than having nothing. And the truth was, if I even started to imagine that their Teachings were not The Way, I would have to admit that Hiroto was right—that I *was* crazy. I would have to admit I had pushed everyone I loved out of my life and that I had radically altered everything about me because some strangers had told me to.

In late November, shattered and suicidal, I woke up with the sudden urge to go back to Colorado. I still owned a condo there, the one my mother had used when hers was rented. She had left it to my brother and me, but I bought him out of it shortly after she died. It was still filled with her belongings. I had not been there in over five years because Lakshmi and Vishnu had advised me not to go.

"It will bring back the old you," they had told me.

I decided to go. *Maybe it will help me find my way,* I thought. Maybe it would ease the pain. I planned a trip for five nights.

On the fourth day, I had a snowboarding accident. I was racing down the mountain at top speed when I hit a rock that was covered with snow. It threw me into the air, and I landed headfirst, tucked my neck, and miraculously rolled out of it unscathed. I sat down and started laughing. It was unbelievable and so scary. I decided to go back to my mom's condo and lay low for the rest of the day. I tried to nap, but got the urge to get up and get rid of my mother's stuff. I put it all in bags, thinking about my life while I purged. By the time I was done, I was sure I needed to quit school, leave New York, and move to Colorado to start a new life.

I had a phone call scheduled the next morning with a woman who reads the Akashic records (a library of everything that has happened and will happen in the many lives of a soul). A friend had told me about her months prior, and I had scheduled an appointment; however, the first appointment I could get was months away, and *months away* was now suddenly *tomorrow*. I had been told I would be allowed to ask five questions.

When the theosophist called, she asked my full name and birthdate and said she would open the records and I could ask my first question.

"What happened to me yesterday?" I asked. "Why do I suddenly feel like the life I am living is all wrong and I want to start a totally new life, *again*?"

"Renee," she said. "Ski trips are interesting. Accidents happen all the time. Nobody would have asked questions. You had an opportunity to leave this life, and you decided not to. I like to call it an *Opt Out*. Each soul schedules them throughout its lifetime in case it needs a big rest and wants to return Home; these are the accidents that seemingly occur out of nowhere. When you decided to stay, you decided to get on your True Path."

As she was saying this, I pictured myself tucking my chin and rolling out of that fall. If I had not tucked my chin, I would have broken my neck and died instantly. I hadn't told her I was on a ski trip or that I had had an accident. I suddenly remembered the last thing I had done before flying to Colorado: I had rewritten my will. I had removed Lakshmi and Vishnu, and I had gotten the revision notarized the morning I got on the plane. As I thought this my skin rippled with goosebumps. I had prepared myself to transition to non-physical. I had prepared myself to Leave.

"Why were my Spiritual Teachers so mean to me? Why did they send me away?" I asked next.

"Renee, they did not have your best interests in mind," she said. "They were doing shadow work. They hated how bright you were, how bright you *are*."

I needed validation, and she was giving me that, but I was not ready to hear that Lakshmi and Vishnu were working against me.

"Their spiritual names are masks that they hide behind," she continued. "They are not good people. They spread doubt and fear. They spread paranoia. They think they are spreading light, but they are doing the opposite." She was right. They had filled my mind with doubt, with paranoia. They had shattered my intuition.

I returned to New York more confused than ever. While lying on the floor one morning, sobbing over the lawsuit, I finally admitted to myself that I was in a cult.

Yes, I know you and every other person in my life already *knew* this, but I, unfortunately, had yet to figure this out.

After hearing what my attorney had told me about the e-mails attached to Hiroto's counterclaim, I had not allowed myself to read them, thinking it would be too devastating, too embarrassing, but I pulled them out and read them all. I saw how demented my thoughts had been, how I had truly believed Hiroto was a "Magnificent Being trapped in Maya" and I was "a Bodhisattva sent to save him and pull him out." I sounded exactly like Lakshmi and Vishnu. My e-mails were filled with hatred and accusations and weird concepts from the cult.

"I'm losing my mind," I thought. I began therapy that week.

As if they sensed my newfound clarity, Lakshmi and Vishnu sent me a letter via certified mail. The must have found my mailing address through my tax records; I had rented a mailbox from a mailroom, as they had instructed. The letter arrived in a brown envelope, the kind I used to mail for them. It contained a note:

Renee,
Eternity is your Teacher now. It is no longer appropriate for you to attend Lakshmi's events.

I was officially set free. I felt so relieved.

I had *no* idea that the hardest part of my entire journey still lay ahead.

PART 4
ALONE

"Only when it's dark enough can you see the stars."
—Ralph Waldo Emerson

Chapter 31
Colorado

In January 2013, six months after I filed my lawsuit, I took a leave of absence from NYU and moved to Colorado. I was sure the move would make me feel normal. And by normal, I mean happy and resilient and optimistic about life and able to interact with others without worrying that doing so would harm me in some way. Instead, I got to Colorado and broke apart even more. Without the structure of New York and school, I became lost. I had no idea how to fill my days and no energy to do much more than sleep. And I was so afraid. I didn't trust anybody anymore. I had no idea who was going to screw me over next. I was terrified of running into people I knew and having to explain why I had disappeared and what I was doing with my life. I was now so completely different from the fun free spirit that they used to know. How could I possibly explain the change?

I hated Hiroto for making me afraid of men. I hated him for refusing to return my money. I hated him for not showing up to work and for lying about me in his counterclaim, and I hated him for pretending to be something he wasn't.

"How could he do this to me?" I asked myself over and over again. I started fantasizing about him getting an STD or getting in a motorcycle accident that would break his pelvis, or even about him getting diagnosed with cancer. I would fantasize about him losing all his money—my money—and becoming homeless. My mind was mired in dark, angry, vengeful places. I called friends in New York who knew Hiroto and asked how he was doing, hoping to hear he was doing terribly. Instead they told me the studio was beautiful and full of people. Hiroto was doing well, surrounded by my money in the beautiful studio that I built, and I was lying in a heap on the sofa, unable to get up or go outside. It all seemed so extraordinarily unfair.

My hate turned to Lakshmi. I hated her for pretending to be something she wasn't. I hated her for teaching me to erase myself, for convincing me to throw away everything—and everyone— that made me who I was. I hated her for talking me into spending my prime hidden away in sack-like clothing. I had given six years of my life to this woman, and now it felt as though I was damaged beyond repair. I hated her for brainwashing me into believing I was a witch and a sorceress and that I was manipulating people with my energy. My mind overflowed with all the ways she damaged me. My face contorted with them. I could not forgive her.

Then my hatred turned to Vishnu. I hated him for making me believe I was so incredibly flawed, for training me to believe that everything and everyone was going to steal my energy and pull me off my path to Enlightenment. I hated him for making me paranoid. I had stopped hugging people, because Vishnu told me I shouldn't blend my energy with other peoples'. I had stopped wearing bikinis to the beach, because he told me men would fantasize about me and put energetic lines into me. I had stopped going out dancing because Vishnu told me people would watch me and I wouldn't be able to get them out of my attention. I hated him for making me believe old friends would hold me back or that I could not invite anyone to my home and that I could never stay with others. I hated him for making me believe that if I slept past sunrise or did not wake up often enough throughout the night, I would get "energetically raped on the dream plane." I hated him for making me believe that I had to meditate for an hour every morning, as soon as I woke up, or I would mess up my karma. These beliefs were not going away; they didn't instantly disappear. I was so pissed off that I couldn't just immediately go back to normal.

My thoughts cycled back to Hiroto: I had given Hiroto everything—*everything*—and he had shit all over me, said I was "the devil," said I ruined his life. Then they circled back to Lakshmi and Vishnu: I had trusted and loved and adored Lakshmi, and she had hated me and brainwashed me. I had trusted Vishnu, and he had turned me into his slave and concubine. Then, in a flash, the self-doubt resurfaced. I started to believe all of them. Maybe I was a witch. Maybe I was the devil. Maybe I was a sorceress that was using my energy to manipulate people. Maybe I was irrevocably flawed.

Hiroto, Lakshmi, Vishnu. The triple knockout punch. Lakshmi and Vishnu had shattered me just enough to allow Hiroto perfect access. And he came along and shattered what was left.

My anger consumed me. My thoughts of suicide returned. I did not fit into the world at all. Nobody understood me. Nobody else cared about Enlightenment. The world was cruel and people were cruel and there was no reason to go on living. I had no purpose. I had nothing to believe in. I had run out of hope.

The pain was fierce. All the parts of myself I had pushed down over the past six years were bubbling to the surface. I had *no* idea who I was anymore. I had *no* idea how to find out. I had *no* idea what brought me joy and no idea which way to turn. I wanted to undo the last six years, to go back to the free-spirited girl I was before I joined the cult. But I could not, and that caused me unbearable mental anguish. The more I suffered, the more hate I felt. The more hate I felt, the more exhausted I became, and the more exhausted I became, the more I stayed inside, alone, with nothing but the demons in my head to keep me company.

The cycles of hate, anger, and rage felt like acid inside of me, killing me from within. They left me fragile and weak. There were days where my task was just to stand up in the shower and not collapse: "You can do this. Breathe. Feel your feet planted in the ground. Be here, now. You can do this. Just make it through this shower." And all I wanted to do was sleep. And cry. And sleep. Only when I was sleeping did the pain go away.

I had calls every week with my therapist in New York. I would tell her, "I know this happened for a reason, and I know it is part of the Divine Plan, but I am just so angry and filled with hate."

She told me I had to stop looking for the saintly approach to healing and had to allow myself to feel the rage. "Emotions should be feelings in motion," she would say. "You have to let them move through you. You have to let them out."

She encouraged me to journal. She encouraged me to scream into pillows. She encouraged me to buy a punching bag and take my anger out on it. I punched my punching bag until I could no longer raise my arms. It helped. I screamed into pillows until my voice gave out, the screams turning into inhuman shrieks in a desperate attempt to release the rage I had felt toward Lakshmi for years but could not—would not—admit. How dare she claim to be teaching Enlightenment, teaching spirituality, teaching meditation, when all she really wanted was a plethora of broken souls lying in worship at her feet?

Into my pillow I screamed, "Fuck you, Lakshmi! Fuck you and your fucking dharma. Fuck you, you fucking piece of shit liar."

My therapist was right. It helped a lot. Oh my God, to express what I had hidden inside me for so long was such a relief. To allow my emotions, these seemingly dark emotions, to finally flow through me brought a sense of joy and a sense of self that I had forgotten existed; it empowered me.

When I wasn't talking to my therapist or screaming into pillows or punching my punching bag, I ate. Somehow, I ended up with two family-sized slow cookers. I made meals like cheesy tuna-stuffed baked potatoes and chocolate peanut butter fudge pudding cake for eight people. And then I would eat it—*all of it*. Not in one sitting, of course, but I still ate all of it. And I sat . . . and sat . . . and sat—for *months*. And I got fat, for the first time in my life. I didn't even notice the change in my body. I didn't have a full-length mirror, and I was living in sweat pants and pajamas.

In mid-February, I got in touch with Kate. She was now living in the Middle East, married and pregnant. "I'm traumatized by the cult, too," she said. "I need to see you. I didn't want to admit it really was a cult until I knew you were out of it, because you believed in it so much, but they really fucked us up. I have to come see you." She jumped on a plane to come visit. We had not spoken to each other in close to five years.

When she arrived, we spent days talking about everything that had happened. Lakshmi had taught us that we should never get married and we should never have children. If we did, God forbid, have a child, we should never let it breastfeed; it would be sucking from our heart chakra, draining all our energy. After years in the cult, it was difficult to trust our own feelings and intuition.

We googled *brainwashing techniques* and discovered they had followed every single step. Overloaded schedule to create sleep deprivation. Check. Induced Alpha mind-state through meditation, speaking cadence, or music. Check. Environment of isolation (all normal social reference points unavailable). Check. Assault on identity. Check. Guilt. Check. Self-betrayal. Check. This list continued.

"How did they do this to us?" she asked. "We are both so strong and independent. It amazes me that this happened to women like us."

Kate said that after she left the group she went back to traveling the world as a journalist. She said it was the only way she could find herself again but that she still struggled with doubt about getting married and having a baby. Seeing how Kate got her life back gave me strength. I began exercising with her, and I began eating better. The change gave me more energy.

She talked me into going shopping. I felt alive again. I got excited about buying clothes. I pulled a handful off the rack and went to the dressing room. I took my clothes off, turned around to look at my backside in the mirror, and saw it: Dimples! *Everywhere.* My arms! My legs! My ASS! All my muscle had disappeared and had been replaced with cellulite. Every part of me was huge and pasty white and soft and full of dimples. My eight-pack stomach had been replaced by *rolls! Rolls of fat!* Yes, I had noticed these but I told myself it was just because I was sitting down and my stomach was scrunched up. I stood there, amazed, my smooshy white dimpled ass bulging and sagging out of my tiny black G-string. I cried. And then I put all the clothing back on the rack and left the dressing room utterly dejected.

When I came downstairs, Kate took one look at me and said, "What is wrong?"

"I'm fat!" I wailed.

She laughed. "Oh, Honey," she said. "We all get fat. Look at me." She lifted up her shirt to show me her huge belly. "And I'm sure I have a camel toe. These pants are *so* tight."

We both started laughing and left the store. But deep within, I was now even more depressed. Kate was gorgeous and gregarious and men stopped to stare at her as we walked into stores and restaurants. I, on the other hand, was fat and wounded and could not even imagine being confident enough to talk to strangers.

As soon as she left, I pulled out the slow cookers and ate some more—and sat some more. I simply could not muster the energy to change anything. I couldn't bear to make myself stop eating; it was seemingly the only source of comfort I had. Somehow, it filled the emptiness. Each bowl of pudding cake felt like a warm hug. Each tuna-stuffed cheesy potato felt like my father holding me and telling me everything would be okay. And I couldn't bear to force myself to exercise. I just didn't have the energy or the willpower. All I could do was trust that one day I would get the energy to start exercising again and that the fat would all go away and that I'd get my hard, sexy, sleek body back.

Meanwhile, I tormented myself. I began to google every single beautiful actress I saw in a movie—their great bodies and great faces and great skin and great hair.

"I used to look like that!" I whined.

This fueled my anger at Lakshmi and Vishnu.

"I spent the best years of my life dressed like an old lady. I gave up sex. I gave up dating. Now I'm old and ugly and gray and I can't get those years back!" I wailed. Every time I looked in the mirror, I just saw an old tired gray woman. Add to that the dimples and the weight and I was revolting. My dating life was over. I was doomed to be alone and angry and damaged and hateful forever.

And I was still fighting the lawsuit. Every time I got an e-mail from my lawyer telling me we were no closer to a settlement, the anger tore me apart from the inside out. I had escaped to Colorado to heal from the hurt but had only lost myself to anger. My therapist helped me realize I was having such a hard time letting it go because ultimately I was angry with myself. *I* had gone into business with a guy I had just met, *I* had decided we didn't need to sign a contract, *I* had agreed to getting the loan in my name. Suddenly, after almost a year of agony, I realized I had the key to my own handcuffs, and I could free myself any moment I chose.

In April, I called my lawyer and told him I wanted him to do whatever it took to end my lawsuit.

"You *can't* let this guy win," he said.

I said, "I have already won. I get to wake up every morning and be me. He has to wake up every morning and be him."

He told me that as 50 percent owner I had the power to dissolve the company. I did not want to do that. The company was all Hiroto had. I had to forgive Hiroto. I had to move on.

I heard a saying once: good people bring out the best in others; bad people bring out the worst. Fighting Hiroto brought out such an angry, hateful, mean, nasty side of me. That may have been the scariest part of the entire experience for me. I was turning into a monster: hating Hiroto, hating Vishnu, hating Lakshmi, hating everybody. I wanted to be me again. I wanted to trust again. I wanted to love people and life again. I could not take the business away from Hiroto. I would never be able to live with myself. If I was ever going to heal, the fighting had to be over.

My lawyer said, "It's so unfair . . . "

And, again, I told him I didn't care.

I felt better after hanging up the phone. Finally deciding to let go was an incredibly powerful decision for me. I got myself into that mess, I could get myself out. The experience was an expensive life lesson, but one I clearly needed to learn. I would never get into a legal battle again. I would never go into business with someone I did not know well again. I would never try to save somebody again. And I would never date a guy who did not cherish me ever, ever, *ever* again.

I forgave Hiroto. I asked God to please let me never see him again, in this life or any other. And then I let him go. Every now and then, I'd get a wave of anger and google him and hope to see that something horrible had happened to him, but those waves slowly dissipated and eventually went away altogether. With my decision to forgive him, I regained a huge piece of my heart and a large chunk of my power. Some of my energy returned. I felt lighter. I felt stronger.

Now, I had to figure out how to forgive Lakshmi and Vishnu. And—most difficult of all—I still had to figure out how to forgive myself.

Chapter 32
Mirrors

I decided to drive to California and spend six weeks on the beach. I yearned to get my fun free-spirited self back and I thought maybe this was the way. My California house was leased to tenants, so I rented a studio apartment. I loaded my car with beach clothes and self-help books. I packed *Falling Upward* by Richard Rohr and *This Time I Dance* by Tama Kieves and *Living Beautifully With Uncertainty and Change* by Pema Chodron and *Ask and it is Given* by Ester and Jerry Hicks.

I thought maybe, now that the lawsuit was over, the ocean would heal me. Maybe I could return to California and jump back into my old life and my old self. I had run over all my surfboards with my car once I knew I was moving to New York, in an effort to kill the surfer girl within me. It felt like maybe now was the perfect time to resurrect her.

After thirty minutes on the road, I stopped for lunch. Sitting at the counter, eating a slice of pizza, I got an e-mail from my lawyer; the settlement papers were attached. My heart sped up. My hands started shaking. I jumped in my car and found a copy store. Still shaking, I went to a computer and printed everything out. I signed the papers and overnight-shipped them back to him. I walked out to my car, got in the driver's seat, and started crying—and laughing. It was over. Life was about to get fun again. I felt a thousand pounds lighter as I drove west.

I spent the first night in Arizona. I had been there so often with Lakshmi and Vishnu that, for some reason, it felt right to start there. I went to the same hotel I used to stay in. I cried a lot; I wanted to be back with them. I missed the good times we had had together, the magic of our path. I missed thinking I was on my way to Enlightenment and believing I was with a tribe of people just like me. I walked around the center of town, terrified I'd run into them. My emotions swirled from anger and hate to love and forgiveness, rapidly changing from one extreme to the other.

I got in the car the next morning and drove to Sedona. I had never been there before and arrived at twilight. I could barely see the red rocks, but I could feel them blasting me with white light. I began to dissolve, the same feeling I had when I touched the pyramid in Egypt. I had to squeeze the steering wheel and sing loudly to stay alert and in my body. The energy there was off the chart. I picked a hotel nestled in the base of a red mountain, took a shower, ordered room service and got in bed. As I drifted off to sleep I could feel the energy of the land pulsing through me. I dreamed of ancient Indian warrior chiefs, male and female; I saw their beautiful, kind, wise, weathered faces and felt them holding me in wombs of light, as if rocking me to sleep in a hand-made cradle of love. I dreamed of magnificent beings all around me, reminding me I was much stronger than I knew. I woke up in the morning with strength and clarity: I would heal. I would come out the other side of this, and I would come out stronger and wiser than I could ever imagine.

I began to chant to myself: "This will turn out better than I can possibly imagine. I don't know how, but I know it will."

I chanted it to myself all morning long. It became my mantra. I headed west. Fortified.

The next stop on my tour was a place in the desert I had visited at least twice a year with the sangha. Lakshmi and Vishnu had told us it was a sacred site for our tribe. I felt like I might gain some clarity there; it used to feel so loving and magical. We had always been told never to go there alone, but I thought that doing so might empower me and help seal in my mind the idea that I was now my own Teacher, that I could go wherever I wanted.

I got there as the sun was setting. The desert sand was washed in pink and purple, reflecting the pastel sky. It was beautiful, and it took my breath away. I checked into my hotel and went up to the room. Suddenly, I had to go to the toilet. I took a huge shit and then realized, while sitting in the bathroom, that I had to get the hell out of there. It felt so wrong; I couldn't sleep there.

I walked back down to the front desk, checked out, got in my car, and drove the rest of the way to the beach, laughing the whole way about the fact that I had just gone to our sacred site to shit and leave.

I navigated the twisting desert roads in the dark, arriving in California close to midnight. It had been three and a half years since I had left and it felt amazing to return. I checked into a hotel and left my balcony doors open, smiling as I drifted off to sleep to the sound of the ocean and the humid air on my skin.

The next day, I woke up refreshed. I squeezed into an old bikini and went straight to the ocean for a swim. None of my beach clothes fit me anymore, so after breakfast I went to buy new bathing suits. I pulled my usual style off the rack, tried it on, and cringed. There was no way I would ever fit in this style of swimsuit again. It looked obscene on my now fuller and larger body. I looked for one with more fabric. It looked just as bad. Nothing looked good on me. I began to sink into despair, and then remembered my chant. "This will turn out better than I can possibly imagine. I don't know how, but I know it will." I repeated the mantra a few times to myself in the dressing room. Then I bought a wetsuit and a surfboard and headed to the beach to paddle out.

As soon as I hit the water I was gasping. Me! I had surfed almost my entire life! Now I was like a beached whale squeezed into a neoprene wetsuit. It was disgusting and depressing. I began to cry. And then I caught myself and chanted my mantra. I spent an hour in the ocean, doing my best, burning calories, making myself stronger and thinner. Chanting to myself the whole time. Next, I moved into the apartment I rented and, that night, I went to a yoga class, the first in close to three years. When I got back to the apartment, I ripped off my clothes and looked in the mirror. I didn't look any stronger *or* thinner!

Then it hit me: It was going to take a while to get my body back, and it was going to take a while to get my mind back. I had to *undo* all the damage I had sustained over close to seven years. As the days rolled by I knew I couldn't push myself; I had done that for too many years, and it had backfired. As soon as I put pressure on myself to make better food choices and limit my intake, all I wanted to do was eat as much sugar and fat as possible. I had to let myself eat as much as I wanted, whatever I wanted. Otherwise, I would simply deprive myself for a few days, obsessing the entire time about what I really wanted to eat, and then I would give in and gorge myself on it a few days later. It made more sense to just eat what I wanted to eat when I wanted to eat it. I trusted that, as I slowly got my mojo back, I would make better food choices. I had always known what foods my body needed and exactly how much. No matter what was in front of me, I ate until I was full and then I stopped. Some days, I wanted salads; other days, I wanted a burger and dessert, but my body always told me what to eat and I never overate. Now, I had no idea how much food was enough food. I had no shut-off gauge. It terrified me. And I wanted only thick, gooey, filling foods, because they comforted me in a way nothing else at the time could.

As a thin, fit model and dancer, I was used to getting a lot of male attention. Now, no men noticed me. And I noticed them not noticing me. I had never before felt that my self-worth was tied to what I looked like, but suddenly I realized it was. I felt ugly and old and fat and worthless. I became even more insecure, more introverted. I spent most of my days on the sofa, watching people walk by my window. I rented a lot of movies. I cried a lot. I spoke to my therapist once a week.

To make everything worse, my apartment was a 1970s man cave. It was a studio near the beach, decorated in grey Formica and animal-print furniture. I called it *the man-ther den*. It had a raised platform bed and switches on the nightstands so the owner could control all the lighting from the bed. Worst of all, it was wall-to-wall, floor-to-ceiling mirrors—for the fattest time in my life! Every single direction I turned, I saw my fat belly and my fat ass and my fat thighs and my dimples, dimples, dimples. I could not escape them.

One day, I finally laughed and stopped looking. I reminded myself that I didn't have to care what my body looked like. My insecurity was based on my perception of what other people were thinking of me. I told myself that we love people who are kind and who make us feel good; we don't care if they are pretty or ugly, old or young, fat or thin. I had to find a way to be kind again.

But that epiphany did not last long. I was still terrified I would run into someone I used to know. How on earth could I explain that I had shoved her out of my life, abandoned him, in order to become Enlightened? I looked terrible. And I had turned my life into a shit show. What was I going to say if I ran into somebody I used to know? "I joined a cult and now I'm all fucked up and fat?" I did not want any of my old friends, or anyone I recognized, to see me this way. I walked into stores with a hat on and my head down. On the really bad days, I stayed in bed and cried. I watched movies and I screamed into my pillow and I wrote in my journal.

But on good days, the positive self-talk continued. I told myself that once my mind got strong again, my body would follow. And I chanted my new mantra: "This will turn out better than I can possibly imagine. I don't know how, but I know it will." My process was three steps forward, two steps back, four steps forward, one step back. It was definitely not the "full steam ahead to healing" that I had pictured when I imagined going to California to jump back into my old life. In fact, "jumping back into my old life" did not seem to be working at all. I was terrified of running into my old life. My old life simply did not fit me any longer.

I started going to yoga and surfing almost daily. I didn't push myself. I surfed where there were no people and basically no waves. I took it easy. And if I wasn't in the mood, I wouldn't go. No more forcing myself to do anything.

It dawned on me I had to learn to be kind to myself. And I had to be patient. I had been *so* hard on myself for *so long*. I had been so mean to myself. I had pushed and pushed and pushed myself for so long. Pushed myself until I broke. In college I danced until my feet bled through my pointe shoes and I broke bones in my legs and then I danced some more. I took so many classes and forced myself to do so well in them that I got diagnosed with Chronic Fatigue Syndrome. I never allowed myself to feel I was good enough or strong enough or smart enough or pretty enough. It had to stop. This behavior *had* to stop.

So, for the first time in my life, the only movement I wanted to do was nurturing movement: yoga—gentle, flowing, dancing yoga—and surfing. I refused to beat myself up on a spin bike. I refused to jar my body running. I refused to bang my joints apart in a karate class. I had thought I would move back to California and surf and dance and get my old body back quickly, but my spirit wanted something different. It wanted me to stay slowed down.

So my ass was getting bigger. And my thighs had cellulite. And my belly was a muffin top. But I was not going to starve myself. And I was not going to force myself to exercise. I was not, in any aspect of my life, going to deprive myself any longer, and I was not, in any aspect of my life, going to beat myself up any longer. So if nurturing myself meant having a fatter ass and fatter thighs, then so be it. But deep down I knew it didn't. Deep down I knew I was giving birth—to a new me, to my life's work. And if I were pregnant with a child, I would listen to my body. I would eat what I wanted to eat, when I wanted to eat it. I would rest as much as I needed to rest. I would expect my body to change as the new life grew inside of me. It is a price I would be more than willing to pay. And I knew it was up to me to trust, and to know, that my body would balance out eventually.

Holding onto that "thin" version of my young self was bringing me unbearable pain. Yearning to be her, wanting to get the same male attention she got, judging myself based on my physical looks and the reactions I got from strangers was *so incredibly painful* I just could not do that to myself any longer. It did not matter. It could not matter. My sense of self-worth *could not* be based on my looks any longer. It's a shame that it was in my twenties and thirties, but as a woman entering my forties, to hold onto physical appearance as my sense of power, as my sense of self-worth, was so damaging in the most extreme way. I vowed to let it go. I vowed to do whatever it took to let it go.

As I went through this time in my healing, I experienced waves of pain and anguish followed by waves of bliss and serenity that coincided perfectly with when I clung to my past version of self and when I embraced my emerging new self.

One side of me said, *I want to be thin, tiny, ripped, surfing my old surfboards, getting noticed in the water, turning heads, sexy.* This side of me screamed in agony. She hated the world. She noticed the flaws with everyone and everything. In fact, she didn't really even want to be here anymore.

The other side of me, the fuller, rounder, introverted middle-aged woman, loved being alive. She loved the feel of a cool breeze on her skin, of walking with a long skirt tickling her legs. She loved the sparkling blue of the ocean and the bright pinks and fuchsias of the flowers. She loved watching the birds and the dogs and the babies. She loved seeing people just be people.

One day, I finally understood what was happening to me: The old version of me, the young sexy surfer, was dying—had died—and this was not a sad thing, did not need to be a sad thing. It was her time to go. I had spent the past three months so *angry* about her dying, so angry that they had killed her. So angry that "those terrible experiences with those terrible people" had killed her. But the truth was, it was her time to go. And, oh my God, it made perfect sense why she—why I, when I was seeing through her eyes and in her state of mind—did not even want to be here. Her time was done. I had to let her go. She *wanted* to go.

I realized I had been eating away this sexy young version of myself: the sex kitten. She had been fun, but she had caused me *a lot* of pain. Without realizing it, I had been eating to make myself less attractive, less desirable. The weight was forming around my second chakra, my thighs and my stomach, as a way to protect myself. I was eating to make myself invisible. I needed to. In order to heal, I *had* to go within. I had to change—a metamorphosis, like a caterpillar turning into a butterfly. My mother had been so envious of and so threatened by my beauty and my sexuality. Lakshmi had told me to hide it and screamed at me for using it to pull Vishnu away from her. Vishnu had accused me of using it to make my male sangha mates fall in love with me. Hiroto had noticed it immediately and entered my life because of it. Subconsciously, I wanted it to go away. As a child, I had been shy and introverted. As a preteen, I had been nerdy and prude. But when my father died, I discovered that the bad girl side of me was powerful. I had learned that side of me got a lot of attention. That side of me was popular and desirable and hot. Men loved me. I was used to walking into a bar and walking out with any man I wanted. It felt good. But it was soul-crushing. It was a façade. *It was not real.* Some part of me knew this and was over it. The wiser part of me that wanted to heal, that needed to heal, was ready for change. The sex kitten had to go. The woman had to emerge.

Chapter 33
Surprise

I was changing; I was changed. I should have been so excited. My God, it had been my goal for the past seven years! I had been so sure I needed to change completely in order to become Enlightened. But instead, I was devastated. Now that it had happened, the reality of it was killing me. I was willing to accept the fact that the new me was fat, but I was struggling to accept that the new me was so timid and so shy and so alone and so incredibly *afraid* of the world. I had to find a way to accept it; I had to find a way to embrace who I had become.

For starters, embracing her meant not caring what the world thought when they asked what I was doing with myself and I said, "healing." Embracing her meant refusing to disempower her by yearning for a man to fill the void and, instead, trusting that the right one would appear when the time was right, when she'd had enough solitude to build the new foundation she needed to build for herself. Embracing her meant listening to her when she said she wanted to be alone, away from the world, and sit in silence for an entire day. Embracing her meant letting go of the past, forgiving those that "killed" her old self, and accepting the fact that all that happened to her was life moving her toward her wholeness. No one really killed anyone. Her old self's time was up and those people and those experiences just helped shatter the mold so that oftentimes self-absorbed, spoiled, immature Renee could be set free and that compassionate, kind, patient, womanly Renee could unfold in her place. Slowly I began to love this new Renee. I began to love how still and patient and kind she was. I began to notice how she no longer needed to be the center of attention, how happy she was to sit back and allow others to shine. I was well on my way to recovery.

And then I found out I had herpes. It was time for my yearly checkup and I asked to have a full exam, including blood work. My doctor told me she would call if I had abnormal results, and that a nurse would call with my STD results as they came in. A nurse called me a few days later and said my blood tested negative for HIV. She said it would take a few more days for the rest of my results to come in. A few days later, she called and told me I tested negative for most of the STDs, but I still had to wait for the herpes results. The next day, I got a call from my doctor. Immediately, I knew what that meant. I had tested positive. And then, before she even spoke, I remembered a night with Vishnu . . .

––––––––––

We were in his bedroom. He was going through his closet, looking for a shirt.

"I used to have herpes," he said, his back to me, his left arm reaching for the shirt.

I was speechless. This man had made me get every single blood test possible and fax him the results. He had made me get a pap smear. He had made me circumambulate a sacred site *three times* to clean my energy field. He had even told me to take an Epsom salt bath and put my fingers inside my vagina to "clean out energetic lines left by other men." He had insisted I be as clean as possible in every possible way before he screwed me. *And* he had insisted I get on The Pill so he did not have to use condoms and could ejaculate inside me. And now, after sleeping with me for over a year, after having unprotected sex with me for over a year, he casually mentions he *used* to have herpes. That son of a bitch.

I came back to the present. My doctor was talking.

"You tested positive for herpes," she was saying. "Would you like me to prescribe medication? Would you like to come in and talk with me?"

I sat down and started to cry. I was just healing. I was just forgiving. I was just starting to move on with my life and now this? How could it be? I had been so promiscuous my entire life and now, at age thirty-nine, after becoming ordained as a monk, I end up with herpes? I was shattered *again*.

I decided not to get on medication. If my body wanted to purge a virus through my skin, I wanted it to be able to. I started getting outbreaks. They were tiny. The first few times I thought a spider had bitten me. Then I realized it was herpes. I had no idea why it took so long to appear. Maybe just knowing I had it in my blood caused me to manifest the symptoms. I was furious. My hatred for Vishnu *flared*. My anger burned. Now I was even more damaged, even more broken, even more undesirable in the eyes of men. There was no way I was *ever* going to tell a guy I had herpes, so I just gave up the idea of dating. Every time I thought about it, I got angry and depressed and filled with hate.

I returned to Colorado, the months rolled by, and I struggled to let go of my anger. Waves of it would wash over me, *still*. I had been so sure I'd be on my way to the new me and my new life, but I wasn't. I was still in therapy. I was still mad. I was still introverted. I was still broken.

PaRt 5
iNtO the LiGht

"Listen. Make a way for yourself inside yourself. Stop looking in the other way of looking. You already have the precious mixture that will make you well. Use it."

—Rumi

chapter 34
Tango Lesson

When I was learning tango in the United States, I was mostly taught crap. I had no idea it was crap, but it was crap—an American version of an Argentine social dance. I loved it and I danced it terribly. Then, one day, a young Argentine couple from Chicago came to teach a workshop at the dance studio where I worked. They amazed me. He was *so* handsome, dressed in baggy, hip, multi-pocketed pants, with a chain hanging down the side, and big thick chunky silver rings covering his hands. She was gorgeous—tiny, with similar baggy pants, rolled up to her knees and sexy strappy little high heels. Her short hair was dyed a purple red, and she wore dark nail polish and red lipstick. And they danced the most *beautiful* tango I had ever seen: slow, sensual, rhythmic, yet with dynamic flashes of leg when you least expected it. He held her so close and with so much love. There was no "flash and trash" here. No sloppy, open embrace. No jabbing of his legs in between hers and knocking her off balance. No struggle. No fight. No tight sequined slit dress. Just love and rhythm and impeccable technique. When the song was over, they simply stopped in an embrace—no dip, no flip, no garish split. I had never seen anything like it. I had to learn.

I took as many lessons as I could while they visited. And then I tried to practice, but I couldn't. No one else danced that way. I went down to Argentina to practice, and no one danced that way there either.

At our next lesson, I asked the young man, "How can I practice this if no one else dances this way?"

He said, "You practice on your own."

"Why would I spend so much time learning this way if I can't ever dance it with anyone?"

He looked at me with his warm golden brown eyes and said, "Renee, now that you know tango can be danced like this, how could you dance it any other way?"

I was stunned. He was right. And so I practiced. On my own. I practiced and practiced and practiced. For *years*. And I went back to Argentina and danced there and kept practicing with all the old men, all the men with *panzas* (bellies), all the men who were more than happy to hold a young girl close and let her practice this slow different dancing with them while they wrestled with her and tried to jab their legs in between her feet and knock her off balance.

And then one day, years later, something miraculous happened. I was at my favorite *milonga* in Buenos Aires, after almost nine months of being away, and I danced my first set of tangos with a man who held me close and moved slowly—so slowly, in fact, that I could effectively dance as I had been practicing. It was the best set of tangos I had ever danced with someone besides that male instructor.

In Argentina, a man asks a woman to dance by making eye contact with her from across the room. If she wishes to dance, she holds his eye contact, and they meet on the dance floor. They do not talk; they simply dance. Once the first dance is over, they talk until the next dance begins. (Back in the day, this was the only time young chaperoned couples had to converse without being overheard.) However, if the woman does not wish to dance, she looks away when a man looks at her from across the room. In this way, the man's delicate ego can be protected; he can say to himself, "She just didn't see me."

After the beautiful set of tangos with the new amazing dancer, I sat down and noticed a young, *hot* guy was looking at me. I looked back. We met on the dance floor. He held me close and danced exactly the way my young instructor had. I was in heaven.

When the song ended, he said in Spanish, "Wow, you are a beautiful dancer! Are you Argentine?"

"No," I replied, "Norteamericana."

He told me it was extremely rare for a young North American dancer to dance as I did. We danced three more tangos (the usual set), and he walked me to my table and thanked me.

I sat down and looked up: Another young, hot guy was looking at me. We danced. He held me close and danced with me in that same slow style. My night continued like this until my feet were so sore I could dance no more.

And so it happened. A magical door into an unknown world of young, handsome, incredibly talented tango dancers had opened for me. But the key to that door was this: *I* had to get to that level of ability in that style of dance before I even noticed them, before they even noticed me.

When I asked them why I had never seen them before, they said they had never seen me either, yet we had all gone to the same *milongas* for years. All I had seen were old men with large bellies who smelled like alcohol and cigarettes and dirty hair. And I was willing to dance with these men because I loved tango and I thought only old men danced tango. I had no idea I could dance tango with young, handsome men who smelled amazing and didn't beat me up on the dance floor.

I also realized I had never watched; I had just been dancing with all the bad dancers. The bad dancers stay in the center of the dance floor, bumping into each other, while the good dancers dance around the outside edge. So all I saw from the center were the other bad dancers. I was so intent on improving my own dance that I never stopped to just watch.

My entire tango world had shifted from "hell" to "heaven" once I brought myself up to the level of "heaven" dancing. I had held the key to my own liberation in my lawsuit and here, in the world of tango, *I* held the key, as well. Couldn't this be true— *mustn't* this be true—for anything in life? Finding a partner, finding a job, finding a house or apartment or even magical wonderful new friends—weren't these the same? If I did the work, if I was willing to change and evolve and grow, to let go of behaviors and ways of being that no longer served me, wouldn't I, in effect, be raising myself to a new level in life, be opening myself up to wonderful new possibilities?

Yes! I thought as I remembered this tango experience. *Yes! I believe I would. Yes! I believe I will.*

chapter 35
awakening

My therapist, in one of her group talks, mentioned the poem "Song of a Man Who Has Come Through" by D. H. Lawrence. One day, on a whim, I decided to google it and the last four lines broke through to me in a way nothing else yet had:

What is the knocking at the door in the night?
It is somebody wants to do us harm.
No, no, it is the three strange angels.
Admit them, admit them.

Maybe because there were three angels, maybe because I was finally exhausted by my anger, maybe because I was so desperate to heal—who knows, but somehow, I finally, *really*, got the fact that the intense anger I could not let go of was not anger at Hiroto and Lakshmi and Vishnu—the intense anger I could not let go of was anger at myself. *I* was the one I had to forgive.

If I truly had the faith I professed to have, I had to believe that Lakshmi, Vishnu, and Hiroto had been Three Strange Angels come to change my life in unique and incredibly powerful ways. *They were not mistakes.* My decision to walk with them had not been a mistake. I had needed to change. I had needed to be broken open. I had needed to be shattered so that I could blossom and expand and grow. I suddenly realized that this is the whole point of a spiritual path. We need to be broken apart in order to grow. I realized that it is the fire of life that purifies us. It is the pain, the breaking apart, that softens us and allows us to have compassion for our fellow humans. We need the fire, we need the pain, we need the breaking apart in order to stop, in order to slow down, in order to awaken.

I suddenly saw the beauty of being broken. It made me stop. It was making me stop. It was giving me the time to contemplate what truly mattered in life, like health and friends and family. It was making me turn to the little things I love, like a warm cup of coffee in a pretty porcelain mug, sitting in front of the fire reading, watching the snow fall. These simple things, these tiny luxuries were responsible for pulling me out of the dark and into the light. These tiny steps.

I suddenly realized how utterly important friends and family are—and kindness. As I was healing, a smile or kind word from a stranger could bring me to my knees in gratitude or infuse me with the energy to keep on going, while a rude comment or mean look from a stranger could crumple me with sadness. I knew I should be stronger than this, that I shouldn't be so affected by others. I had studied Buddhism for seven years! I should be detached. But I wasn't. In this utterly fragile state, I was affected by everything—and everyone. I suddenly understood that I had to *stop making it about me*. It wasn't that nobody understood me; it was that I wasn't taking the time to understand anyone else. I was so consumed by myself and my own pain that I was not paying attention to anyone else. I had been utterly self-obsessed. We all go through the same struggles. We all just want to feel love and approval. We all gravitate toward pleasure and run from pain. We are all damaged in our own way.

I finally saw the key to unlocking my fear of strangers, of being out in the world, and the key to unraveling much of the pain inside my mind: Turn my focus *outward*. Again, I held the key to my own liberation: I had to focus on others, bring joy to others, listen to and try to understand others, not the other way around. And I could do this in simple ways: I could walk into a store with a smile on my face, notice the salespeople, smile at them, allow them to show me around. It was my job to make *them* feel appreciated. I had wanted so desperately to be a saint, to spread light. This was one simple way to do that, to be back on my path of Enlightenment. I couldn't control what other people thought about me, but I could certainly make sure I was open and kind. And, because I was stopped and shattered and broken, I had time to listen to them, to really see them.

I suddenly realized I could leave a larger tip at a bar or restaurant or in a taxi, I could hold open a door for someone, I could stop and smile at and listen to strangers even though I felt like shit, I could leave fifteen minutes earlier and not be in a rush, not be an asshole behind the wheel of my car, let people merge in front of me in traffic. I realized there were so many opportunities, so many little ways, for me to spread light every single moment of every single day.

And, most liberating of all, being so incredibly shattered made me stop *judging*. If I could join a cult, if I could become brainwashed, if I could fall in love with and go into business with a man who was so . . . damaged, who was I to judge anything? Suddenly my super-strong, rigid opinions about everything softened. I realized my way was not always the right way. I realized I had *no* idea what other people were going through. I had *no* idea what made them tick, why they did the things they did. Who was I to judge anyone? Who was I to believe I knew what was right for anyone else? Judging was exhausting and depressing. It made me stiff and self-righteous and mean. Accepting was easy; it took no energy. I realized I could redirect all the energy I wasted wanting others to change, wanting the world to change, focusing on what others did that I didn't approve of . . . I could redirect all the energy I wasted judging others and use it instead on myself: to improve and uplift myself, to create a life I loved. And I noticed that as I worked to heal myself, as love and light and acceptance began to flow through my heart again, I simply stopped noticing what others were doing or not doing. I stopped caring.

Oh my God, it made a *huge* difference. I slowly began to enjoy going outside. I slowly became less afraid of others. I started building friendships again. And I decided it really was okay to tell people the truth: that life had kicked my ass and I was taking time to find myself again.

A few weeks later, I was talking to a friend who had survived cancer, trying to convince her that she was truly healed—that just because the medical community used the term "in remission," she had the right and the power to instead think "entirely healed."

"I believe disease is a result of negative emotion stored in the body, blocking the flow of life-force energy. The destructive, angry thought patterns need to change; the emotion needs to be dealt with and released. If it is not, the body cannot heal," I said. "But you have changed. You have softened. You have purged so much of the anger and fear that you used to carry. You have forgiven. The disease has served its purpose. You can thank it and let it go."

As those words came out of my mouth, it strengthened my belief even more: These seemingly horrible experiences are created by the hand of the Divine in order to push us toward expansion. If we listen and learn and squeeze the juice out of them, we grow, we change, we blossom.

I was not supposed to be the person I was before the cult, before Hiroto. Thank God, because that person was long gone. Now, I just had to figure out who the new me was.

Well, for starters, the new me was fat and the new me was introverted and the new me was invisible and the new me had herpes. I had forgiven Hiroto, and with that, I had regained a huge piece of my heart, my power, and my sanity. But I still had a long way to go. I could not get over the herpes thing. I *hated* Vishnu for that. I started with the self-talk again: If I believed disease was given to us for a reason, then I had herpes for a reason. I had to believe that, on some level, my soul chose it, and that once I accepted it and stopped fighting it and took the time to understand why, and made the appropriate changes, my body would heal itself and let the dis-ease go. And if I was going to forgive, if I was going to let go, I had to take responsibility for it. The more I thought about it, the more I realized having herpes was protecting me from having reckless random sex, from sleeping with men that were not good for me. Herpes was helping me get rid of the sex kitten. Herpes was helping me put on hold an entire facet of my life: dating and men. I needed healing. I needed to mend my soul from the inside out. I had always struggled with my relationships with men; I had often used sex to get what I wanted. It was time for this behavior to stop.

I had to figure out why I had allowed Vishnu to have unprotected sex with me without first insisting *he* get tested and show me the results. I had to figure out how I got myself in the cult in the first place, why I allowed myself to be used by Vishnu and Lakshmi and then by Hiroto. What was lacking in me? What was broken in me?

I began to see that as the daughter of an alcoholic, I had become addicted to emotionally unavailable men who were also addicts. I was drawn to them because their push–pull love cycle reminded me of my mother's. But I was also drawn to them for another reason: most addicts are incredibly sensitive and lonely people. Life has caused these people to feel isolated. They feel less-than. And because they feel unable to bond with other humans, they bond with an addictive behavior, something that temporarily eases the pain of life, something that is always there for them. I wanted to save them. I wanted to open their hearts again. I could see that they, like my mother, were beautiful wounded souls and I yearned to bring that beauty to the surface, to show them the world was a safe and magical place, to remind them that they are extraordinary and worthy and so deserving of love. Instead, I always got crushed; I always got pulled down with them, because my wounds caused me to become instantly attached, to try to squeeze love from someone unable to give it. A part of me felt that if I could save a man that was emotionally unavailable, if I could melt his heart and get him to open and get him to love me, then somehow I could make up for the fact that I was never able to save my mother. But I realized I needed to remind myself that *I* was extraordinary and worthy and so deserving of love. It was not my job to save them; it was my job to save myself.

I admitted to myself that by choosing these men, I was bringing to the surface a wound I had since childhood: judging my self-worth based on the attention I got from an emotionally unavailable loved one. It was far past time for me to stop recreating the pain of a wailing four-year-old desperate for her alcoholic mother's attention. I didn't have to wait anymore for something or someone out of my control to come fix my life, to come fill this void, to love me. Again, I held the key to my own liberation. The only thing keeping me trapped in the pain of the past, in a life I didn't love, was . . . *me.* I was going to save myself. And I was going to start *right now.*

Chapter 36
Warrior

I turned back to the little things that brought me joy. I continued to nurture myself. I *knew* self-love was the key. Determined to get my life back under control, I called NYU and started the process of finishing my degree. Even though it was a task given to me by Lakshmi, I was going back to school. I *loved* NYU. I *loved* New York. As soon as I was reenrolled, I signed up for Body Pump classes and started doing Power Yoga. Yes, I had accepted the fuller version of me, and she had served me well for over a year, but I was tired of being soft and lethargic and flabby; I was ready to get strong again, in body and in mind. I made a play list called "Back in Black." It started with AC/DC's "Back in Black" and then went to Ozzy Osborne's "Crazy Train" and Marilyn Manson's "The New Shit." I added Eminem's "Lose Yourself" and Ludacris's "Get Back." I played it loud in my car, on repeat. I was done being a victim. I was ready to become a warrior.

I had to start school in April, on the Global Study Tour, with a new class, in South Korea. I had to show up as the new girl. It wasn't easy. Especially after being out of school for over a year. Especially after spending almost all of that time sitting alone in the mountains. Especially having no idea who I was. When I landed in the middle of the new MBA class, some students were nice and welcoming; others ignored me. When people asked me why I took a break from school, what made me leave, I told them that I had been in a cult and had gone into a radically failed business venture and then moved to the mountains to heal and figure out who the hell I was. When they asked why I decided to get my MBA, I said, "Because my spiritual teacher told me to." When they asked why I finally left the cult I said, "Because I was screwing my guru's boyfriend, and she threw me out." I was so totally fed up with pretending to be anything besides my true self that I couldn't twist the truth even a little bit.

To my complete surprise, most of them were fascinated by the story and couldn't wait to hear more. Not only were they interested, but most of them also instantly offered their own very private stories of struggle: divorce, recovery from addiction, embracing their sexuality, and so on. Most of them accepted me immediately. When they invited me out after class and I told them I was not really ready to socialize, they were incredibly understanding. My honesty and their acceptance was a huge part of my rise out of the dark and back into life. And I believe that in my willingness to be vulnerable with strangers I invited them to be vulnerable back. I lowered the walls on my side and it gave them permission to do the same, causing instant, real bonds with amazing people that I may not have bonded with otherwise.

The study load was exhausting, but it gave me something to focus on. I had to keep up with the other students; I couldn't wallow in self-pity anymore. It also helped me forgive Lakshmi; I was going to school because of her. I allowed myself to see the myriad ways in which Lakshmi had pushed me to change and to grow. The truth was, in many ways, she *had* liberated me.

I eventually felt strong enough to spend time with my brother and his family. I vowed to tell him the full story and I did as soon as I saw him. One evening, while I was sitting at a bar with my sister-in-law's sister, the handsome bartender asked how often we got to see each other.

I said, "We haven't seen each other in seven years." When he asked why, I said, "Because I joined a cult and pushed everyone I loved out of my life."

He laughed.

Then my brother chimed in, "She's not kidding. It's true."

Everyone at the bar got quiet. They all looked at me like I had just landed from outer space. And then, seemingly at the same time, they all said, "Seriously? We have to know the story."

After that, I began to realize my story had worth. It was interesting. I grew less afraid of having people know the truth about me. I began to own it. This brought my power back even more. I was no longer afraid to run into old friends; in fact, I started trying to find them online. With each old friend that came back into my life, my sense of self, my power, increased. They reminded me that I was loved. They all forgave me for disappearing. Many of them broke down crying when they saw or heard from me.

"I'm just so glad you are okay," they would weep. "I was so worried about you. I thought I might never see you again. You mean so much to me."

A few jokingly said they were going to kick my ass for joining a cult, but they all surrounded me with so much unconditional love. They understood that I had changed, and they welcomed, embraced, supported, and encouraged this newer, softer, more introverted version of me.

The idea that Lakshmi had implanted so deeply in my psyche, that I was a sorceress and a witch, that I was evil, that I was manipulating people energetically, slowly began to fade. The belief that I was lovable, kind, compassionate, and giving began to rise more forcefully to the surface. With my old friends back by my side, my self-confidence grew, and I became happier, kinder, more loving—an upward spiral of light.

That summer, I went out to a restaurant in Colorado and, on a dare, got up on the bar and started dancing. People stopped eating, stopped talking, and turned to stare, and then almost everyone in the bar started dancing. A bartender turned the music up. The party had ramped up ten thousand notches. A super-sexy, muscular, tattooed guy, at least ten years younger than me, handed me a shot. As he was helping me off the bar I said, "That's my first shot in seven years."

"Why?" he asked.

"Because I was in a cult and got ordained as a Buddhist monk."

"Seriously?"

We were smooshed together, body to body, in the middle of the dancing crowd. I looked up at him. "Yup," I said back.

"You are the most interesting person I have ever met," he said, with a sparkle in his eyes.

My body was coming back, my sense of self was rapidly returning, and apparently, it was time to start dancing again. Dancing had been stripped away early in my years with the cult. I had forgotten that my fearlessness of dancing when no one else was dancing liberated others, encouraged them to do the same. I had forgotten how that one simple action always turned a mundane event into a party. And I had forgotten how incredibly *good* it felt to dance! It was, after all, my God-given gift.

In January, I was invited by Jaana Kunitz, world champion Latin-ballroom dancer, performer, choreographer, and fitness celebrity, to be a backup dancer in her teacher-training videos. It was a huge honor, and it forced me to get back into dancing shape. For the month of February, as I struggled to learn her routines and build my aerobic capacity, I kept trying to get myself fired, telling Jaana I couldn't do it, that I was too out of shape, that I did not dance well enough, that she should hire someone half my age and much more talented, but she refused to let me off the hook.

She tirelessly coached me through iPhone videos, constantly encouraging me when I wanted to give up. "I want you," she said. "You *can* do it. Keep trying."

When I showed up to film, I realized the only other dancer besides Jaana and me was a finalist on *So You Think You Can Dance*. I had to hold my own next to these two. Two hours into filming, I pulled my hamstring and threw out my back. I quietly mentioned both to Jaana and then got painkillers from a cameraman. The only reason I made it through the video shoot was because I had been training at an altitude of 8,000 feet and was now filming at sea level.

I walked (well, hobbled) back to my hotel room at the end of that day changed. I caught my reflection in the mirror. I was different; I was a dancer again. A huge chunk of my spirit came flooding back, a huge piece of my soul.

This change gave me the courage I needed to drive by my house the following day. I had been afraid to return there. I knew I had to sell it. I could not bear to even look at it—so many painful memories. I called my real estate agent and told her it had to go. I was willing to lower the price; losing so much money in New York had taught me that emotional and psychological freedom was *so much more important* than money. The house *absolutely* had to go. She put a "coming soon" sign in front of it that afternoon. My heart sang with relief. I was a dancer again, and my ashram had to go.

I returned to Colorado. I had not dated in close to three years. I wanted my sexuality back. I had to figure out how to incorporate sensuality with the "new" me. I couldn't be celibate forever. I was a dancer; I used my body to express myself. What better way to express love of another than through the physicality of sex? I signed up for pole-dancing class and then I began snowboarding in earnest. I was no longer afraid to fall, and I was no longer afraid to sit next to strangers on the chair lift. It had taken me two years to get to this point, and the freedom that came along with it was blissful. I now had the energy and the confidence to ride all over the mountain on my own. My love of snowboarding returned. I could not believe that, for the last year, I had been terrified of doing more than the one run by my house, and I was so scared of strangers that I only went to snowboard at 8:45 a.m., as soon as the mountain opened, so I could ride the lift by myself. I had been embarrassed that the lift operators saw poor sad old shy broken me every morning by myself, never with friends. I kept my head down and never looked at them. Now I smiled and said "hello" to the lift operators. I danced a little while waiting for the chair if they had music playing. I high-fived them as I whizzed into the singles line and rode up with strangers, listening to them tell me about their lives the whole way. It is amazing how much joy interacting with others brought to me; it is amazing how liberating it felt to trust people again; it is *amazing* the change in my world when I decided, rather than seeing everyone as "being in my way" or "draining my energy" or "out to get me," to see everyone as a friend I had not met yet . . . to see them as angels being sent to remind me I am not alone. And it is amazing how just being me suddenly, after so much time of not being me, brought me more joy than I ever could have imagined. *It brought me to nirvana.*

The more I smiled and the more I talked and the more I danced and snowboarded and went to yoga, the happier and fuller and larger my life became. And as I became happier, I radiated that light and love and joy to everyone I met. A happy me was a radiating me. A happy me was an accepting me. A happy me was a nonjudgmental me. My key to becoming saint-like, to having patience and compassion and radiating love and light and peace and God, was—oh my God—just doing the things that made me *me!*

Part 6
Whole

"Just let go. Let go of how you thought your life should be, and embrace the life that is trying to work its way into your consciousness."

—Caroline Myss

Chapter 37
Wild Monk

Slowly but surely, I was assembling my pieces. It seemed like I had so many of them, they would never fit back together. I felt like I had split identities: One side of me loved being a monk and living a quiet life of contemplation and solitude. Another side of me loved men and sex and dancing and drinking and surfing and snowboarding and being naughty. One side of me wanted to leave society all together and spend my life alone with religious books and devotional chanting and sunrises and my cat and God. The other side of me wanted to move back to New York and be a best-selling author. How could I be such an extreme dichotomy? Which side was going to win out? Who was I, really? Which parts of me were real and which were façades? I still could not tell . . .

With pole-dancing class and going to bars again, the "bad girl" started shoving her way to the surface. She wanted back in my life, and she wanted back with a vengeance. In order to become whole, this side of me *had* to come back. I had shoved her away for so long, covered her in sack-like clothing. I had run over her surfboards with my car and burned all her leather jackets and platform heels. Even in my healing, I had decided the young, sexy, wild, fun girl had to die.

Not completely true.

The sex kitten had to die, but the untamed side of me had to remain.

She is a part of me. A *powerful* part of me. Her passion is the manifestation of the spiritual in physical form. Her desire is the summoning of Life Force Energy moving through her. She is freedom. She is a rule-breaker. She is unbound.

The difference is this:

I am now all of it. I am the older, wiser, slower, more grounded, kinder, more compassionate monk woman, *and* I am the sexy, fun, dangerous, pole-dancing, leather-wearing, freaky wild child. I have found a way to combine them and to honor them both. It's not easy. Most people who first meet me dancing on a bar are shocked when I tell them I am a monk and an introvert. They can't understand how I can be so fun and wild and free and still want to spend most of my time alone at home in silence. Most people who meet me in yoga, when I am centered and quiet and shy, are shocked if they happen to see me out at night wearing leather pants and knee high boots, spinning around a stripper pole. I have stopped trying to be one or the other. I am all of it. Sometimes I need to be wild. Most of the time I need to be contained.

I'm proud to be me.

I'm proud of all I went through.

I'm proud of every single decision I made, because it was the best I could do at that time.

And, the most important of all: *I would not undo any of it.*

chapter 38
GRADUATiON

May 19, 2015, I sit in the backseat of a taxi, bumping along FDR Drive on the east side of Manhattan. I have just landed at LaGuardia airport and am on my way to a hotel in Soho. A huge smile spreads across my face.

I did it. I fucking did it. I, Renee Linnell, ex-professional dancer and bikini model, have just graduated from the Executive Masters in Business Administration program at NYU Stern. I cannot believe it.

As the taxi rattles along in rush-hour traffic and the hot humid air from the open window hits me in the face, I realize it was all worth it.

I lean back into the dirty leather seat and look at the river. I feel peace. I feel a deep, deep peace—all the way to the depths of my soul. And I feel joy. I feel overwhelming joy. And I feel a sense of accomplishment that I cannot describe. Tomorrow I, along with over eight thousand other graduates, will walk into Yankee Stadium dressed in purple.

I close my eyes, overcome with gratitude. I am so incredibly grateful. Grateful, at long last, to be returning to the entirety of myself; grateful to be, *finally*, rising from the ashes like a phoenix.

I hold this vision in my mind: a phoenix, large, graceful, power-ful . . . rising from the ashes in victory, wings spread wide, chest arched and open, head held high. Unashamed. Unafraid. My skin tingles with goose bumps. I feel stronger than I have *ever* felt, more grateful than I have *ever* felt, and free.

EPiLOGUe

It has been five years since I moved to Colorado. I never imagined it would take this long for me to heal. But, I have to say, I feel as if I've been rebuilt from the ground up. As if every single piece of myself that came back, came back stronger, more grounded, more sure of who I am and what I want, more appreciative of all life has given me, and more Free. I learned so much and for that I am truly grateful. I'm not as needy as I used to be. Not as insecure. I give more than I take. I spend time every day in silence. And I try my hardest to always be kind.

I did not just survive the burn zone that first night I met Lakshmi, I lived in and survived the burn zone for close to ten years. Like the Samurai sword, I endured being held in the flame, being pounded down and flattened by life, and I came out the other side as a version of myself that I truly love.

————

I will never understand what Lakshmi and Vishnu wanted. I will never understand how Lakshmi could flood a room with Light and be so hateful at the same time. I will never understand if Vishnu was just a narcissist that craved power or simply a wounded and confused man filled with self-hatred and desperate to believe the lies about his "magnificence." And I am still trying to figure out how to undo the lingering paranoia left in my mind by their incessant teachings on the occult. But I do know that Lakshmi *did* push me toward freedom. She *did* teach me to grow up. She *did* help me to expand my life in magnificent ways.

Lakshmi and Vishnu taught me to fear others. To separate myself from them. To push them away. To disdain anyone that was not on the same path I was on. I became isolated. I became cold. I became distant. I became self-righteous. I became judgmental. I became mean. They taught me to hate myself, to hate every part of myself that was "unspiritual," to hate every part of myself that was human. The more I hated myself, the more I hated others, and the more I hated others, the more I attracted hateful people into my life. This is how I got so incredibly taken advantage of in New York; this is how I let hate begin to consume me.

Mind control is no joke. It is *incredibly* damaging. Planting seeds of self-doubt and hatred in other people's minds is the antithesis of spreading light. And it amazes me that it could happen to me, that it could happen to my friends, that it can happen to anyone if we allow others to tell us who we are.

In New York, I had a quote on my desk from St. Catherine of Siena. It said, "Be who God meant you to be, and you will set the world on fire."

I would look at that quote every day and say to myself, sometimes out loud, but always in great emotional pain, "I don't know who God meant me to be. I have no idea what to be, what to do with my life. I am so unhappy, and I feel so small. If I knew who God meant me to be, I would do it. I would love to set the world on fire." And then I would go about my day.

One day, my eyes landed on that quote and *Love* popped into my head. Simply the word *Love*.

And then I got it.

God meant me to be love: a walking, breathing, living manifestation of love. God meant for all of us to be love. When we love ourselves, we love others. And when we love others, we bring out the best in them; we create a beautiful safe space for the vulnerable, gooey, raw parts to come out from behind the ego and shine.

And the truth suddenly showed itself, after I had spent a lifetime searching: *Love.*

My search for God led me through hell and back. I destroyed myself. I destroyed all I loved. And the most important thing I got out of all of it at the end was this: when I love, I feel God. When I'm grateful, I feel God. When I'm giving and kind and patient and caring and compassionate, I feel God. The rest doesn't matter. *Nothing* else matters. And the key to feeling love and kindness and patience and compassion is loving and accepting—completely accepting—myself.

God made me. S/he wants me to be me. With all the flaws and cracks and broken bits. And s/he wants me to be happy. S/he wants all of us to be happy. And s/he wants us to love each other. When we love each other, we create heaven on earth. When we don't, we create hell. It is up to us. It has always been up to us.

At least, after all my searching, this is what I now believe. It doesn't mean it's true. It doesn't mean I know exactly what God wants. It doesn't mean anyone else has to believe it. But imagine if everybody did: instead of suicide bombers we'd have anonymous acts of love, generosity, and kindness. Instead of "sin and confession and redemption" we'd have joy and fun and self-acceptance and play. Instead of altercations with grumpy strangers that provoke "What's your problem, asshole?" we'd understand a mean person is suffering and say, instead, "Are you okay, can I help?" or at least walk away without being mean back, without perpetuating the cycle of hate, understanding that a mean person is a person in pain. Instead of holy wars, we'd have holy love fests.

I look back on all I went through and I can't believe I put up with being treated so badly for so long. Now that I'm out the other side, I find the whole story mind-boggling. But maybe that's the whole point of a spiritual path, of this journey on earth: to come into this world perfect; to lose ourselves through childhood; to allow ourselves to believe we have to look, walk, act, talk, dress a certain way to fit in, hold a certain job to be important, make a certain amount of money to have self-worth

. . . to walk that path until it breaks us, and then to slowly come back to our authentic selves at the end.

A part of me believes we have all been brainwashed to some degree. Anytime we believe we are unworthy, we have been brainwashed. Anytime we believe we are ugly or stupid or *not good enough*, we have been brainwashed. Anytime we believe we need to buy another product to be happy or hide our sexuality to fit in or cut into our face and body in order to be beautiful, we have been brainwashed. We are bombarded with messaging that tells us we are not okay the way we are. It is time for messaging that tells us the opposite: there is room for all of us, with all our diversity, and each one of us is incredibly worthy. By believing in and loving and being true to ourselves, we add our light to the sum of light, and we shift the consciousness of this planet from fear to love. Is there anything else more worthy of our time?

People hear my story and ask what I learned as a monk; they ask whether I found Enlightenment. They ask me about religions and spiritual paths. They ask me what to believe. This is how I respond:

When you are walking toward fear and hate and judgment and condemnation and isolation, you are walking in the wrong direction. When you walk toward faith and love and community and acceptance and kindness and compassion, you are on the right path.

———

I can't know The Way that is right for you; I am not you. But I do know that if you get quiet, if you allow your mind to go still for just fifteen minutes every day, even if you just *try* to allow your mind to go still for fifteen minutes each day, you will begin to hear the Wise Voice within, the one you were born with, the one that is always there guiding you. You already know the answers you seek, you just need to get still enough to listen. No guru can replace your own Inner Knowing, no one outside of yourself should. Follow your heart, follow your dreams, follow your passions. They are given to you for a reason, implanted inside of you on purpose. They are the key to your destiny. And above all else, find a way to be more playful, more childlike, less serious. Give yourself a break. Trust the unfolding. Love yourself; be amazed by yourself. You are a magnificent creation of the Divine.

ABOUT the AUTHOR

Renee Linnell is a serial entrepreneur who has founded or cofounded five companies and has an MBA from New York University; before that she was a model and professional dancer. Currently she is working on starting a publishing company to give people from diverse walks of life an opportunity to tell their stories. Linnell divides her time between Colorado and Southern California. For more information please visit www.reneelinnell.com.

Author photo © In Her Image Photography

ACKNOWLEDGMENTS

"Set your life on fire. Seek those who fan your flames."
—Rumi

First, I have to thank August Gold, my therapist. Without you I would probably not still be here. Next, I have to thank Cherise Fisher, my editor, who turned 500 pages of my journal entries ("vomit," as you lovingly called them) into a book. Third, I have to thank Fauzia Burke, who is not only the world's best marketing consultant but also a great friend and a fantastic coach. Next come Brooke Warner and the team at She Writes Press: thank you for believing in my story and for doing such a wonderful job polishing it . . . and for being so *amazing* to work with. Thank you to Cait Levin for keeping my project on track, to Mimi Bark for the *beautiful* cover, to Heidi and Tara of In Her Image Photography for making me feel like a goddess and for capturing so many amazing photos for my covers and my branding, and to Sanyu for introducing me to Cherise. And now the ladies—Shawna, Luann, Adrienne, Jane, Julia, Sachi, and Allison—who tirelessly listened to me talk about "working on my book," who read numerous manuscript versions, and who made me keep going each time I wanted to quit. I thank you from the bottom of my heart; you make me feel so safe in this world. Thank you to Bruno for being my rock and for always making me laugh; to Sharon C for telling me I had to write a book; to Jason G for making me pull my manuscript out of the trash and look for a publisher; and to Jaana for making me dance again and for believing in me and for being so wild and crazy and sparkly and for reading and endorsing my manuscript. Thank you to Madisyn Taylor of DailyOM for reading my email and being willing to not only respond but read an entire MS sent to you by a stranger and then endorse it. Thank you to Meredith Rom for your wise guidance and for also taking the time to read my MS and write such a lovely endorsement; to Diane R for offering to proofread and instead losing yourself so completely in the MS that you quit proofreading a few chapters in; to Aaron S, my "party coach," who got me back into the bars and back into the world; to the Sarasota Book Club ladies, who offered to beta test my manuscript and gave me wonderful feedback—I think I implemented all of it. Thank you to Nathan at GLBG for your edits, you helped make my book so much stronger; to Richard C for your legal advice, your fabulous NY accent, and your fantastic humor about the whole thing; to Jonathan K for your support and legal guidance. I have to thank Gary, my brother and womb-mate, for never giving up on me and for saying, "I don't care how weird you get or what kind of a cult you join, you are not kicking me out of your life, I am your family," and Tameka, my sister-in-law and my soul sister, for supporting and loving my brother and for giving me great marketing advice. I have to thank Kristin A and Kasey G for forgiving me for ruining our debutante party; I was selfish and a jerk and I am so sorry. Thank you to all my NYU classmates (A13 and J15) and professors; you supported me and encouraged me more than you know, and without you I would still be "just a dancer." Thank you, Jeff C, for offering to proofread and for taking me in off the street when I was basically homeless in Hawaii. My list could go on and on. Thank you to everyone who has ever been kind to me, I am still here on this planet because of you. And a *huge* thank-you to all of my friends who allowed me to push you away and go radio silent for almost eight years, and then welcomed me back with open arms. I could not live in this world without you. Thank you to every single person who has ever fanned my flames.

SELECTED TITLES FROM SHE WRITES PRESS

She Writes Press is an independent publishing company founded to serve women writers everywhere. Visit us at www.shewritespress.com.

Manifesting Me: A Story of Rebellion and Redemption by Leah E. Reinhart. $16.95, 978-1-63152-383-0. When Leah Reinhart was six years old, her family joined a cult in Oakland, California—and she spent much of her life afterward trying to break free of the damaging patterns she was taught there.

Uncovered: How I Left Hassidic Life and Finally Came Home by Leah Lax. $16.95, 978-1-63152-995-5. Drawn in their offers of refuge from her troubled family and promises of eternal love, Leah Lax becomes a Hassidic Jew—but ultimately, as a forty-something woman, comes to reject everything she has lived for three decades in order to be who she truly is.

Fourteen: A Daughter's Memoir of Adventure, Sailing, and Survival by Leslie Johansen Nack. $16.95, 978-1-63152-941-2. A coming-of-age adventure story about a young girl who comes into her own power, fights back against abuse, becomes an accomplished sailor, and falls in love with the ocean and the natural world.

Lost in the Reflecting Pool: A Memoir by Diane Pomerantz. $16.95, 978-1-63152-268-0. A psychological story about Diane, a highly trained child psychologist, who falls in love with Charles, a brilliant and charming psychiatrist—ignoring all the red flags that will later come back to haunt her.

The S Word by Paolina Milana. $16.95, 978-1-63152-927-6. An insider's account of growing up with a schizophrenic mother, and the disastrous toll the illness—and her Sicilian Catholic family's code of secrecy—takes upon her young life.

Not Exactly Love: A Memoir by Betty Hafner. $16.95, 978-1-63152-149-2. At twenty-five Betty Hafner, thought she'd found the man to make her dream of a family and cozy home come true—but after they married, his rages turned the dream into a nightmare, and Betty had to decide: stay with the man she loved, or find a way to leave?